A
CENTURY
OF
CHRISTIAN
SCIENCE
HEALING

A
CENTURY
OF
CHRISTIAN
SCIENCE
HEALING

The Christian Science Publishing Society

Boston, Massachusetts

Contents

Foreword   vii

1 The Beginnings *1866–1883*   1

2 The Tide of Healing   15

1883–1914   18
1914–1945   72
1945–1965   146

3 The Horizon of Healing   235

Healing and Salvation   237
Practical Aspects   239
The Whole Man   243
Healing in the Churches   246
The Healing of the Nations   249
Christianity and Science   251
The Second Century   255

Foreword

ONE HUNDRED YEARS have elapsed since the discovery of Christian Science by Mary Baker Eddy. The significance of that event has been attested by a mounting tide of spiritual healing through the intervening years. As a result, a unique body of testimony to the healing power of God has become available, gathering weight and volume with every year.

No aspect of religious experience bears more directly on the often-asked question: Is Christianity relevant to a scientific age? With the revived interest in spiritual healing in the traditional churches during recent decades, the cumulative evidence which Christian Science has to offer becomes a matter of deep concern to all who wonder whether the New Testament promises are valid today. With contemporary developments in physics, biochemistry, and psychotherapy challenging men to explore more vigorously the relation of matter to mind, the practical experience of Christian Scientists yields a kind of datum not to be found elsewhere.

The present book puts on record something of the character and variety of Christian Science healing during the past century. This record has a broader purpose than the commemoration of a cherished denominational anniversary. By offering a representative sampling of the mass of testimony available, it opens up an area of religious experience still not generally understood, bears concrete witness to the healing dimension of present-day Christian discipleship, and presents the phenomena of spiritual healing not under the category of miracle but at the level of a reasoned understanding of spiritual law.

For a full, systematic presentation of the basis of Christian Science healing the reader must inevitably turn to the Christian Science textbook, *Science and Health with Key to the Scriptures* by Mrs. Eddy. The present volume, however, should furnish anyone unfamiliar with the subject at least some insight into the grounds for the Christian Scientist's conviction that Christianity properly understood is demonstrable Science.

The book is not a study in medicine or in church history but in human lives radically grasped by the Christ. Seen in perspective, the flow of healing through the century has a bolder sweep than many Christian Scientists themselves may have appreciated; but the deepest purpose of all such testimony is to give praise to God.

Christian Scientists are not primarily concerned with bodily health; in fact they undoubtedly give far less attention to their bodies than do most people. The words "health" and "healing" as used in Christian Science apply to the demonstration of spiritual wholeness in all the aspects of human living. The healing or rectification of all the ills and evils of the human condition is seen as the progressive coming into evidence of the kingdom of heaven, the order of true being.

In her book *Rudimental Divine Science* Mrs. Eddy writes (p. 2): "Healing physical sickness is the smallest part of Christian Science. It is only the bugle-call to thought and action, in the higher range of infinite goodness." The bugle call rings out clearly in Christian Science literature, for, as Paul says in 1 Corinthians 14, "If the trumpet give an uncertain sound, who shall prepare himself to the battle?" But the higher range and wider concern implied in Christian Science use of the word "healing" are clearly evidenced in the total body of testimony over the century and they are appropriately reflected in the present volume.

The following explanation of the book's structure may help to clarify its purpose.

The first chapter briefly describes the event in Mrs. Eddy's life which led to her discovery of Christian Science and eventually to her founding of The First Church of Christ, Scientist, in Boston, Massachusetts — The Mother Church — and its branches throughout the world. The period covered extends from Mrs. Eddy's healing in 1866 to her founding in 1883 of *The Christian Science Journal*. This monthly publication, together with the other periodicals which she later founded, contains testimonies of healing in each issue. In their totality, these testimonies constitute an important reservoir of source material on spiritual healing.

Foreword

The second chapter draws on that material as well as on various other sources to present a picture of Christian Science healing through the years. The healings chosen for inclusion are not necessarily the most striking; in fact, a conscious effort has been made to strike a balance between healings that would ordinarily be accounted "miraculous" and those closer to the level of common experience. Not all Christian Science healings are rapid, and examples have been included of cases which took years of prayer and regeneration of character before yielding.

To represent adequately the full diversity of Christian Science healing, a book many times the size of this one would be necessary. The selections in chapter two give no more than a glimpse of the tide that has risen since 1866. It is the quality of individual experience rather than the quantity of testimonies published that is of first importance; but it may be of some interest to note that approximately forty-five thousand testimonies have been published during the past eighty years. These are available to the general reader in the bound volumes of the Christian Science periodicals.

The third chapter considers the significance of this subject in the full context of Christian life and in relation to evolving human society. No one recognizes more readily than do Christian Scientists how far they still have to go to demonstrate the kingdom of God in its fullness — and in the face of an increasingly sophisticated materialism challenging spiritual values at every point. This last chapter examines some of the exigent demands to which Christian Scientists and all Christians are summoned by the bugle call of spiritual healing.

Mrs. Eddy herself faced consistently toward the future as she worked for the establishment of God's kingdom on earth. At the time of her retirement to Concord, New Hampshire, to plan for the continuity and development of the Church of Christ, Scientist, she wrote her students in Boston, "I am still with you on the field of battle, taking forward marches, broader and higher views, and with the hope that you will follow" (*Miscellaneous Writings*, p. 136). In paying tribute to this devoted woman whose vision, love, and sacrifice have brought the wonders of early Christianity into countless lives as active, glowing reality — as provable, contemporary fact — we are mindful of the words of Proverbs 31: "Give her of the fruit of her hands; and let her own works praise her in the gates."

This book has been prepared under the supervision of the Manager of Christian Science Committees on Publication. We are grateful to the members of his staff whose faithful labors have made the book possible, and to the Christian Scientists who have permitted the use of their testimonies in its pages.

The Christian Science Board of Directors

Chapter One

The Beginnings

1866-1883

Chapter One

The Beginnings

1866-1883

A CENTURY AGO a woman living near Lynn, Massachusetts, experienced a sudden healing from serious internal injuries caused by a fall on the ice.

A Lynn newspaper the day before had announced her situation to be "critical." Her friends despaired of her recovery. Her husband, who was away on a business trip, had been called home by telegram. Her minister had been sent for. The doctor who had attended her since the accident three days before saw nothing more to be done.

At this crucial point the woman asked for her Bible and turned to one of the healings of Jesus. As she read, the presence and power of God seemed to flood her whole being, and she rose, healed.*

The woman was Mary Baker Eddy (then Mrs. Patterson) and the incident marked the beginning not only of a great religious movement but of a great modern revival of Christian healing.

Healing had been a vital part of the Christian gospel in the apostolic age; indeed, it had persisted through the first three centuries of Christian history and had occurred as an occasional, unpredictable phenomenon in Christian experience through the intervening fifteen hundred years. But a century which prided itself on being scientific had relegated such healing to the realm of miracle and holy legend. Blind faith might be permitted to believe that it once had been possible; but rational enlightenment posited a universe governed by law, and miracles as a capricious setting aside of law had no place in such a universe.

* For interesting evidence relating to the experience see Clifford P. Smith, *Historical Sketches from the Life of Mary Baker Eddy and the History of Christian Science* (The Christian Science Publishing Society, 1941), pp. 54-61.

A Century of Christian Science Healing

An effort of imagination is necessary to recall the mental climate of that day. Though in some respects the scientific materialism of the nineteenth century persists today, the twentieth century has learned to accommodate itself to the idea of spiritual healing, even though it has frequently tried to explain it in psychological rather than Christian terms. The development of psychosomatic medicine and of psychotherapy in general has emphasized the importance of mental and emotional factors in disease, and this has at least accustomed people to recognize that physical healing may result from profound mental changes in the individual. To the Christian, his most profound relationship is with God, from which follow his relations with his fellow men; and in the Christian church today there is an increasing willingness to admit that a setting right of one's basic spiritual relations may result in physical changes which at one time would have been accounted miraculous.

This was far from being the case in 1866. The self-confident, mechanistic materialism of natural science had no room for anything but purely physical causes. Though the medicine of that day is accounted primitive by today's standards — as today's medicine will be accounted primitive a century hence — medical men were shocked at the concept of healing through prayer. Theology, too, was shocked that "miracles" which properly belonged to a remote age should be thought of as possible in the modern world.

Mrs. Eddy agreed that miracles as infractions of universal law were impossible. Like the natural scientists of her day and ours, she was deeply convinced that law governs all things. If Jesus had healed, if she herself had been healed by divine power, it was the result of law.

Even before her healing on February 4, 1866, she was certain that there was a law of God which, properly understood, would bring healing to every sort of physical and moral ill, and that this was the law which had governed the healing work of the Founder of Christianity. Through years of search and experiment she had come to an increasing conviction that causation is mental and that God's remedy for sickness must therefore be mental and spiritual rather than physical.

Now, in 1866, at forty-five years of age, she began the great work of following out the implications of what she had glimpsed at the time of her own healing, and of sharing her discovery with the world.

In the textbook which she later wrote, *Science and Health with Key to the Scriptures,* she explains her early steps in these words (p. 109):

"For three years after my discovery, I sought the solution of this problem of Mind-healing, searched the Scriptures and read little else, kept aloof from society, and devoted time and energies to discovering a positive rule. The search was sweet, calm, and buoyant with hope, not selfish nor depressing. I knew the Principle of all harmonious Mind-action to be God, and that cures were produced in primitive Christian healing by holy, uplifting faith; but I must know the Science of this healing, and I won my way to absolute conclusions through divine revelation, reason, and demonstration."

From the beginning she put strong emphasis on "demonstration," on practical proof of the validity of Christian faith and understanding. Jesus had said, "He that believeth on me, the works that I do shall he do also" (John 14:12), and "By their fruits ye shall know them" (Matthew 7:20). He had expected his followers to prove their discipleship by their works, and this was to be a continuing activity. "If ye continue in my word," he declared, "then are ye my disciples indeed; and ye shall know the truth, and the truth shall make you free" (John 8:31, 32).

If God, or Truth, was the divine Principle of all spiritual healing and regeneration, then healing could not be regarded as a personal gift. It must be open to all Christian *disciples,* or students. From 1866 on, Mrs. Eddy had abundant proof of her own ability to heal through the Christ-power, but an even greater test confronted her. Could she teach others to heal by the same method? If Christianity was truly Science, then it must be teachable, and it must be provable by any sincere learner.

Very quickly she found that she was able to impart the understanding which enabled others to heal — at first with some admixture of material methods but, after three or four years, by the purely spiritual means which she herself had used from the beginning. The success of these students drew others to study with

5

her, and so began the movement which has resulted in the world-wide spread of Christian Science today.

Only after nine years of practical demonstration of Christian healing did Mrs. Eddy publish *Science and Health,* in which she set forth the Principle and rules of Christian healing as she had discovered them up to that time — as well as the larger metaphysical implications of her new view of God and man.

That was in 1875. Four years later, under her direction, a group of her students voted to "organize a church designed to commemorate the word and works of our Master, which should reinstate primitive Christianity and its lost element of healing" (*Church Manual,* p. 17). This was the beginning of the Church of Christ, Scientist.

The healing of physical disease is only one element in the total message of Christian Science, as it is only one element in the New Testament; but it is an essential and indispensable part of each. In *Science and Health* (p. 150) Mrs. Eddy writes:

"To-day the healing power of Truth is widely demonstrated as an immament, eternal Science, instead of a phenomenal exhibition. Its appearing is the coming anew of the gospel of 'on earth peace, good-will toward men.' This coming, as was promised by the Master, is for its establishment as a permanent dispensation among men; but the mission of Christian Science now, as in the time of its earlier demonstration, is not primarily one of physical healing. Now, as then, signs and wonders are wrought in the metaphysical healing of physical disease; but these signs are only to demonstrate its divine origin, — to attest the reality of the higher mission of the Christ-power to take away the sins of the world."

From the outset Mrs. Eddy realized the importance of public testimony to the healing power of Truth. She could readily agree with the words of A. Bronson Alcott, the Concord philosopher, in a letter to one of her students: "A method so contrary to received opinion, and a faith so spiritual as hers, must of necessity encounter popular prejudice, and its truths proved by unquestioned facts, and many such." *

* Alcott to Daniel H. Spofford, March 15, 1876. Archives of The Mother Church.

The Beginnings

The first edition of *Science and Health* contained signed testimonies by some of those whom she herself had healed, and soon letters began to come to her telling of healings which had taken place simply through a reading of the book.

Today the last chapter of *Science and Health,* entitled "Fruitage," consists of one hundred pages of testimonies of this latter sort. They bear witness not only to hopeless physical diseases cured but also to the moral and spiritual regeneration which Mrs. Eddy saw as being at the heart of Christian healing. In a very real sense the book is inseparable from its fruitage, as the Bible itself cannot be judged apart from its profound effects on the minds and hearts and lives of people throughout the ages.

In the early years of Christian Science few people turned to it except in desperation, when all else had failed. Mrs. Eddy's own earliest demonstrations of the power of God to heal the sick and the dying were brought about in the face of almost total skepticism. Many who saw these healings were content to accept them as unexplainable wonders, without asking what they proved about the nature of God, man, matter, and disease. A single instance will illustrate this point.

About the time she was writing *Science and Health* she knocked one drizzly day at the door of Charles E. L. Green, a young businessman of Lynn, and said that she was looking for quiet lodgings. As Green described the incident thirty-four years later, "We told her that we had no rooms to rent. She said she knew that, but desired to get in that locality, but my wife told her we had no room to rent, and then said, 'You will have to excuse me, I have a sick child.'"

The child, Josephine, then three-and-a-half or four years old, was suffering from what Green described as brain fever. He had been called back from a business trip because of the gravity of her situation. On being told this, Mrs. Eddy immediately asked if she could see the child and after a little discussion the parents gave their assent. In Green's words, "Mrs. Eddy went into the room and stood at the bedside. She took the little girl's hand and spoke with her in a low voice. In about twenty minutes or half an hour she said, let me dress the child." Uncomprehending but somehow willing to trust her, the parents allowed her not only to dress the child but also to take her outside for a short walk. As Green later said, "We had confidence in that woman."

Their confidence was justified, for the little girl was well from then on. When the doctor arrived the next morning he was baffled to find her fully recovered, but dismissed it as inexplicable — in modern phrase, a case of spontaneous remission. The parents, too, told the story with wonder through the years,* but never felt impelled by it to find out how such healing could be possible.

It became clear to Mrs. Eddy that her own time must be given to teaching, rather than healing, in order to speed the progress of Christian Science. Though she continued to heal when need arose and many remarkable instances of this are recorded by her biographers,† her chief effort was to kindle in others the spiritual understanding that heals. In order to do this successfully the student must learn to say with Jesus, "I can of mine own self do nothing. . . The Father that dwelleth in me, he doeth the works" (John 5:30; 14:10).

In her classes in Boston during the 1880's she would sometimes inform the members at the end of their third or fourth day of instruction that she wanted each of them to go out and heal someone before the class met again the next day. With rare exceptions each of them did exactly that, though many of them were strangers in Boston. One of them, returning to his lodging house, told his landlady that he had no idea where to find a sick person, whereupon she said, "You can heal me: for I am totally deaf in one ear." Full of joy he ran up to his room and turned in thought to "the realm of the real" — the kingdom of God — where deafness could not exist. Instantly the woman felt a report like a pistol shot in the ear and ran up after him, calling, "I am healed." The next day fifteen of the sixteen members of the class were able to report healings accomplished since the preceding day's session.‡

* The Archives of The Mother Church contain accounts of this healing by people to whom Green told it, as well as Mrs. Eddy's own recollection of the incident. The words quoted above are from Green's own account.

† See, e.g., Smith, *Historical Sketches*, pp. 69–87 and Irving C. Tomlinson, *Twelve Years with Mary Baker Eddy* (The Christian Science Publishing Society, 1945), pp. 46–65.

‡ Archives of The Mother Church. See also the account by C. Lulu Blackman

The Beginnings

Much of the healing of that period has never been recorded. One of Mrs. Eddy's students who in 1884 responded to a call to help someone in Littleton, New Hampshire, wrote her from there:

"There is a perfect *rush* of patients. Three M.D.'s are sending me patients. . . I am turning away ten or a dozen patients every day that I cannot find time to see. . . It is God that is doing this work, but when it is done I shall be so glad to go home. It is late in the night. I have no time to eat drink or sleep."

Later she wrote that during her eleven-day stay in Littleton she had treated as many as seventy patients a day, giving each one a few minutes only, and that most of them were healed quickly.*

Although Mrs. Eddy herself was devoting her whole time now to teaching and writing, she continued to heal almost spontaneously in the midst of her busy life. A typical incident which occurred in the 1880's is glimpsed through a letter written to her many years later and published in the *Christian Science Sentinel* of July 18, 1908:

Leominster, Mass., July 2, 1908

Dear Leader: — I had an uncle by marriage who was a helpless cripple and who was deformed. All his limbs were withered, and on very pleasant mornings a special policeman would wheel him out on Boston Common in his wheel chair. One morning a number of years ago, he sat there in his wheel chair as you were passing through the Common, and you stopped and spoke to him, telling him that man is God's perfect child, and a few other words. Later, after you had left him, he declared you had helped him. The next morning he looked and looked for you in the same place, and morning after morning continued to do so, until one day you came. Again you repeated to him what you had said before, and this time he was healed and made perfect, — every whit whole; and after that he was able to go into business for himself and provide his own living. No doubt you will remember the whole circumstance. His bones had hardened so that when sitting or lying down his knees

in *We Knew Mary Baker Eddy*, Second Series (The Christian Science Publishing Society, 1950), pp. 8–11.
* Archives of The Mother Church. The quotation is from a letter by Julia Bartlett to Mrs. Eddy on April 9, 1884.

were drawn up and rigid, his brother having to carry him up and down stairs, and feed him and care for him all the time; but after he was healed through your spoken word, he was able to be as active as other men and earned his own living; and whereas before he could not even brush a fly from his face, he regained the use of his hands, and became more than an ordinary penman.

It was you, dear Leader, who spoke to him of the healing Christ and set him free, when you met him so long ago on Boston Common and many times I have desired to tell you about it, and to express to you my gratitude for the many benefits I also have received from Christian Science. Words can never express it.

With deepest love, in which my husband joins me,

Your loving student,
Mrs. *Charlotte F. Lyon.*

The phenomenal early growth of Christian Science is explainable only in terms of its healing work. Success, however, brought opposition as well as attention, and there were struggles and failures as well as healings and victories for those early students. After Mrs. Eddy founded *The Christian Science Journal* in 1883, this official organ of her church served as a means for giving practical encouragement and help to those who were striving to demonstrate Christian Science consistently. Before long, testimonies of healing began to appear in the *Journal,* and later they became a regular monthly feature of it, as they also did of the weekly *Christian Science Sentinel* when it was founded fifteen years later.

These monthly and weekly accounts of healing have continued to appear ever since in an increasing, ever-widening flow of testimony to God's redemptive, healing power. Written out of heartfelt gratitude to God rather than from a desire to "make a case," they are nevertheless verified before publication and in their totality constitute an unmatched body of evidence for the efficacy of spiritual healing.

The earliest published testimonies were often short, simple statements, signed only with initials, but useful today as records of the first fresh impact of Christian Science on the times. A random example of this sort of testimony is found in the June, 1885, issue of the *Journal*:

The Beginnings

"Am a journalist by profession. Broke down two years ago from overwork in Philadelphia. Physicians called it nervous exhaustion. Forbade me to touch a pen for a year. My wife has been more or less under medical treatment for fifteen years. Doctors' bills made a serious inroad on our small savings. I grew worse, instead of better. Then change of air was recommended, and I was absent in all a year, with no good results. Came home discouraged, to find my wife restored to perfect health through Chr'stian Science. Never heard of such a thing, only in a general way, and should have ridiculed it but for my wife's most remarkable cure. This was six weeks ago. Today I am a well man — eat, sleep and work as of old. Have not touched sedatives or medicines since my return. Christian Science has done it; and how ministers of Christ professing the meek and lowly spirit of their Master show such bitter animosity against a belief whose beginning and ending is based upon God and His promises — prayer and its fulfilment — is something I cannot understand."

C.

In succeeding years, as the church became better organized, a regular editorial procedure for testimonies was established. No longer was it possible for such a sketchy little statement as the one just quoted to be published. Each testimony must appear in print with the full name and home city of the testifier, indicating his willingness to attest to his statements before his own community; and a reasonable number of years must have elapsed since the healing in order to establish its permanence. In accordance with Mrs. Eddy's wishes, nothing which might be construed as reflecting on the medical profession or as critical of other denominations may appear. Emotional outbursts without solid evidence of regeneration and healing are not acceptable.

Each incoming testimony must be verified by three church members who know of the healing or can vouch for the integrity of the testifier. In many cases the accounts refer to medical diagnoses and prognoses, to X-rays, biopsies, operations, hospital records, and so forth; and the permanence and completeness of a healing are sometimes established by a subsequent — and usually compulsory — medical examination for insurance purposes, entry into the armed services, or some other special reason, as well as by the living of a normal, active life for many years. Further particulars on any aspect of a case may be sought.

A testimony reaches its turn to be edited about six to nine months after it is received, and at this stage it is processed to be set in type. When the time comes for publication, galley proofs are sent to the testifier and the verifiers. Each is required to submit a signed statement that so far as he knows the facts related are authentic and no condition has arisen which would render undesirable the appearance of the testimony in print. In order to protect the reader, no testimony is published where investigation turns up any unfavorable information. Date of publication of the account is ordinarily from one year to eighteen months after it is first received. A complete file for every testimony is kept for three years after its publication.

This process applies to accounts of healing published in the Christian Science periodicals, including *The Herald of Christian Science* in its various foreign-language editions; it of course does not apply to accounts in secular newspapers, magazines, and books, a few of which are quoted in the present volume.

In the case of testimonies presented on the radio and television series "How Christian Science Heals" and its successor program "The Bible Speaks to You," additional details have been carefully sought through long, investigatory interviews with the persons concerned.

In the early days it was frequently said, without too great exaggeration, that the ranks of Christian Science were "recruited from the graveyards" — and a great many people still turn to Christian Science only when all hope of recovery through other methods has been abandoned. But with the maturing of the movement and the existence of many second- and third-generation Christian Scientists, such healings have been increasingly supplemented by experiences which reveal Christian Science as a total way of life. Spiritual guidance through the complex problems that confront men in an age of revolutionary change is no less an evidence of the healing Christ than is the healing of an inoperable cancer or a fractured pelvis.

This does not mean that striking healings are less frequent today.

The Beginnings

On the contrary, any impartial examination of the evidence must convince the investigator that the volume of such healings enormously exceeds that of fifty years ago. But equally important to Christian Scientists are all the other evidences of the Christ-power in their lives: the sense of meaning and purpose gained, the enrichment of human values, the purifying and strengthening of moral character, the harmonizing of personal relations, the solving of business and professional problems, the unselfing of endeavor, the gaining of a sense of man's unity with God. All this is "healing" in the fullest sense of the word.

In the earliest days of Christian Science, as at the present time, the purpose in giving public testimony in regard to healing has been to glorify God. It was her all-encompassing sense of God as Love which gave the impetus to Mrs. Eddy's great lifework; it is in scientific witness to the power of divine Love that the value of testimony lies.

When Mrs. Eddy herself lay helpless in bed on February 4, 1866, her healing came as she read in Matthew 9 of Jesus' raising up the palsied man. That account concludes, "But when the multitudes saw it, they marvelled, and glorified God, which had given such power unto men."

Chapter Two

The Tide of Healing

Chapter Two

The Tide of Healing

MANY OF the experiences recorded in this chapter could have taken place at any time during the past century. The basis and rules of Christian Science healing have not changed since Mrs. Eddy discovered them. But social circumstances and modes of expression do change, and in the telling of each experience there is inevitably something of the flavor of its period. These testimonies record not merely the logistics of healing but the flow of human lives.

For purposes of convenience and readability, the chapter is divided into three sections.

The first covers the period from the founding of *The Christian Science Journal* in 1883 to the years just after Mrs. Eddy's passing in 1910. This was the period in which Christian Science gained a firm foothold in the United States and began to expand into other countries. The founding of *The Christian Science Monitor* in 1908 presaged that broader involvement with the world's affairs which Mrs. Eddy had foreseen from the beginning.

The second section covers the period of history roughly delimited by World War I and World War II — years when international developments and collective problems began to impinge more directly on the individual. The testimonies in the Christian Science periodicals during this period show a growing variety of backgrounds and situations, the increasing international composition of the movement, and finally the demonstration of Christian Science through the grim events culminating in total war.

The third section covers the remarkable years which have brought in the atomic age, the space age, the age marked by an explosion of knowledge as well as a population explosion, by a crisis of identity as well as a crisis of Christian faith. All these concerns are reflected in the testimonies of this period in one way or another, and the relevance of Christian Science healing to the new age is implicitly evidenced.

It is useful to remember that a published testimony of Christian Science healing is normally an outpouring of spontaneous gratitude rather than an endeavor to present an academic case study. In order to include as broad a variety and as large a selection as possible, within the limits of general readability, some of the accounts have been abridged, but always in the testifier's own words and retaining all details germane to the case.

1883-1914

In 1892 the *Journal* published several articles by Captain Joseph S. Eastaman telling of his life of adventure on the high seas and of the events which led to his first encounter with Christian Science in 1884. The series was entitled "The Travail of my Soul." The following account is from the last of these articles:

AFTER an interval of five years, each month of which furnished material for a chapter by itself, I started on my way home from Peru; to save, if possible, the life of my wife who for six months had been very low, and under the doctor's care. On my arrival, I found her much lower than I had supposed; and the consultation of physicians, immediately secured, only made it apparent that she could not live long.

One evening as I was sitting hopeless at my wife's bedside, a lady friend called and asked: "Captain, why don't you get a Christian Scientist to treat your wife?" To my inquiry as to what that was, she replied that she did not know, but had heard that they healed many cases without medicine. "Anything that will heal my wife I will get, if it takes all I own in the world," I replied.

In the room, at the time, was my nephew who also was under medical treatment. At close of the lady's call he exclaimed: "Uncle, if Christian Science is good for Manie, it must be good for me too!" I assented, and in a day or two his wife took him (he could not see his way) to a Scientist, under whose treatment he at once placed himself. His teeth, salivated by free use of mercurial remedies, had restricted him entirely to the use of spoon-diet; but on his return from the first treatment, he gritted them together and exclaimed: "There, Uncle! I can eat something now." This renewed my determination to look into the matter, in spite of my wife's protests and fears that it was Spiritualism. Accordingly, I accompanied him on his next visit to the Scientist's and myself had a talk with the healer.

At this interview I learned, for the first, the existence in Boston of a College whose president and principal, the Rev. Mary B. G. Eddy, was the founder of Christian Science; also, that Christian Science was not for one or two chosen only, for other practitioners were to be found. To my nephew I said: "If this healer can do so much, his teacher must heal instantly. I will take you there; then when you are healed, Manie will see what it is, and I will get the founder to come to the house and heal her." So, like a drowning man grasping at a straw, with alternating hopes and fears besieging me on the way, I led him to the College.

In answer to my request for a personal interview, Mrs. Eddy kindly granted us an extended audience; though to my appeal for help, she made the gentle announcement that she herself did not now take patients, but had instructed students who were well qualified to heal. At this, my heart failed utterly; for I felt that none less than the founder was equal to the healing necessary in our case. As I was about to leave, she turned to me and, with much earnestness, asked: "Captain, why don't you heal your wife yourself?" I stood spellbound. Never for one moment had the possibility of *my* becoming a healer dawned upon me. I did not know what to say, or think. Finally, I stammered out: "How can I heal my wife! Have I not procured the best medical aid, — and, to leave nothing untried, added to that my own medical knowledge? What more can I do?" Gently she said: "Learn how to heal." Without hesitation, I returned to the parlor for particulars. It seemed, then, that it must require years of study to learn Christian Science, and she whom I was trying to save would not long be here; but when I heard that the entire term required but three weeks, I gathered courage, and asked about tuition fees, which proved to be very reasonable. In twenty minutes more, I had arranged to enter the class about to open on the third day following.

My wife proved much averse to the plan; having, in addition

to her fears with regard to Spiritualism, due caution on account of the already heavy financial drain occasioned by her prolonged illness. I was ready to spend every dollar to save her, however, and continued firm in my resolve to go through the class. Thus the 22nd of December 1884, ended "the travail of my soul," since it proved to be the day of my birth in Christian Science.

The class included many highly cultured people, all more or less conversant with the rudiments of Christian Science; while I, a sailor, with only a seaman's knowledge of the world, and no faintest inkling of the field to be opened up before me, felt very much out of place indeed. However, God had called me there, and I had long since been schooled to say: "Thy will be done." To that first and last and most important question, "What is God," the students replied variously, according to their own thought, or to the technicalities of SCIENCE AND HEALTH, — which I had not yet procured. When the question came to me, I stammered out: "God is all, with all and in all; everything that is good and pure, — I don't know but it is the very breath I draw." The teacher smiled encouragingly as my answers followed one after another, and I was strengthened to go on.

Every day during the term, questions were asked and answers made that puzzled me not a little; but to all of my own simple and earnest queries, the patient teacher replied clearly and satisfactorily. The many laughs enjoyed by the class at my expense did not trouble me, therefore; for evidently my teacher knew that I would not profess to understand when I did not. The simpler my questions, the more pains she took to explain clearly; and thus were brought forward and cleared up many points that otherwise might not have been touched upon. In consequence, that has been admitted to be one of the best classes, as a whole, that has ever graduated from the College. All, except one, went into active work in the Master's Cause, and the majority bid fair to remain "faithful to the end." For myself, I am sure I did not want Christian Science in part; I wanted every bit of it.

How much was due to my own changed thought, I cannot tell; but after Christian Science was recognized in our home — even before I entered the College — my wife began to recover. Soon as I understood the rudiments, I began to treat her; and, so quickly did she respond to the treatment, that she was able to avail herself of the kind invitation of the teacher to accompany me to the final session. That one lesson dispelled her every doubt as to whether Christian Science had any kinship with Mesmerism or Spiritualism — for which she had strong antipathies. She became, then and there, a staunch friend to the Cause; eager to join the next class, that she too might become a Christian Scientist, and help to bless mankind.

My first active efforts in the Cause, aside from healing my wife, were made among my personal acquaintances, ship-owners and merchants. In response to my friendly arguments some let me relieve their suffering, while others only laughed at me for enlisting in such foolishness. My first patient was a wealthy ship-owner. He was happy over the success in getting rid of his ailments; but pride made him keep the good news to himself, instead of aiding others by his experience. Next, however, he engaged me to treat his wife and daughter, who, on recovery, freely introduced me to their suffering friends. Here virtually, though I knew it not, began my practice.

— *Journal,* Vol. 10, pp. 68–72
(May, 1892).

A subsequent article by Captain Eastaman, entitled "Early Lessons in Demonstration," told of some of his cases of healing. Later the Christian Science periodicals established an editorial policy which does not permit a practitioner to describe his own cases in this way. A testimony must be written by the person healed, and the name of the practitioner is not made public. An excerpt from Captain Eastaman's article is included, however, to illustrate this type of early testimony and because independent corroborative evidence of the healing exists:

DURING MY EARLY LABORS, a lady having five tumors around her neck, after having taken nitrate of silver till she was the color of a mulatto, came to me for treatment. Also, the throat was so swelled inside that she could only take liquid food, and her physicians agreed that she must soon die in great agony. In a few weeks the tumors all disappeared, leaving only the trace of the instrument where one had been lanced; and her complexion was restored to its natural hue. After many weeks, all trace of the wound also disappeared, and she returned home a happy woman. About ten days ago this same lady, bright and healthy as one could wish, called at my office and assured me she had been perfectly well from that time to the present. Only a practitioner in the same line of work, can tell the happiness that such testimony after so many years brings me. This lady and one other at that time successfully treated for the same claim, have sent me many, many others, who in turn have sent their friends for healing.

— Journal, Vol. 10, pp. 156–157
(July, 1892).

Corroboration of the foregoing case occurs in a letter written to Captain Eastaman by the young woman several years earlier and published at that time in the *Journal*:

I THINK it my duty, for the benefit of suffering humanity, and the credit of Christian Science, to make the following statement. I have been afflicted for years with five tumors about my neck, and one on my cheek, and have been under the physician's care for months. Last September my doctor told me, with tears in his eyes, that there was no help for me, that I might choke to death at any moment. The medicine he had given me had caused my flesh to turn quite dark, and broke down my health entirely. I felt as though I carried a mountain-weight of sin about me. I was advised to come to you, by Mrs. ————, and am thankful to say, to-day, that the tumors are all gone. My original whiteness has returned.

The Tide of Healing

My health is entirely recovered, and I feel happy and light-hearted as a little girl. Hoping that these few lines may induce others to put themselves under this treatment, I am,

respectfully and thankfully yours,

Marguerite Jones.

363 Pearl St., North Albany, N. Y.

— *Journal*, Vol. 3, p. 213
(February, 1886).

The foregoing material centers around the experience of a single Christian Scientist, illustrating the way in which the early healing work got under way. The testimonies which follow are presented without introductory remarks except where a brief explanation is needed:

Dear Journal: Please find room in your columns for these few lines; for mortals must know what happiness I have found in Christian Science. I have been quite deaf all my life, the infirmity being hereditary. I suffered when a child with my ears, for months together, so I could not attend school. About five years ago, some machinery exploded. A piece of the iron hit the side of my head; and the drum of my left ear was perforated with five holes, and my head was injured inwardly. For this I have been doctored most of the time. During five months my ear discharged blood and matter. There were times when I suffered greatly. Over one year ago the pain in my head became constant. I wished someone would shoot me, for life was a burden. I could not work, I could not read, and there was no hope of a cure.

I was told to go to Mrs. ————, a Christian Scientist of our town. I said to her that if I could only be relieved in my head, it would be all I would ask, for I could not expect to recover my hearing. The doctors all said that was impossible. Mrs. ———— said to me that all things were possible, through God. The second day after my treatment I received my hearing. I am lifted out of the darkness into light. I am a new man, free from dyspepsia of nine years' standing, free from all pain. I have my hearing, and am able to do as hard a day's work as any man in the county. Last, but not least, I appreciate God as I never could before, and realize that all things are possible.

Gustav Gericke.
Grand Junction, Colorado.

— *Journal,* Vol. 5, p. 525
(January, 1888).

I WAS a great sufferer, and also blind. I was persuaded by a friend to try Christian Science. I went to Maquon, Ill., and received treatment. My health began to improve, and then my sight came. Now I can say I am well, and can see, without glasses, to read and sew, and to thread a fine needle. Tongue can't express my joy that I can see my children once more!

Mrs. S. E., Trenton, Neb.

— *Journal,* Vol. 8, p. 129
(June, 1890).

I AM SEVENTY-SIX years of age, and I have practised medicine forty-eight years, and have been very outspoken in denouncing Christian Science. About three years ago my health began to fail. I tried all remedies known to me, but received no permanent relief. I called other physicians, who also failed to cure me, and after all material remedies had failed, I realized that I was failing rapidly. My wife asked me if she might call Mr. R. to which I consented. When he came I said to him, "I am almost gone. Everything has failed me."

He replied, Doctor, you are now ready to receive Christian Science. I replied that I had no confidence in that kind of treatment, and that I had been very bitter against the cause. He said, "That makes no difference," and added if it was my wish he would treat me. I said you may go on. I rested well that night, and the next morning realized that I was a great deal better. The following morning I was so much better that I did not feel like staying in the house, so I got up, walked a half-mile, attended to my horse, worked in my garden, and sawed and split wood all day. My health and strength have been improving ever since and I am now well. My wife and I have since gone through a class taught by Mr. R. I am delighted with the teachings of Christian Science. I love it, and I intend to live it, and cheerfully recommend it to all.

A. M. Overman, M. D.
Spearfish, So. Dakota.

— *Journal*, Vol. 11, pp. 136–137
(June, 1893).

The following affidavit was presented in connection with a legislative hearing on a bill which would have affected the practice of Christian Science healing:

AFFIDAVIT

Commonwealth of Massachusetts, } ss.
    County of Suffolk.

Joseph G. Mann, being duly sworn, on his oath states:

In November, 1886, I was accidentally shot with a thirty-two calibre revolver, the ball entering the left breast near the nipple. I immediately became unconscious, was carried into the house and laid on the nearest bed. On our doctor's arrival the family were informed that I had received a fatal wound; indeed so serious did he consider the case that he felt unwilling to father its responsibility alone. Accordingly three more well known and eminent physicians were summoned post haste. One of these was known in the city whence he came as a skillful surgeon. All four are to-day in the field of practice and their standing is considered as good as any in the medical profession, and in the community in which they live they are known as honest men. They examined the wound closely and carefully and concluded it would be useless to probe for the ball for if they should attempt this, or in any way stir me, I would die on their hands. They further concluded, that judging from the excessive bleeding, both internally and externally, and the peculiar color of the blood, the ball had touched the heart, and was probably lodged in the pericardium.

The doctors informed the family that they were unable to stop the flow of blood, and should they attempt this from without, I would still bleed inwardly, and thus bleed to death.

After a few hours they held a council in an adjoining room, and then told the family there was no hope, saying to father: "Mr. Mann, we are sorry, but we can do nothing for your son." In his sorrow and desperation father implored them to spare nothing that money might afford, send for any other help that might bring hope; but they said it would be useless.

With this verdict the three departed. While our family physician still lingered he kept the family informed that I was gradually dying; the body was growing cold, and before he left the house the eyes were becoming set and the death perspiration stood on the forehead. As he went out he said to our grieving friends that death was so near, the pulse was scarcely perceptible. All human help had now left, and the last hope of the family went out with it. So sure were the doctors of my death that they themselves told our friends and relatives, by the way, that they would never see me again alive. Telegrams were written and held ready to spread the news that I was dead.

In this last moment, Christian Science was providentially brought to our door. The family had never heard of this (to them) new method of healing and refused to admit the Scientist; for, as they said, they wanted no one to experiment on the dying whom the *doctors* had given up as hopeless.

They were assured, however, that the patient should not be touched or given medicine; and that "man's extremity has been (is) God's opportunity." Within about fifteen minutes after Christian Science had been admitted into our house I began suddenly to grow warm again under its treatment. My breath was again revived and normal. I became conscious, opened my eyes and knew

I should not die, but would live. That same evening I sat up in bed and ate a little steak and toast. The excruciating pain I had felt during intervals of consciousness while dying, was all gone and I was steadily and rapidly growing strong and well. Notwithstanding the great loss of blood, I was strong enough the next day to have my blood-saturated garments (which had dried during the night and had to be removed by cutting) exchanged for clean ones. Beyond washing the wound and body to cleanse them from the blood, no attention was given them. The doctors on hearing that I had not died, predicted that gangrene and other evils would yet set in, especially on account of the excessive internal bleeding, and this would certainly produce death. I however continued to improve. The same power that had brought me to this point of recovery, forestalled also the bad results which the M. D.'s expected. The second day I was out of bed and dressed the greater part of the time; and the third day found me up bright and early and about with the family as though the accident had never occurred.

That our mourning had been turned into joy is true, indeed; and to prove to my many visitors that I was really healed and quite like myself again in so short a time, I took my part with the family in singing our familiar church hymns; all were agreed that my voice was strong and sound. Relatives who had come to attend the funeral rejoiced with me instead. The wound healed inwardly and outwardly without any apparent inflammation, swelling, or suppuration; and meanwhile, from the fourth day on, I walked out to visit friends, rode with the family in carriage and sleigh over rough roads, and in all kinds of weather without sustaining the slightest ill effect therefrom.

Christian Science not only perfectly healed me after the medical doctors had failed and had given me up, but through what understanding I have gained, I have ever since been kept well. When I was first healed I experienced a little soreness during the first few weeks of my being about, but this soon entirely disappeared, and not a sensation from the wound have I felt since.

In the village which bears witness to my healing, is the home of my father, John F. Mann, where he has resided for upwards of forty years. I have no doubt that he, or any honest man, who was a citizen of Broad Brook, town of East Windsor, Hartford Co., Conn., where my healing occurred, will give his testimony to any reader who might wish further evidence than my statement of it.

Any who would personally inquire into this case are kindly invited to call on me at 418 Columbus avenue, Boston, Mass.

Joseph G. Mann.

Subscribed and sworn to before me this 27th day of February, A.D. 1894.

(Seal) Walter L. Church, *Notary Public*.

> The above affidavit is quoted in the reminiscences of Calvin C. Hill as published in *We Knew Mary Baker Eddy*, Third Series (The Christian Science Publishing Society, 1953). Mr. Hill, a close friend of Joseph Mann, added the following details from his own personal knowledge (pp. 35–37):

AT THE TIME OF the healing related in the foregoing affidavit, Mr. Mann was twenty-two years of age. When the physicians gave their verdict that death was inevitable, the grief of the family was intensified by the fact that it was a brother-in-law who had accidentally shot him when the two young men were target-practicing with thirty-two calibre revolvers. When life returned the joy of the family was correspondingly great, and their gratitude for healing in Christian Science was profound. It turned three brothers and two sisters to active interest in Christian Science.

The first thing Joseph Mann said when he returned to consciousness was, "Is this something I can learn, and do for others?"

He immediately began to study the Christian Science textbook, and many, upon hearing of his healing, went to him for help, and he healed them.

The Tide of Healing

When Mrs. Eddy was informed of his healing work she invited him to attend her class, which he did in 1888. Shortly after, he established his practice in Boston, and his sister Pauline joined him to keep his home. Ten years later, hearing of Mrs. Eddy's need for an overseer on her Pleasant View estate, he volunteered his services and left a growing practice in order to help her. In this same year Mrs. Eddy invited him to be a member of her last class, the well-known "class of seventy."

One day, when Mrs. Eddy was having a conversation with Joseph Mann, she questioned him in detail about his remarkable experience and especially about the regeneration which took place in him while he stood in the vestibule of death, a change which had come of an experience almost equal to his having died and then been resurrected.

Mrs. Eddy summarized the incident conclusively, I was told, in these words: "Joseph, you have had a *wonderful* experience; you were thrown violently out of the house, and picked yourself up on the outside; go not back into it."

Christian Scientists sincerely respect the unselfish efforts of doctors, surgeons, psychiatrists, and others concerned with alleviating suffering. If they themselves prefer to rely wholly on prayer and spiritual understanding for healing, that is because of their experience and basic convictions; but they in no way oppose the use of medical means by those who prefer them. In the words of Abraham to Lot, they would say, "Let there be no strife, I pray thee, between me and thee, and between my herdmen and thy herdmen; for we be brethren" (Genesis 13:8. See also *Science and Health,* p. 444).

While some testimonies in the early days of Christian Science made a pointed contrast between the writers' experiences with medical and with spiritual treatment, the good will of Christian Scientists is well expressed by a testifier in the *Christian Science Sentinel* (Vol. 25, p. 714) who had previously consulted some twenty doctors in regard to the aural vertigo from which he was then suffering: "I should like to say a word here in praise of doctors and nurses, who, in my experience, stand on a high rung of the ladder of human material effort to lighten the burden of suffering humanity. I am sincerely and deeply grateful to all those good, kind people with whom I came in contact during the period of the terrible affliction."

The following newspaper interview is included in this book to represent honestly the atmosphere of the time, in which several similar incidents were recorded by the press:

Mᴜᴄʜ to the wonder of some and the disappointment and displeasure of others of his patients, who had received successful treatment under the old school of practice, Dr. Frank W. Haviland, a well-known physician and surgeon of Harlem, quietly added to his sign of M. D., the words Christian Scientist, and refused to practise, even among his old patients, anything but the new Christian Science treatment, says the *New York Evening Telegram* of December 26.

Dr. Haviland is a regular graduate of the old school of medicine from the Brooklyn Medical College. After a successful hospital practice, and a residence of fifteen years in Harlem, where his success and popularity had built up a large practice for him, such an announcement on his part offered much ground for comment. Knowing of at least three cases in one neighborhood, where he had successfully performed difficult operations under the old treatment, it seemed to me that an interview to get the doctor's reasons for his radical change of practice would furnish some very interesting reading to his friends, patients, and the public generally.

With this idea in view, I called at Doctor Haviland's handsome residence, No. 210 West One Hundred and Twenty-Third street, yesterday, and met with a very kind and courteous reception. After learning my business, the doctor at once consented to an interview, saying, by way of premise, that as the principal thought of his life was to do good to his fellow creatures, and as he was now satisfied that he was able to do more good than ever, through his new practice, he had no hesitation in making the whole matter as public as possible.

The Tide of Healing

The manner, appearance, and conversation of the doctor indicated a man of intellect, educated up to a high degree of knowledge. Our conversation was continued as follows:

Q. Doctor, have you contributed anything in writing, through the public press or otherwise, in regard to this new faith or your adoption of it?

A. No; except an article sent out in answer to Ingersoll and Moody. Otherwise I have only given explanation of the new science in conversation — no public teachings of it.

Q. Heretofore have you confined yourself entirely to the older school of medicine in your practice, and may I ask from what school and from what college you were graduated?

A. Yes; I practised the allopathic. I graduated from Long Island College, Brooklyn, in 1881.

Q. How long have you practised the old system in New York and elsewhere?

A. The old system since 1881. After graduating I had considerable hospital practice. I practised here in New York, and had practised in the New York hospitals. I have been practising in Harlem for fifteen years last July.

Q. How came you to embrace this new faith with such devotion, and in what respect do you believe that Christian Science is better than the old practice?

A. My attention was first directed to Christian Science about nine years ago, and, being interested in any and all methods that offered relief to the sick, I at once purchased the text-book of the Science, *Science and Health with Key to the Scriptures*, by Rev. Mary Baker G. Eddy. I perused this book carefully from beginning to end. I then laid it aside with a promise that I would some day make a study of it, for I observed the fact that it contained much that required sober thought and pure desire for a higher spiritual life than most people are willing to live. I was at that time interested in medical jurisprudence and was desirous of finishing certain work in that line before taking up so deep a subject as divine metaphysics, which is the foundation of Christian Science. During several years following I made it a point to learn more about the practical results of treatment in the Science, and from all the information gathered

I came to the conclusion that if what I had heard was true the Science was far in advance of anything else in the healing art.

Several years ago I took up the study of the subject, with the determination to reach an unprejudiced opinion concerning its merits or demerits. When talking with Scientists, I of course opposed every point which they brought forward in its favor, and when arguing with its opponents I took a positive stand for the Science, and in this way brought out every argument for and against the subject, both as a subject and a Science. I must say that I was not religiously inclined, and was often blocked in my arguments by some quotation from the Bible, but having studied the metaphysics very earnestly I always had admirable weapons of defence, and finally brought out many points that I could not get by reading.

I attended the Sunday services and the Friday night experience meetings, and tried to live right. I found that the mode of living had more to do with gaining an understanding of the subject than reading and arguing, and one day the whole matter seemed to unfold itself to my consciousness, and since that moment I have had no shadow of a doubt concerning the absolute truth of the principles.

I took a course of lectures from one of New York's prominent Scientists, and, having an abundance of material upon which to demonstrate, I applied every understanding of the Science and religion to the healing of the sick and was more than pleased when most of my cases responded promptly.

Now firmly convinced of the truth of the principle and its application to simple diseases, my only doubts were regarding its application to cases of a more severe character and under a variety of conditions and circumstances. To investigate this part of the subject required more than ordinary study and patience, and the highest possible sense of justice. I watched the work of good Scientists on cases that I selected for them, and on every case that I could learn of where the facts of diagnosis and treatment were clear, and with but one exception, I was satisfied that the Science could do more than any method known to medicine or surgery.

The one exceptional case was surrounded by conditions of such a peculiar and intricate nature that I could not get at the bottom facts without meddling in affairs of a strictly private nature, and even in this most unfavorable case the patient was brought out of a state of profound coma that ordinarily ends in death within a very short time.

— Chicago Inter Ocean, Jan. 17, 1897.

Quoted in *Journal,* Vol. 14, pp. 598–603 (March, 1897).

As I HAVE READ of many cases of quick healing in the *Journal,* I thought my own case might encourage some one who, like myself, did not get help in a short time. Between eight and ten years ago a disease began to trouble me which the doctors cannot cure. I then heard of Christian Science, and thought I might get help there. I also sat in class during those years, and took treatment at different times from five or six Scientists, who were doing good work. Finally I was taken down to my bed.

I again asked for help in Science, but did not seem to get on well. My husband became alarmed and wanted to call a doctor, and finally did so. The doctor looked at me a few minutes, asked some questions, and said he did not think he could help me, but would try. He asked my husband to ride up to the drug store with him to get the prescription filled. On the way my husband asked him if he would call the next day. He replied that he could do no more and that I could not live more than a couple of weeks any way. I got no better, but continued to grow weaker.

My husband, now thoroughly alarmed, was willing to turn again to Christian Science for help (*I* had never willingly left it), and went for a Scientist who had helped me for other troubles. We saw a change the next day, and right along afterwards, and in three months from that time, I was entirely healed.

I hope this may encourage some one who, like myself, does not get help at once, to cling to the Truth, even though the way may seem dark at times.

Mrs. Carrie Swartz, Eau Claire, Wis.

— *Journal,* Vol. 14, pp. 350–351 (October, 1896).

A Century of Christian Science Healing

I ALWAYS eagerly await the arrival of the *Journal* and *Sentinel*. In the autumn and winter of 1894 my wife became interested in Christian Science to the extent of reading literature and attending services. Although I saw marked changes for the better in my wife's health, I was bitterly opposed to my then conception of what Christian Science was, and refused to attend services or investigate.

This state of affairs continued until some time in March, 1895. My wife announced to me one evening that she had invited the pioneers of the work here to visit us, and that they would be here on that evening. Of course I knew what it meant and was enraged, and I swore harder at the cow when milking that evening than common.

The evening was pleasantly spent. I made every effort to keep Christian Science from being mentioned, but like Banquo's ghost, it would not down. I saw that the Scientists were not ignorant, superstitious people, as I had conceived. I promised to attend services, and did so. I soon purchased *Science and Health*, and very soon found myself interested, in fact, proving its statements.

In the four years past we have had many beautiful demonstrations of healing, but the physical benefit is not to be compared to the reformation in morals. I had always been a man of the world. I was addicted to drinking and swearing. I had tried on different occasions to quit the use of profanity, but in vain. To Christian Science I owe all.

George M. Kochler, Bunch, Iowa.

— *Journal*, Vol. 17, pp. 512–513
(October, 1899).

M ORE THAN ten years ago, while practising medicine in Chicago, I became sorely afflicted with what was diagnosed under various names from nervous dyspepsia to cancer of the stomach. At first

The Tide of Healing

I took my own medicines. Then I employed other doctors to dose me. Afterwards I gave up practice and traveled. I improved for a time, then became much worse and put myself under the care of one of Chicago's best physicians, as a last resort I then thought. After treating me for several months, he said to me, "I don't want you to feel alarmed, for no doubt I can keep you along for another year, yet it would be well for you to put your property in your wife's name; for it would be much better for her should anything happen to you." I took his prescription and paid for it, but did not get it filled.

I went home and told my wife what he had said. She had been trying for many months to induce me to try Christian Science. I knew she had been healed of a seemingly very serious difficulty. Yet I felt that it was all right for others, but my case seemed to be an exception, and it could do me no good. She said, "Now you are ready for Christian Science treatment." I was. My last straw was gone. My last human prop had vanished. I went to a Christian Science healer, and in a few weeks I was free to eat whatever I desired with impunity. I then gained in strength and weight rapidly, and in a few months I was as well and strong as ever.

A. W. Paine, M.D., C.S., Los Angeles, Cal.

— Journal, Vol. 17, pp. 207–208
(June, 1899).

I HAVE just received a position as ticket agent for the Chicago and North-Western Railway Co. This has been a demonstration to me, for it came to me without asking. I have been studying Science for three years. I was an inmate of the Home for Aged and Disabled Railway Men, suffering with locomotor ataxia, but Christian Science has brought me from my back to be able to take this position.

Frank C. Prichard, Ravinia, Ill.

— Journal, Vol. 17, p. 661
(December, 1899).

A Century of Christian Science Healing

Repeatedly testimonies which tell of physical healings emphasize that the writers consider the physical freedom gained to be secondary to the spiritual and moral benefits received. A few typical comments from longer testimonies are gathered below:

WHEN I am asked, "What has Christian Science done for you?" I reply, "Christian Science has given me an abiding faith in the power of Good." I would not exchange this blessed gift for all that the world can offer. I look up with steadfast hope and courage since "I know that my *Redeemer liveth!*"

Evelyn White Nolte, Weston, Mass.

— *Journal*, Vol. 19, pp. 525–526
(November, 1901).

PREVIOUS to investigating for myself, I had thought with much skepticism that Christian Science was simply another proposed method for curing sickness, but I have found that I was quite wrong, not only in my skepticism as to the healing, but in thinking that this was its only purpose. For through the study and practice of this Science not only have my health and morals been improved but I have been raised from a worldly, godless agnostic to a God-loving Christian.

Louis H. Jordan, Toronto, Ont.

— *Journal*, Vol. 20, p. 561
(December, 1902).

I WAS hungry for love, but I knew we must give love if we would get love, and I did not know how to love till I learned the way in Christian Science. The way is that which Jesus revealed; the foot-

36

steps, self-sacrifice, toil, strife with all that is unlike God; and the reward, now and always, clearer glimpses of Good, God, and the certainty that, no matter how wrong things may seem to be, God is All-in-all.

Catharine Verrall, Brighton, Eng.

— *Journal,* Vol. 19, p. 718
(February, 1902).

ONE OF the greatest changes I notice in myself is, that I have a greater respect for other people's beliefs and opinions where they are sincere; formerly, I had very little.

J. F. Argue, Florence, Colo.

— *Journal,* Vol. 21, p. 44
(April, 1903).

THE GREATEST JOY that has come to me has been in the help I have been able to give to others, for in doing this I have reaped the reward which Jesus promised to them that would go forth unto the world, preaching the gospel and healing the sick.

Maude L. McLaughlin, Chicago, Ill.

— *Journal,* Vol. 22, p. 311
(August, 1904).

Christian Scientists do not claim to have reached the degree of spiritual understanding and inspiration which enabled Jesus always and instantaneously to heal the sick; and they are aware that even in his case the Bible states that when he came to Nazareth "he did not many mighty works there because of their unbelief" (Matt. 13:58). They are grateful for the extraordinary success they have had in healing and preventing disease, but they know they have to make further spiritual progress to fulfill the possibilities of their Master's promise: "He that believeth on me, the works that I do shall he do also; and greater works than these shall he do; because I go unto my Father" (John 14:12).

Today the record of Christian Science in healing every sort of disease is well established,* and there are large numbers of families who, over many decades and often through several generations, have relied exclusively and successfully on the ministrations of Christian Science for their health needs. In the early days, however, people usually asked for Christian Science treatment only as a last, desperate resort.

Then, as now, thousands were healed after all hope had been virtually abandoned. But the death of a patient, even if he had previously been given up by medical science, was likely to result in court action against the practitioner or family of the deceased. These cases tended to bring forth a large number of voluntary witnesses to the efficacy of Christian Science healing under the most severe conditions.

Such an instance was that of The People vs. Merrill Reed *et al.* The hearing in Los Angeles, California, in November 1902, resulted in the acquittal of the defendants.

Among those who testified in behalf of Christian Science on this occasion were a justice of the Supreme Court of California, a railroad executive, a stock broker, a journalist, a physician, a civil engineer, a court reporter, a county assessor, several manufacturers, and individuals from other segments of society. From the voluminous testimony given, the following brief passage from the interrogation of Silas P. Eldridge is selected:

Q. What is your business, Mr. Eldridge?

A. I am a hod-carrier.

Q. Are you a believer in Christian Science?

A. I am.

Q. When did you become a believer?

A. It has been about four years now, or a little over.

Q. Were you treated for bodily disease by means of it?

A. I was.

* See pages 239–243 of this book for a more detailed discussion of this subject.

The Tide of Healing

Q. You may state to the jury, Mr. Eldridge, what the nature of your trouble was and the treatment, and what the result was.

A. My disease was sciatic rheumatism. I had it very nearly all my life. When I was a boy I used to have it for six months at a time that I couldn't walk and couldn't get around at all; and I suffered terrible pains and it kept growing worse and worse till I got so that it was impossible for me to get around at all. I had to give up work, and when everything else failed I tried doctors — numerous doctors, different doctors.

Q. What length of time were you under medical treatment, about?

A. Well, about ten years that I was under treatment, taking medicine all the time.

Q. Very well.

A. I kept growing worse and worse until I got so I could not get around at all, and then after the doctors failed to relieve me in any way and I had got tired of taking medicine, I tried Christian Science; and I would say too that my limb was one eighth of an inch smaller around than the other. The flesh had simply shrunken away, and I became so that I could not get around, and there was pretty near a year that I could not get around at all. And then Christian Science found me.

Q. You took treatment, did you, by Christian Science?

A. I was entirely healed through Christian Science.

Q. I say you took Christian Science treatment, did you?

A. I did, sir.

Q. How long a time did you take Christian Science treatment?

A. I think I was being treated about three months.

Q. Were you finally cured of your troubles in that time?

A. I was not thoroughly cured at that time, but in a short time. I was free then. I went to work then, before that time. I went to work in about a month and a half after I commenced treatment. I was not entirely healed then, but by keeping on and reading *Science and Health,* I have been entirely restored.

Q. Making a study of *Science and Health,* you recovered your health completely?

A. Yes, sir.

Q. Have you been well ever since?

A. I have been well ever since. I have never lost a meal in three years and a half.

— *Journal,* Vol. 20, pp. 704–705
(February, 1903).

> It is sometimes assumed that Christian Science is effective only in cases of functional or neurasthenic disorder. While there is abundant evidence to the contrary, the unhappy individuals who are suffering from diseases that might be classified medically as neurasthenic in origin are fortunately not excluded from help by Christian Science, as some of the following illustrate:

On the 24th of March, 1902, I was working on the new station, South Eastern & Chatham Railway, Bexhill, glazing the covered platform, when I suddenly slipped and fell onto the concrete platform below, injuring my spine. I was taken to Hastings Hospital and detained one week, being sent out on the 31st, Easter Monday. The house surgeon told me to come again on Thursday, which I did, and then he told me to rest. The next time I went I saw a new house surgeon, who told me I was giving myself wrong treatment and that if I did not want to be deformed I must exercise my back and muscles as much as possible, for I was at the age when my back would set. The next time I went he told me he could not do anything for me, that I must get an out-patient's letter and see one of the doctors. He said I could come next day at noon and he would speak to one of them. Next day I attended and saw one of the doctors, who said he could not examine me without a letter. I asked him if he would hear me, and I told him all. He said the walking about was wrong, and that I needed rest. He also rang for the house surgeon and told him that he had given me wrong treatment, and that it might injure me for life. The house surgeon said it was a case that had come into the hospital before he came there, therefore he did not know the extent of the injury. I attended there for eleven weeks as out-patient, getting worse and weaker every week. I took drugs in the form of liquid and pills, also used a lotion for the back, the last two weeks. After the ninth week my doctor told me that I should have to go into the hospital again and have my back straightened, and that in the mean time I must lie in bed until they sent for me, as there were five beds wanted before mine.

During this time I wrote to a cousin at Eastbourne, and through her efforts I got into Poplar Hospital, London. I entered this institution about the 18th of June, and was in bed for three or four weeks, when I asked the doctors if I might get up. Whenever I asked them if I should ever be able to do my usual work, they would not tell me, but turn away, or say that there was plenty of time later to think of working, that what I needed now was to get fit for it. I was given medicine to make me eat; also pills and plasters, then massage treatment, until at last they said I must have a surgical jacket to keep me straight, for I was bent double, and though I could get my back straight with levering myself up with my hands, I could not do so without. The only rest I got was when I was on my back. I wore the jacket, which was made of "chemicalized" felt and steel supports, about one month before I came out. Though I was not well, I asked if I might leave, as I thought there were others who needed the treatment more than I did. I left about the 18th of October, 1902, and I went again to be examined in February, 1903, for the last time, for, though my doctor there would have liked me to stay, the hospital was full and I could not do so.

I was examined at the London Hospital on the following Saturday, but I never heard what the report was until lately. They called it traumatic neurasthenia. I was troubled with cold feet and hands, bad circulation, sleeplessness, no appetite, etc., and every stride I took brought me pain.

It was not until the 11th of June, 1904, that I was told I could be healed and be even better than I was before the accident. One day I called on a gentleman whose son asked me if I should like to to be healed. I thought at the time that he was joking, but he was in earnest. I replied, "Ah, if I could only be well, and climb the roofs as I once used to do!" Before I left, his father gave me two or three copies of the *Christian Science Sentinel*, which I read through and through, and he asked me to come on the following Friday for treatment, which I did, and during the four weeks' treatment I felt better in health than I had been for over two years.

On the 18th of July, while seeking orders, the thought came to me that I could walk without my surgical jacket, and on the 19th, when I got up I dressed without it. I then ripped it in two pieces, so that I should never rely on it again for support. I wished to keep on trusting in God, who is all Love, and who knows no evil, therefore evil cannot come from God. On this day I walked about twelve miles, also treadled a fret-cutting machine about three hours, and was not so tired as I had been when I wore the jacket. I have never felt that I needed it since I took it off. I can now say that I am thoroughly well. I sleep in peace, eat anything and enjoy it, and, though I am working from early morn till late at night, I never feel overtired.

Arthur Brook, Bexhill on Sea, Sussex, England.

— *Journal*, Vol. 22, pp. 777–779
(March, 1905).

I WAS A MISERABLE WOMAN, suffering daily with headache which the best doctors could not cure. I also had organic troubles which made it impossible for me to do my work at times without terrible pain. Doctors told me that I ought to go to a hospital and undergo an operation, they said I would never be well until I did.

I was very nervous and despondent. I had been taught to read the Bible and attend church. I went to different churches, talked with ministers and other good people, investigated every religion I could hear of, but was always disappointed.

They all told me I ought to love God, and then told me that it was by His will that I suffered, and that it was right to doctor for the troubles. I could not see why, if they believed that sickness was sent by a divine God for a good purpose, they should wish or dare to call in some man to undo what God in His wisdom had done.

I read the Bible, but it seemed to contradict itself, and to tell of a God who made mistakes and corrected them in anger afterwards. At last I gave up and decided that there was no God or heaven, I was sure only of the hell here on earth. I was never satisfied and was on the verge of suicide when a neighbor asked me to go to a Christian Science meeting with her.

I went, and was impressed first by the happy and loving faces about me, and then by the way in which each one seemed to lean on the promises of the Bible and the loving Father as revealed by the life and words of Christ.

As we walked home at the close of the meeting, I asked the Reader some questions, and was satisfied by her sensible answers, that those people had found what I had been wanting all my life. I went home, and putting aside all my doubts and fears, I asked the loving Father to show me if this were the right way, and pledged myself, if I found my headaches healed, to try to understand and live for God all the rest of my life.

I was so sure that Love would make everything right, that I went to sleep happier than I had been in years. I awoke the next morning, well and strong, with the glorious assurance that my Father is Love, and that He had heard my prayer.

That was my healing five years ago, and I have had no need for drugs since. I never asked to have the other troubles healed, they simply disappeared at that first meeting.

I cannot put into words my gratitude to God. I am also most thankful to Mrs. Eddy for her pure and noble life, and to the dear ones who helped me out of the darkness of doubt and despair.

Anna I. Sperry, Sandy Hook, Conn.

— *Sentinel*, Vol. 5, p. 561
(May 2, 1903).

FROM my earliest recollections I was well and happy; not a wave of trouble ever passed over my mortal sense of life till I reached the age of thirteen years. About this time I was suddenly snatched from the tender care of kind parents, from my brother and sister, taken away from all trace of civilization and plunged into an Indian camp, a helpless captive among savages in whom no element of the cruel and revolting seemed lacking.

The instructions of my devoted mother and her teachings were to me a heavenly benediction during the dark days of my captivity among the Indians, keeping me from despair and strengthening my faith and hope in life eternal.

I would often cry out to God, to deliver me from this awful bondage. I cried and God answered, for I was delivered.

When the name Christian Science first sounded on my ear, I was again a captive, though not among the Indians. For fourteen years I was under a doctor's care, confined to my bed for months at a time, unable to sit up or walk.

I could not reconcile my sufferings, misfortunes, and sorrows with what I believed to be our heavenly Father's will. Up to 1888, when I turned to Christian Science, neither *materia medica* nor prayer was able to heal my disease or give me rest and peace; but thanks be to God for the great discovery by Mrs. Eddy of the long-lost key to the Christ-healing, I can now say that I am well and happy in the joy of spiritual understanding which I have received through the faithful study of the Bible and *Science and Health*.

For the physical relief which I have gained through Christian Science I am sincerely thankful, but when all the horrors of an Indian massacre that had haunted my memory for thirty years were wiped out of consciousness, my cup of joy and thanksgiving to God was full and running over. The very heavens seemed open for a moment, and I caught a glimpse of the reality of good and the unreality of evil. In this spiritual understanding of God — the new birth — old things indeed passed away and all things became new, — the universe and man spiritual and not material. With this new sense of God and man I could understand how Jesus was able to say, "Father, forgive them; for they know not what they do."

In the course of eighteen months after I was healed I accepted an invitation to go to Grand Forks, N. D., to assist a Scientist in her work at that place. After my arrival in Grand Forks I was asked to treat some patients absently. Nothing was said at this time regarding these people, except that they had asked for Christian Science treatment. Their names had been translated into English and I was not aware that any of my patients were Indians until it was made known after the healing was done. I could indeed say, like Peter of old, "Of a truth I perceive that God is no respecter of persons." God's will was plain and I was then ready and willing to carry the glad tidings of great joy even to the Indians.

In due time I made several journeys to the Indian reservations in North and South Dakota, visiting the Indians in their homes and camps, the Government schools and churches. In September, 1892, I appeared before a number of Sioux Indians who had congregated together with religious thought in the Presbyterian church. At the close of the Sunday services the Indian pastor invited me to come forward; he introduced me to his people and interpreted the words which I spoke. Having good reason to think it possible that some of my captors were before me, I assured all those present that notwithstanding all I had suffered from their race, who had exterminated all my people and carried me away into captivity, that through the revelation of Spirit, of Truth, and the will of our Father-Mother God, that all the former fear and hatred toward the Indian had passed out of my mind. They all seemed deeply affected, and as these words were interpreted the profound stillness that pervaded the room was broken by a low, pathetic murmur from all present. The most intense interest was also manifested when I told them that I now looked upon the Indians as God's children, as well as the white man; that with our Father-Mother God there was no difference between them and the white people; that He desired His children to love one another as He loved us, and that they should all live in peace and harmony and go to war no more one with another. As these words were interpreted the low murmur of approval that again ran through the audience showed that the heart of the savage had become subdued, that it could be touched by feelings of our common humanity, and even respond to utterances of truth.

This interview was closed by all the Indians coming forward and shaking my hand, giving the Sioux salutation, "Ho," in token of their appreciation of what had been said to them, and the bright gleam of their eyes revealed a far more pleasing thought than that which I had seen some thirty years before. On another occasion I had the privilege of placing in the hands of the Indian children in the Government school at Pipestone, Minnesota, sixty-eight Bibles, in each of which I had written the pupil's name and, "On earth peace, good will toward men."

The news of my return among the Indians spread with great rapidity over the reservations and a deep interest was manifested everywhere I went among them. They looked upon me with awe, and regarded my feelings of good will toward them as wonderful, so they conferred on me the name Winyantokcha, signifying wonderful woman. One of the three friendly Indians was found who had been sent out under the directions of the governor of Minnesota at the time of my captivity, and who negotiated for my ransom. This Indian, now seventy-one years of age, had escorted me over a long and perilous journey from the camp of my captors to the capital of Minnesota, where I was formally delivered over to the governor. This Indian, accompanied by his interpreter, paid me a visit some two years later. While he was here I had the privilege of reading to him from the Bible and *Science and Health*. A copy of *Science and Health* was given them to carry to their children who were educated well enough to read.

When I turned to Christian Science for physical healing I had a sincere desire to learn how the miracle was done, that I might be able to help others. This prayer has been answered in the healing of many types of disease after the patients had been given up to die by the attending physician.

Abigail Gardner Sharp, Arnolds Park, Okoboji Lakes, Ia.

— *Journal,* Vol. 24, pp. 490–493
(November, 1906).

Something of the early impact of Christian Science is indicated by the many stories of healing which appeared in American newspapers during the first decade of the century. Though sometimes amusing in the typically journalistic slant they were given, these stories contribute to the general picture of the period. Following are several news stories from 1907–08:

The Tide of Healing

HEALS PREDECESSOR; LOSES $10,000 JOB

CHARLES K. URQUHART, formerly manager of the National Packing Company at South Omaha, has lost by his own act a $10,000 job in Chicago because he is a Christian Scientist.

Urquhart was transferred from South Omaha to Chicago to succeed, first temporarily and then permanently, the Windy City manager, who was supposed to be ill of a mortal disease.

After Urquhart reached Chicago, he visited his predecessor, who told him he had tried all kinds of physicians and remedies. Death seemed ahead.

Urquhart suggested Christian Science, which was not included in the list of failures.

The suggestion was taken. It cured the sufferer and Urquhart was out of a job, which his patient again assumed.

Urquhart is now in St. Louis, manager of the National Packing Company branch there, whither he was transferred after his healing exploit.

— Omaha (Nebraska) *Daily News*
(July 26, 1907).

MAYOR IS NOW A CHRISTIAN SCIENTIST

*Hamilton Official Says He Has Religion— Gamblers Fear Lid
Will Go On*

HAMILTON, O., May 6. — (Spl.) — Mayor William F. Thomas, in a public speech Sunday, before a large audience in the Jefferson Theater, announced he had embraced Christian Science and proposed to join that church. He said his Bible, which had been under the dust of the book shelves for years, was his daily solace.

CURED HIS SON

The Mayor gave as his reason for embracing the Christian Science religion that his young son had been cured by it. He said the boy had never been as other children since his birth — that he had been weak and anemic and that he had, at Mrs. Thomas' solicitation, finally placed the child under a Christian Science practitioner, with the result that the son was cured.

The audience assembled to hear a lecture by Judge Septimus J. Hanna, Colorado, one of Mrs. Mary Baker G. Eddy's most eloquent supporters. Mayor Thomas introduced him.

The politicians and gamblers of Hamilton are now wondering what is going to happen. The Mayor has always been looked upon as "liberal." There is fear that he will clap the "lid" down tight.

— Cincinnati (Ohio) *Post*
(May 6, 1907).

THIS PRIMA DONNA MAKES CONVERTS

Miss Ethel Balch, of Beggar Prince Company, Averts Swollen Nose

IS CHRISTIAN SCIENTIST

The teachings of Mrs. Mary Baker Eddy have been given an impetus in the Beggar Prince Opera Company this week.

To be sure, Christian Science had already a strong foothold among the members through Miss Ethel Balch, the prima donna, who is a devoted adherent of the belief. Miss Balch attends the Science church regularly on Sunday mornings and six members of the company already accompany her just as regularly.

But there were some more in the attitude of the Missourian, and these said, "Show me."

Miss Balch "showed" and she did it very effectively on Monday evening at Boyd's theater during the production of "The Mikado."

It happened this way. The plaudits had been long and loud after one of the acts and Miss Balch was bowing to her hearers just in the spot where the heavy drop curtain is wont to descend.

LOOKED BAD FOR NOSE

So occupied was the prima donna that she did not hear the signal that was given, and the big curtain descended right on the bridge of her delicate little nose.

It was a staggering blow dealt by some hundreds of pounds of weight, and managers, stage managers and company bewailed their fate at missing the services of the prima donna for some time.

Not so Miss Balch.

"I will be all right tomorrow," she said with assurance in her tones.

"Look at the swelling of your nose," exclaimed someone. "It's getting bigger every moment; you won't be fit to face an audience."

"You will have eyes as black as a prize fighter's," mourned someone else.

"My nose will be in perfect condition; so will my eyes. I shall play my part just as usual," asserted Miss Balch with so much certainty in her tone that it carried some conviction with it. Managers decided to wait and see.

The morrow came and with it Miss Balch, who wore a nonchalant air just as though nothing unusual had happened.

Members of the company stared, they could not believe their eyes.

It was surely Miss Balch with a perfectly normal nose, not a scar on it, and eyes that were as serene as though no drop curtain had ever come within a mile of them.

The skeptics were "showed."

Now Miss Balch is preparing to act as escort to a score instead of a half dozen next Sunday.

— Omaha (Nebraska) *Daily News*
(May 29, 1907).

CHRISTY'S SIGHT IS RESTORED

Famous Artist Is Once More Able To Draw

SAYS THAT CHRISTIAN SCIENCE SAVED HIM FROM BLINDNESS

Creator Of The Dazzling "Christy" Girl Was Approaching Total Darkness And Says He Was Healed in Three Weeks

[SPECIAL CORRESPONDENCE.]

New York, Nov. 17. — Back to the world of light and life and work; back from the dusk of creeping blindness which for a year and a half had shadowed his life and the lives of his wife and child.

A Century of Christian Science Healing

Howard Chandler Cristy, famous artist, has resumed the work which made him famous. When he had to quit it, because of his failing sight, he was a stranger to Christian Science; to-day he studies its teachings, and seeks to become a member of the church founded by Mrs. Eddy.

Christy tells in simple language the story of his healing. "Last March," he says, "I was almost blind. For a year and a half my sight had been failing, and I had done no work. I groped along the walls when I went about the house; I could not read the headlines in a newspaper. My wife, a Christian Scientist, suggested to me, as she had many times before, that I take Christian Science treatment. I had always laughed at Christian Science, but my plight was now become so serious that I grasped at any straw, and I consented.

"Twenty minutes after my first treatment I realized that I could see better, and my nerves were entirely calmed — the fear of blindness had left me. Three weeks later I took my last treatment. I was cured."

With Cristy's healing a great load is lifted from the heart of a beautiful and a brave woman — the "Christy girl." Her husband's future, her husband's work, her husband's ambitions were her life. The year and a half of his threatened blindness were dark days for her, too. But she, confident in her religion, believed firmly that some day he would be saved through the faith that kept her strong of heart, and so it proved.

— Albany (N.Y.) *Times-Union*
(November 17, 1908).

THE MUSICAL DIRECTOR WAS CURED BY CHRISTIAN SCIENCE

Crippled for Years by Rheumatism, Wm. H. Manchette Now Able to Direct Royal Alexandra Orchestra — Staff Inspector Stephen Stops Salome Dance — Notes of Local Stages.

CURED by a Christian Science treatment of rheumatism, which had crippled him for long years, William H. Manchette is now wielding the baton over the orchestra in the Royal Alexandra Theater.

For several years past he has been unable to follow his profession, for rheumatism had practically paralyzed him. Both arms and legs were affected, and he found it impossible to use the baton.

In Milwaukee he consulted some Christian Science healers, and underwent their treatment. He claims that it was effective, and eventually he was rid of the rheumatic plague sufficiently to accept the post of musical director at the Royal Alexandra. Needless to say, Mr. Manchette is eloquent in his praise of the healing qualities of Christian Science.

The past week has been his first as leader of the Royal Alexandra orchestra, and he has given good satisfaction. He succeeded Harry Girard, who filled in very efficiently after Mr. Arthur C. Pell was released.

— Toronto (Ont.) *Daily Star*
(October 17, 1908).

AFTER A NUMBER OF YEARS of constant suffering, resulting in a stiffened joint which rendered walking very difficult, and impossible save only for a short distance, I have been cured by Christian Science to such a degree that a tramp of eight miles over the mountains is a delight, and I am able to go about my business without being burdened with crutches or groaning with pain. In my left knee I had but slight motion, in appearance it did not bear the semblance of a human knee-joint, and not for a moment was it free from pain. Today it is almost normal in size and shape, the knee-cap being both visible to the eye and free from adhesions, and there has not been a sense of pain in it since the first treatment I received from a Christian Science practitioner, about eight months ago. At that time I was a mere wreck in general health; today I am as well and competent as ever in my life.

Having spent twenty-five years of active life in the Christian ministry, I think it but fair to assume that I know what the subjective experiences of a Christian heart are. I surely do know and understand these things from the orthodox standpoint, but let me say that I never had an adequate idea of the real nature and quality of that peace "which passeth all understanding" until, through Christian Science, I found it in the knowledge of the allness of God, and was enabled to understand better the teachings of Jesus the Christ through the light shed upon them by that wonderful book, *Science and Health with Key to the Scriptures* by Mrs. Eddy.

John Z. Armstrong, Ph.D., LL.D., Los Angeles, California

— *Salt Lake Telegram*
(December 28, 1907).

The bracketed statement at the beginning of the following testimony was written by the editor of the *Christian Science Sentinel*:

[A statement of the following very interesting case was sent to a popular magazine which had published the medical opinion that Christian Science has never healed any so-called organic diseases. The magazine did not see fit to publish Mr. Oliver's statement, but we are glad to do so, and venture to quote briefly from a report of this case which appeared in the *Journal* of the American Medical Association, under date of July 27, 1907. The article, which was written by one of the physicians who had attended Mrs. Oliver, began with this explanatory statement: "The following case is reported because it is, I believe, the first instance recorded of recovery from generalized blastomycosis." The conditions are then described in detail, one statement being, "The lesions in some instances, as on one of the fingers, destroyed the bone." The general report bears out the husband's statement, except where it says that she "lived much of the time out of doors." The article gives the names (which we omit) of a number of physicians who attended Mrs. Oliver, and concludes as follows: —

The Tide of Healing

"No medicine was taken after March 23, 1906. In August, 1906, the last sore had disappeared. I have seen the patient several times since, and she is apparently, at the date of this writing, July 12, 1907, in perfect health. She writes me under recent date, 'I am better now than I have ever been in my whole life, and can endure anything and never have an ache or pain.' The diagnosis of blastomycosis was made, not only on the clinical symptoms, including the naked eye appearance of the lesions and the exclusion of other diseases, — tuberculosis, syphilis, etc., — but by the microscopic examination of the pus from the wounds with a cultural development of the blastomyces. The culture experiments were made by Dr. ————. The patient was seen at various times by Drs. ————, ————, and ————. These agreed in the diagnosis of generalized blastomycosis."]

AN ARTICLE appeared in the American Medical Association *Journal,* under date of July 27, 1907, which gave a complete statement of the case to which reference is made. By way of explanation it may be said that according to medical opinion blastomycosis is a so-called organic disease, as unsightly as leprosy and as painful as any form of rheumatic trouble known to suffering mortals. To impress one with the severity of this case, it may be noted that the knife was used some eighty odd times, and that up to the present time there has never been a positive cure of such a case known in the history of medicine. It may also be of interest to know that the patient suffered from this terrible disease for over two years, and was treated by a number of eminent physicians, and that they agreed upon the diagnosis of the case as given in the medical journal already named. The writer of this testimony is the husband of the patient, and the facts herein related can be substantiated by any of the medical doctors who attended the case. The article referred to would give one the impression that the 'out-of-door' life in sunny California had a decided tendency toward the healing of this case, but the facts are that the weather during the patient's stay in California was rainy and disagreeable, which confined her to the house

53

during her entire stay, with the exception of a few hours which were spent upon the porch.

The patient was taken ill the latter part of May, 1904, and was not able to leave her bed except for a short period until taken to California in February, 1906. Upon her arrival in Los Angeles, she was refused admission to all hotels, hospitals, and sanitariums, nor was it possible to lease a house after the owner had ascertained the nature of the disease. At last, as a final resort, it became necessary to purchase a house for her shelter. A remarkable coincidence happened in the purchase of that house. After being turned from door to door, it certainly seemed a miracle to have the owner of that house recommend Christian Science, though she herself was not a Scientist. Like all others who have had to be driven into the acceptance of the truth, my wife scorned the idea of being cured in Christian Science, until she was told point-blank by her Los Angeles physician that her place was at home, where she could 'die among her friends.' Then came the resolution to accept the truth, and she did so right there and then. The physician was dismissed in the forenoon and a Christian Science practitioner called in the afternoon. Up to that time the patient had had little or no natural sleep during the entire illness, and had, during the past several weeks, retained none of her food. At this time she weighed less than ninety pounds, her normal weight being over one hundred and thirty. The rapidity of her progress under Christian Science treatment was almost phenomenal and unless substantiated by responsible people would certainly sound mythical, or, to put it stronger, like a downright falsehood.

March 28, 1906, was the last day that the physician called, and the first day of the Christian Science treatment. It may seem past belief, but after the first treatment in Science the patient drank two cups of coffee and ate several doughnuts and a plate of baked beans for her evening meal. She then slept after seven o'clock the next morning, and without the usual 'capsule,' too. Within a month she returned to Chicago, and although able to walk but little, showed rapid daily progress under treatment by a Christian Science practitioner in that city. In July of the same year she had regained her normal weight, and could walk and stand as much physically as she could prior to her illness. To-day she is the same, after having spent the past year in a trip around the world without a sign of the aches and pains which usually accompany such a feat.

David Oliver, Chicago, Ill.

— *Sentinel*, Vol. 11, pp. 203–204
(November 14, 1908).

A number of magazine articles about Christian Science appeared in the early years of the century. Some of these were written by Christian Scientists and include outstanding experiences of their own. The following example came from a man with professional competence in observing and describing disease. It appeared in *The Midwestern* (Des Moines, Iowa) in February, 1908.

WHY I BECAME A CHRISTIAN SCIENTIST

by Dr. Edmund F. Burton

The author of this article is an alumnus of Rush Medical College of Chicago. He served an internship of eighteen months in Cook County Hospital, Chicago — one of the largest hospitals in the country — and at the termination of his internship was appointed a member of the surgical consulting staff of the same hospital. At the same time he received appointment as instructor on the faculty of Rush Medical College, and held these positions until forced by ill health to leave the north. In Arizona he was Acting Assistant Surgeon of the United States Marine Hospital Service for Arizona. He is licensed to practice in Illinois, Arizona and California and was a member of the American Medical Association until he left medicine for Christian Science work.

I HAVE been asked to tell why I gave up the practice of medicine and surgery to devote myself to Christian Science work. I might commence at the point at which my thought was first turned to the subject, on the morning when I awoke to find that I owed my life to it, but it will perhaps be better to go still further back in point of time and to tell of the occasion and necessity for the help which came to me through this system.

About six years ago I was obliged, on account of tuberculosis of the lungs, to abandon my medical practice in Chicago and to go to Arizona where it was hoped, against expectation, by those who advised this move that the disease might be overcome; but the prognosis was that I would not live more than a few months. I myself had discovered accidentally the presence of the disease more than a year before the time of my leaving Chicago, but had delayed following the advice which I would have given to anyone else, partly with the hope that I could overcome the trouble without the aid of a more favorable climate and partly through dread of the life at a consumption resort. However, during the last two months preceding my leaving for Arizona the hemorrhages became so frequent and profuse that it was no longer possible for me to go on with my work, and I accepted what seemed to be the inevitable. During the year previous to my leaving Chicago I had been depending upon alcohol and opium in different forms to control as far as possible the symptoms of the lung trouble. It was believed both by the manufacturers and physicians at that time that in the form of heroin, (the diacetylate of morphine) opium could be taken without fear of the formation of a habit, and it was principally this preparation which I used.

After reaching Arizona I made use of the best dietary and hygienic means possible, and although for about two months my condition grew worse, from that time on there was improvement and I was able to resume the practice of my profession. The use of opium was abandoned for brief periods several times during the next three years, but never for any great length of time, although the tortures incident to the giving up of its use would seem sufficient to prevent its resumption. It is the common story, however, that the memory of these struggles fades in the presence of the demand for the drug.

I experimented with every means which offered any, even slight, promise of permanent relief, including hypnotism. As a last resort I put myself in the hands of the best known hypnotist in Southern

The Tide of Healing

California in the hope that a new suggestion might relieve me of the old one. I lived in his house, ate and slept in his company and for some time there seemed to be some temporary relief, but the result was the direct opposite of that which I expected and for which I hoped. I went to him to regain my self-control but, as a matter of fact, I lost what little restraint and self-government I had possessed before this experiment. I had voluntarily attempted to yield myself temporarily to the control of another human mind, and that which I had yielded had gone from me entirely. After this my physical and mental condition grew rapidly worse, until within a few weeks there was no reason left. After a period of entire irresponsibility lasting about a week and followed by unconsciousness for something more than forty-eight hours, a number of physicians who had known me for several months, in consultation, pronounced me incurable and told my friends that I had from a few days to a few weeks to live. A private sanitarium to which my wife applied refused to admit me on account of the hopelessness of the case, and they planned that I should be taken the following day to the state insane asylum. During the evening following this verdict a lady suggested with much trepidation the advisability of calling a Christian Science practitioner, and my wife consented that this be done, not with a feeling that anything could be accomplished, but in the same spirit of desperation in which any other harmless although probably useless thing would have been allowed. A practitioner came and remained with me three hours. At the end of the first hour I was sleeping quietly and when I awoke about eight o'clock in the morning it was with a clear mind and the absolute conviction, which has not changed since, that I was free and well. I asked what had been done for me, insisting that a radical change had taken place in my physical and mental condition. Naturally the conviction that I had been healed came very slowly to those about me, and it was months before it was fully acknowledged, but to me there was such a mental change that from the first there was no room to doubt. There is no need here to give figures, although I shall be glad to do so privately to anyone, physician or layman, but I will say so far as I know there is no instance in medical literature of the recovery of anyone taking the amounts of these drugs which I was taking up to the time referred to. And to one who knows the state of the nervous system and of the digestive organs which exists in such cases it is stating it mildly to say that the most remarkable feature of the cure was that there was no period of convalescence. From the time of my waking on the morning following the treatment there was no nervousness or twitching, sleep was natural and quiet, appetite healthy, digestive functions all in good working order and mind clear and composed. The same afternoon I drove my automobile for two hours without weariness or excitement of any kind. During the following thirty days I gained thirty pounds in weight. Within ten days of the time that I was pronounced incurable I undertook a most arduous trip across the Nevada desert, where unusual endurance and physical strength were absolutely necessary and I found that I had an abundance of both. Moreover from the day of the treatment to the present time there has never been any desire for alcohol, opium in any form, cocaine or any other stimulant or drug.

After learning that the condition in which I found myself on this red-letter morning followed treatment by a Christian Scientist I asked to see him again, talked with him and at once commenced the study of the text-book, *Science and Health*. I had not been able to read anything with any degree of understanding for weeks, but found that from that day my mental equipment was normal. Memory, which was practically gone, had returned to a great extent, although improvement in that respect continued gradually for several months. In short, I was not only free from the bondage of the drugs, but was physically and mentally restored to normality, and there has been no other condition since that time. Two months later I was able to lay aside glasses which I had been obliged to wear constantly for several years on account of compound astigmatism, and my vision since has been such that there has been no need to use them. About the same time and without any feeling of inconvenience I was able to abandon the habit of smoking which I acquired in early boyhood and with which I had had many a hard and unsuccessful struggle. At the time of the first treatment, although I considered myself practically free from the lung trouble for which I came to the Southwest, yet there was a quite large cavity involving the upper part of the left lung. Something over a year ago I learned that this cavity was no longer discoverable, but that so far as physical examination could determine there was healthy lung tissue filling the entire space normally so occupied.

For about fifteen months I studied the theory of Christian Science and investigated its results. As I read and investigated I found it not difficult to be convinced that it might do away with the use of drugs in the treatment of medical diseases; partly because I knew that medical men everywhere were coming to place less and less reliance upon drugs, that I myself had found their power most uncertain, and partly because from my own experience I welcomed the doing away with such dangerous tools. As to surgery I was much more slow in believing that mental treatment could be of any use, and it was not until I came to understand the real principle upon which Christian Science is based that I understood that it will eventually do away with operative surgery as well as the demand for it. I myself have seen a broken bone and dislocated joint restored to normal condition and function within a few hours, and that without manipulation, splint or bandage of any kind. I have seen a child of five years freed instantly from a congenital deformity without touch of hand or instrument. I have seen a woman, who, according to the verdict of the best medical talent, was within a few hours of death from cancer, restored to good health and spirits within a few days.

> Material relating to the cancer case named above is to be found in a book written by Benjamin O. Flower, crusading editor of *The Arena*. Though not a Christian Scientist, Flower collected in his book considerable medical testimony as to Christian Science cures:

THE CONFIRMATORY EVIDENCE in the case of Mrs. Belt who was healed of cancer, is exceedingly interesting.

Mrs. Ollie Malone makes the following explicit statement, dated Los Angeles, California, March 26, 1908:

"I hereby certify that I was a special nurse at the Clara Barton Hospital in the city of Los Angeles at the time Mrs. Mary A. Belt was brought there as a patient on or about the first of November, 1906. She was almost continually vomiting and suffering; was unable to eat or sleep or retain anything on her stomach for several days.

[Mrs. Malone's vivid description of the disease is omitted in accordance with the Christian Science conviction that detailed accounts of symptoms are undesirable as tending to produce fears and unhealthy images of thought on impressionable readers and thus sometimes to induce the very symptoms feared.]

"We were not expecting her to live through the night.

"About this time she was treated through Christian Science. Her brother, Mr. W. S. Alexander, remained at the hospital with her practically all the time, day and night, for five days. She appeared to rest easier and not suffering so much pain soon after she was receiving Christian Science treatment, and I think it was the second or third night after she was taking Christian Science treatment, she appeared to have expired.

"I was unable to locate any pulsation. This was about twelve o'clock at night. I immediately looked up the head nurse, and she came to the room with me. She called Mrs. Belt and then tried to locate her pulse. In the meantime her mouth had come open and the jaw turned slightly to one side, every symptom and indication that death had taken place, and the head nurse, in my presence, recorded her death.

"It was then that Mr. Alexander, her brother, stooped in front of her, and, placing his hands to each side of her head, he called her by name, 'Mary,' the second time, and she opened her eyes, and breathed a natural breath, and that morning she turned over on her stomach and had a sleep for the first time while she was at the hospital. Within a few days she left the hospital, and I regard it as miraculous and the most wonderful case of healing through prayer.

"I am not a Christian Scientist, and have told others of this wonderful case of healing, which I could never have believed had I not witnessed the same with my own eyes."

Mrs. Belt's brother, J. B. Alexander, who is not a Christian Scientist, in a statement dated Los Angeles, California, April 1, 1908, confirms the account of Mrs. Belt's suffering and the characteristic symptoms of her case and relates how, after her failure to improve under the hospital treatment, she asked her brother, Scott Alexander, for Christian Science treatment. Mr. J. B. Alexander's statement continues:

"Her improvement seemed slow. A couple of days after she had asked for Christian Science treatment, when I called by as usual, it seemed to me there was then no hope for her. She conveyed to me the idea that she expected soon to expire, and had grasped my hand, but my brother Scott assured us both that all would be well, and I was much impressed with the firmness of his statement.

"The next morning I called by I noted a marked improvement, and learned that she had for the first time in several days had sleep. She soon began to eat and relish her food, and within a few days left the hospital very happy. She soon regained the flesh she had lost, and we all recognized the fact that she has been healed through Christian Science treatment.

"I am not a member of the Christian Science church, although the religion appeals to me as beautiful and consistent with the Scriptures."

Mrs. Belt's own affidavit goes into detail as to her experiences and conditions prior to her healing by Christian Science and dwells at length on her condition before and after taking Christian Science treatment. "I felt that death was near, and told my brother, even if I died, I felt that my soul had been saved. I don't just remember what expressions my brother made, but he would never admit that I would die. He would tell me that life was spiritual and eternal, that in God, in Spirit, we move and live and have our being, and similar statements.

"When I became unconscious, or after I had expired, I do not know for how long, when I became aroused, or awoke from that condition, I felt and knew that I was healed. Such a change had taken place, and I was made exceedingly happy. I was thirsty and hungry and asked for water, which was given me, and I asked for an apple. A half of an apple was found, which I relished, and I turned on my stomach and had a sweet sleep for the first time for about nine days. The next morning my brother brought me a lot of figs and grapes and I had other things to eat, and on that day I sat up in a chair part of the day. The next day I walked about the place, and that evening I had a hearty meal, including corn bread and breakfast bacon, and the next day, with others of the family and friends went up into the roof-garden. The following day, my brother called by with a carriage for me, and we enjoyed a long drive.

"I had been reduced in weight to 105 pounds. Within a few months I regained my normal weight of about 145 pounds."

> — B. O. Flower, *Christian Science As a Religious
> Belief and a Therapeutic Agent* (Boston,
> 1910), pp. 92–97.

The next group of testimonies are taken from a pamphlet presenting the right of Christian Scientists to rely on God for healing:

IN THE MONTH of February, 1906, my little daughter, then ten months old, was taken very ill. After a little time a doctor was called, who after a careful examination first pronounced the ailment bronchial pneumonia, which two days later was complicated by spinal meningitis. He tried various material remedies, without any success, and as she grew worse, frankly admitted he could do no more. After such a declaration I insisted on having Christian Science treatment (as I knew some little about it); but as I was alone in that belief, the suggestion of a baby specialist from the doctor was eagerly accepted by my husband; and one of the best in the city was called. The hope he held out was that if the child's strength lasted until the awful disease ran its course, which would take all the way from a month to six weeks, she might live; but if she did, there was no telling in what condition she might be left, as patients rarely recovered from this disease without some deformity remaining. Later another physician, who had been called from Indiana, confirmed this opinion.

I had Christian Science treatment for her, as it seemed to be right to do after such material laws had been made. (The doctor still came and left medicine, but it was not once given.) After the first treatment the child's body relaxed. The little hands and feet that were so out of shape, in three or four hours had become straight; while her temperature dropped (from 106) three degrees in two hours, and by the next day was normal. The condition of the throat and lungs changed in twelve hours to a natural state, and in three days after the treatment began the child was healed. This was much to the doctor's surprise, and a few days later he admitted he had never known of such a remarkable cure and dismissed the case. There were no bad effects in any way, and today the child is perfect in every way, showing that the truth so beautifully demonstrated has lost none of its power.

It is needless to say that we are more than grateful for all this good that is ours just for the accepting.

Mrs. F. M. Ball, Chicago, Ill.

— Christian Science and Legislation
(The Christian Science Publishing
Society, 1909), pp. 76–77.

Early in the year 1896 our boy of two years was taken ill, and the regular physician was called. The boy grew no better under his treatment, but lay helplessly on his back, unable to walk or stand. After giving this physician a reasonable trial, we called another, and finally a third and fourth, with no better result. All stood high in their profession, yet each diagnosed the case differently. When summer came, and the boy's condition had not improved, we took him to the country to see what good air and nature could accomplish. While there, some one suggested that we consult a spinal specialist. This we did immediately on our return to the city, and the fifth diagnosis was Pott's disease of the spine. The boy was put in the care of the best specialists in Boston, and while under their charge was either kept on his back, strapped down tightly to a canvas stretcher, or incased in a heavy steel brace with an auxiliary head support, which allowed no movement of head or neck in any direction. After several months the boy walked, but in spite of all precautions, grew deformed. At the end of six years' treatment with local specialists we took him to celebrated orthopedic specialists in St. Louis, in whose charge he remained four years. Except for superior mechanical appliances, the treatment was practically the same. A night brace was substituted for the stretcher, but under no consideration was the boy allowed to be at any time, day or night, without support, and I was told by the chief specialist in charge that it would be necessary for him to wear a brace or support until he reached manhood. In the mean time another complication had arisen in the form of acute bronchitis, which developed rapidly and seriously. Again physicians were consulted, both in Boston and New York. This time the diagnosis was similar, the drugs various but ineffectual, and lastly came the verdict that the boy must be taken away from the east winds.

We were preparing to make the change needful to save his life, when Christian Science was recommended to us. At first we ridiculed the idea; then, believing it could do no harm, if not any good, we decided to give it a short trial. A near-by practitioner was found, and the boy put in her charge Jan. 29, 1907. The bronchial attacks ceased from that time, and have never returned. After three weeks' treatment the braces, which he had not been without for ten years, were taken off — they were needed no longer, for the boy was well. During the past year he has grown stronger, straighter, and added between one and two inches to his height. It now seems as if the harder the east wind blows the healthier he gets. He engages in all boyish sports and walks between four and five miles each day to and from school.

Mrs. J. W. Robbins, Boston, Mass.

My attention having recently been called to a book the writer of which attacks Christian Science, challenges proof of its cures, and refers to those who seek such cures as "the adult ignorant" who are in need of state supervision, I desire to tell something of my own experience with Christian Science. A little over a year ago I was a "scoffer" as regards Christian Science, but the healing of my son changed my views entirely.

After years of appeal to the best physicians, and finding "no arm to save," we were at the point of despair when friends recommended Christian Science, and we finally determined to try it, in the hope that the bronchial trouble might be alleviated. Our confidence did not extend to the possible cure of the spinal condition mentioned by my wife, but we placed him in the hands of a good practitioner, burning all *materia medica* bridges behind us. In three weeks he was not only free from the bronchial and rheumatic trouble, but also from the spinal trouble. The braces worn for over ten years were taken off, and the boy was well. This was in February, 1907. In spite of the unusually severe weather of that spring, he had no trouble of a bronchial nature and was absent from school only two days, whereas previously he lost more than half his schooling. Last fall he walked nearly five miles to and from school and even essayed to play "Rugby." He has grown more than ever before in the same length of time. He has had no medicine, nor has he used the braces since February, 1907.

As to "ocular demonstration" in proof of the above, we can show the brace worn so long, the record of growth before and after Christian Science treatment, and also a letter written to us a short time before we tried Christian Science, by the eminent specialist who had the case, telling us that not even the auxiliary head support could, in his judgment, be removed.

John W. Robbins, Boston, Mass.

— Christian Science and Legislation
pp. 97–101.

IN NOVEMBER, 1907, it became necessary for me to have an upper tooth extracted. Owing to the diseased condition of the tooth, and complications, the wall of the antrum was punctured and the jawbone splintered, resulting in the formation of an abscess and proud flesh. One dentist insisted upon immediate treatment, because the conditions had become chronic. Another dentist, whom I had requested to examine the wound, informed me that the case was one for a competent dental surgeon, and recommended an immediate operation.

The fragments of the truth that I had gathered from the study of the Christian Science text-book led me to seek the aid of a Christian Science practitioner, rather than trust my case to surgery, and the divine guidance in this was fully demonstrated. The case was completely met in the first treatment, so far as the pain, etc., were concerned, and in a short time the wound was completely and perfectly healed. During the healing process, seven splinters of bone came out through the gum, without causing any pain. Later, I returned to consult the dentist who had recommended an operation, and after a careful examination he assured me that the healing was perfect. He also told me that the operation necessary in such a case would have been a difficult one to perform and was rarely successful.

Cora R. Sinzich, Chicago, Ill.

[This testimony is accompanied by the following certificate. — Editor.]

Chicago, Ill., Aug. 30, 1949.

Miss Cora R. Sinzich.
This is to certify that I made an examination during the period of the diseased condition, finding a typical antral puncture. That I made an examination about six weeks after, and found that there had been a perfect healing of the gum and of the pathological conditions. That I have made an examination of the gums today, which is about eighteen months subsequent to the second examination, and find nothing to indicate that there was ever anything wrong.

Very truly yours,
Frank E. Cheeseman, D.D.S.

— *Christian Science and Legislation*
pp. 79–80.

The Tide of Healing

IN JANUARY, 1908, my wife was operated upon for a rapidly growing cancer, a malignant form of epithelioma. Three excisions were made. Underneath one a tumor was found and removed. The operation by a chief surgeon and four assistants, with four hospital attendants, consumed two and a half hours. The specimens were examined by the highest authorities, and pronounced epithelioma. Before the wounds were fairly healed, the growth rapidly reappeared, with incidental pain and malignant appearance. After examination, the surgeon declared that another operation was necessary, and that immediately. This my wife positively refused to undergo, stating that when she could no longer endure the pain she would jump in the lake.

My grandfather and his sons had all been surgeons, and for a number of years I devoted all my time to surgery, and up to this time I had never known of a case of cancer being cured by anybody, anywhere. If a so-called case was pronounced a cure — "it was not cancer." I had no hope of staying the disease, and was in utter despair concerning the matter. By a casual friend I was advised to try Christian Science, and was told of a practitioner, to whom I appealed for assistance. He told me to have no anxiety over the matter, and assured me that my wife would be healed and would be perfectly well again. I brought her to see him. The pain soon left her, and she was able to sleep at night for the first time in many weeks. The cancerous growth gradually dwindled away and disappeared; the parts became healthy and healed, and she is now well and strong as ever.

In this connection I feel impelled to relate another demonstration, a case of malignant carcinoma, which was healed by the same practitioner in one treatment. A prominent business man of Chicago had been operated upon for cancer of the breast in June. Six weeks later he sent for me to visit him, stating that he was in a hopeless condition; that the next day he was to go under the knife again, and that he did not expect to live long. After a discussion he concluded to accept my advice and seek the aid of Christian Science, and on the same day, at three o'clock, I went with him to the practitioner. I waited for him in the reception-room, and at half-past five o'clock he came out to me, and grasping both my hands, with tears in his eyes, said, "Forgive me for what I said to you of Christian Science. I am better, the pain has left me, the fever has ceased!" By one treatment he was healed, and in two weeks left for Old Mexico, by way of California, into the wild mining country, in the saddle, requiring great physical endurance, — well and happy and grateful.

I am thankful for the great privilege of writing concerning the above-stated facts, and sincerely hope that an influence for good may be exerted in the minds of all who may read these lines.

C. H. Washburn, Chicago, Ill.

[The following letter from the medical department of the Columbus Laboratories, to the attending physician, is in confirmation of Dr. Washburn's statement regarding the character of the disease from which his wife was healed in Christian Science. — EDITOR.]

Chicago, Ill., Jan. 20, 1908.

Dr. C. E. Sayre, 3946 Drexel Boulevard, City.

Dear Doctor: — Referring to your specimen of tissue submitted to us Jan. 17, from Mrs. Dr. Washburn, we wish to report as follows: —

This is an epithelioma. It is slow growing apparently. There is a fair amount of infection of the epithelioma. The mitosis is very atypical. These sections do not suggest much metastasis.

Thanking you for this specimen, we remain,

Very truly yours,
The Columbus Laboratories.

— Christian Science and Legislation
pp. 81–83.

SIX YEARS ago, on July 4, 1903, I was set free from the ravages of an internal cancer which the doctors in Charleston, W. Va., and in

The Tide of Healing

Lexington, Ky., had pronounced incurable. Three physicians in Lexington agreed that a small chance for my life lay in an operation, at the same time disagreeing in the opinion relative to my being strong enough to undergo the ordeal.

Pending this indecision, my husband, distressed and anxious, sought and found a Christian Science practitioner, who was summoned to me during the middle of the afternoon of the day above noted. Five treatments followed, though I was practically healed by the first one. Within a week's time I was doing the housework, and was able to give my testimony at the following Wednesday evening service.

Mrs. Sarah Runyan, Tuscumbia, Ala.

— Christian Science and Legislation
p. 86.

I wish to witness to the help which Christian Science has brought me. I was cured of an abnormal growth, from which I had suffered for seven years, also of fever and headache. A short time ago the words of our Leader, "Divine Love always has met and always will meet every human need" (*Science and Health*, p. 494), were made very plain to me. I retired at night feeling as well as usual, but about two hours later I awoke with a high fever and was in great pain, so that I could not even make a light. I vomited frequently, continuing to do so all night, and when dawn came I was startled to find I had been vomiting blood. I was entirely alone, and when my servant-boy came at about seven o'clock, he was so frightened that he ran for two native women, and they sent for a doctor; but I refused to take any medicine. I have a Christian Science friend at Huigra, one hundred and fifty miles from here, to whom I sent a message asking for help, and as soon as the message was received I was healed; the pain left, the vomiting ceased, and I went to sleep. By four o'clock in the afternoon I was up, and the boy and the two women were surprised to see me about as if nothing had happened. Truly it was nothing to God's idea, as had been proved with the help of my friend.

I am thankful to God for Christian Science, and grateful to Mrs. Eddy for showing us the way out of human ills.

Mrs. R. H. Hunter, Latacunga, Ecuador, South America.

— *Sentinel,* Vol. 16, p. 475
(February 14, 1914).

The testimonies in the first section of this chapter have been mainly of physical healing. In this respect they are representative of the first half-century of Christian Science. Some of the medical references in them have the horse-and-buggy flavor of that age. But these almost random samples are not offered as clinical evidence or for the purpose of comparison with other methods of healing; they are offered as evidence of the first startling impact of a new awareness of the healing power of divine Love.

Probably a larger proportion tell of quick healings than in the other two sections. This is not because there are fewer or less effective healings later; on the contrary, there are vastly more, but they are part of a widening spectrum of healing involving a greater variety of problems and demands on Christian character. The earlier period reflects the fact that most people turned to Christian Science out of sheer desperation, but in all periods the great substratum of healing has been composed of the little day-by-day overcomings which may seem almost too small to be committed to writing.

The individual whose introduction to Christian Science is through a sudden, remarkable healing learns later the truth of Mrs. Eddy's words in *Science and Health* (p. 4): "What we most need is the prayer of fervent desire for growth in grace, expressed in patience, meekness, love, and good deeds. To keep the commandments of our Master and follow his example, is our proper debt to him and the only worthy evidence of our gratitude for all that he has done." This is the "evidence" which Christian Scientists feel can be furnished only by their lives.

The Tide of Healing

The editorial below is typical of scores that appeared in leading newspapers following Mrs. Eddy's passing:

THE DEATH in her ninetieth year of Mrs. Mary Baker Eddy, Founder and Leader of the Christian Science church and system of faith, is an event that will profoundly stir practically every city and community throughout the United States, so universal was the spread of her doctrines and the congregations of her followers. Already from her adherents have come expressions of regret and outpourings of love — all of these tinctured with a beautiful faith of the orthodox Christian kind which allows the believer in the gospel of Jesus Christ to say over the bier of a beloved one: "She is not dead, but sleeping."

As to the doctrines of Christian Science which Mrs. Eddy promulgated with such success, there is still a wide diversity of opinion, but we think all will agree that there is much that is inspiring and helpful, even to the most orthodox, in Mrs. Eddy's teachings; and the unprejudiced, those not of her faith, but of open mind, must in justice admit that her work, through long years, was always for the betterment and the uplift of mankind.

"God is my life" are reputed to be her last written words; words of strong faith that, could they be reechoed by every man, would make the world a happier and better place to live in. Hers was the gospel of salvation by work aided by prayer, and perhaps the one point on which those outside of her church were unable to follow her was in her positive belief in the efficacy of prayer to resolve all human doubts and cure all human ills. But, even in our inability to follow Mrs. Eddy thus far, we are, after all, but confessing that our faith in God's word was less than hers.

> — Washington, D.C., *Herald,*
> December 6, 1910, quoted in
> *Editorial Comments on the*
> *Life and Work of Mary Baker Eddy*
> (The Christian Science Publishing
> Society, 1911), pp. 32-33.

A Century of Christian Science Healing

1914-1945

In 1903 Mrs. Eddy had founded *Der Herold der Christlichen Wissenschaft*, a periodical in German and English, "to proclaim the universal activity and availability of Truth" (*The First Church of Christ, Scientist, and Miscellany*, p. 353).

Christian Science was already well established in various English-speaking countries and had a number of adherents in Europe, particularly in Germany. Testimonies were coming in to the periodicals from many parts of the world. But it was clear that Christian Scientists whose native tongue was not English would need literature in their own languages to help them advance in the understanding of Christian Science.

In 1918 before the end of the First World War, a French edition of the same periodical appeared, to be known as *Le Héraut de La Science Chrétienne*. Later as other editions appeared in other languages, it became customary to refer to the periodical generically as *The Herald of Christian Science*. At present, monthly or quarterly issues appear in the following languages: Danish, Dutch, French, German, Greek, Indonesian, Italian, Japanese, Norwegian, Portuguese, Spanish, Swedish, and English Braille. In each case the English is printed on the page opposite the translation. In addition, short religious articles in these and other languages, including Afrikaans, Arabic, Finnish, Hebrew, Polish, and Russian, appear regularly on the Home Forum page of *The Christian Science Monitor*.

The testimonies that follow reflect this broadening geographical background. There is some freedom in the chronological sequence in order to bring together testimonies which, though written at different periods, refer to a common subject or historical situation.

It needs to be remembered, however, that while some attempt has been made to choose representative testimonies and arrange them in a meaningful order, the selection has necessarily been somewhat adventitious and there has been no effort to cover all the geographical areas, age levels, varieties of background, and types of disease healed or problem solved. Nor has there been any attempt

The Tide of Healing

to choose the most "impressive" experiences, but simply to convey a sense of the general flow of healing. As already explained, some abridgement has been necessary for space reasons and in the interest of readability.

The following excerpts from a few of the many testimonies dealing with World War I experiences illustrate briefly the sort of help experienced by Christian Scientists on both sides of that massive conflict, and through the dislocations and epidemics that accompanied it.

A Christian Scientist facing a great calamity in which hundreds, thousands, or even millions of lives may be lost does not think that the saving power of divine Love is especially directed toward him. He is convinced, however, that the law of God properly understood and practiced vanquishes every evil circumstance that may present itself, and that this law must be demonstrated individually though it is available universally.

I SPENT twenty-six months on active service, taking part in the battle of Loos, 1915; battle of the Somme, 1916; battle of Messines-Wytschaete Ridge, 1917; and the third battle of Ypres, 1917. In every case I was in the front line, and throughout this time, divine Love was my sure protection. I found Christian Science invaluable in enabling me to demonstrate the truth against the false claims of error in the forms of trench feet, frostbite, etc., during the winters of 1915–1916 and 1916–1917, when on several occasions I spent stretches of eighteen days in what is called "the Salient," thigh deep in mud, and icy cold.

Sergeant E. C. Ericson, M.M., East Surrey Regiment
London, England.

— *Sentinel,* Vol. 20, p. 894
(July 6, 1918).

SINCE THE BEGINNING OF THE WAR I have been protected in many painful circumstances, from dysentery and other ills.

A Century of Christian Science Healing

Whenever I can do so I study the Lesson-Sermons, as I brought my books with me to the front, although at first this seemed impossible.

Georges Finqueneisel, Paris, France.

— *Herald*, French edition,
Vol. 1, p. 318 (August, 1918).

I HAVE BEEN ABLE to do a fair amount of study, and as my understanding of this teaching has increased I have found my troubles and difficulties decrease, so that I am beginning to realize that wonderful peace and happiness "which passeth all understanding," and which defies all inharmonious conditions. I have been in the line many times, on patrol work on No Man's Land very often, and "over the top" once. I have now been made a stretcher bearer, so do not carry arms, but am on a deed of mercy when the battle is raging.

Gilbert D. Adkin, New Zealand Reinforcements.

— *Sentinel*, Vol. 21, pp. 94–95
(October 5, 1918).

IN THE COURSE of the warring years, of which I had spent most of my time at the front, I was buried twice, due to grenades and mines, without suffering any after effects. At the time I was taken prisoner in 1918 God proved to be my protection and my Life. With the exception of a slight injury received on this occasion, which healed in a very short time, I passed through everything unharmed, and after being prisoner for sixteen months returned to my family. During these years of war, thanks to my efforts constantly to think right and to reveal a demonstrable knowledge of

The Tide of Healing

Truth, I was never placed in a position where I was obliged to harm my fellow man.

Hans Struss, Hannover, Germany.

— *Herald,* German edition, Vol. 19, pp. 200–201 (May, 1921).

Having gained our objective we had to intrench and wait for the relief which was due that night. It did not come, however, so we were obliged to wait another twenty-four hours, mostly in the pouring rain and with no food. During that whole time we were in mud up to our knees and often were heavily shelled. The material conditions of fear, cold, and despair had to be very insistently denied. At times all I could do was just to repeat mechanically some phrases I knew by heart. Once while I was trying to work mentally, it came to me very clearly that I had no material body to protect, for man's life is spiritual, and I certainly did not have to worry about protecting the spiritual idea of God; that Love was my eternal protector and I needed no other. I saw clearly that Love was the only means of defense against all evil.

Throughout the whole time after I had done my work, I can solemnly declare that I never felt tired, hungry, or afraid.

Capt. Victor A. Cazalet, London, England.

— *Sentinel,* Vol. 21, p. 494 (February 22, 1919).

I enlisted in the United States Army Ambulance Service, which was organized to serve the French army. When under shellfire for the first time, I huddled at the base of a wall, wanting nothing but to go to sleep and be oblivious to the threat of danger. Here I was, face to face with what I had really enlisted for — to prove the actuality of divine Love in spite of every seeming condition to the contrary. That sense of my purpose woke me out of my dormancy, and the next time the shells burst I found myself standing in the street. Before the smoke and dust cleared out of the air we had our cars going, carrying the wounded French soldiers to the hospital. This was the beginning of a conquest over fear.

That was on the Verdun front. On the Somme front we had fourteen days and nights of incessant activity and of unforgettable proofs of God's care. Never was a patient wounded en route, although we must have carried over three thousand gassed or wounded men those fourteen days. The fellows often remarked about our good fortune. They knew I thought it was divine protection. The proof was plain to me. "Whatever it is, I want a lot of it!" said one of the Irishmen.

On a later front, one quiet day at post, a shell exploded near by, and imbedded a fragment of rock in my shoulder. I was able to man a stretcher and carry more seriously wounded French soldiers to the dressing room and drive them in my ambulance to the hospital, where the fragment was removed from my shoulder. Then I had time to face the error which, undetected, had crept into my thinking. It was a complacent sense of personal immunity, a deceptive counterfeit of that spiritual understanding of God's presence which had been my genuine protection. Jesus' meek words, "I can of mine own self do nothing," restored a sense of true humility; and his amplifying statement, "What things soever [the Father] doeth, these also doeth the Son likewise," renewed the assurance of unity with Principle.

Henry Allen Nichols, Los Angeles, California.

— Sentinel, Vol. 44, pp. 1537–1539 (August 29, 1942).

HAVING PASSED through the war of 1870 and the Commune, and living as we do on a highroad along which the flight of the frightened refugees reminded me of those sad days, I lived through dark hours, and in spite of my dear ones' efforts I could not get hold of myself. I had laid our Christian Science literature aside and devoured the newspapers, which did not help me at all, but in my moral and physical distress I again turned to God and to the study of Christian Science, and this was my salvation. Now I know that we are all the children of one Father, God. Not only have we lacked nothing, but we have been able to help others more unfortunate than ourselves and to see that God is the source of supply for all our needs.

Mrs. C. Renault, Cloyes, Eure et Loir, France.

— *Herald,* French edition, Vol. 1, p. 444 (November, 1918).

IN THE SPRING of 1914 I was told by one of the best medical men in London that it would be many years before I could ever lead a normal life, that my spirit and vitality would wear me out. At that time I had been in bed more or less for eight months and tired for eight years. I got my healing in Christian Science, and when the war came on in August I started a life of activity which has gone on without ceasing, for five years. We have had a military hospital on our place and twenty-four hundred wounded have passed through it. The chief surgeon told me before sailing for Canada that in all of his experience he had never seen a woman able to do more.

The joy of knowing that God is good, and the spiritual knowledge, are of course far greater than any physical healings. Above all is that wonderful sense of knowing that through our understanding of Christian Science we can help the whole world.

(Mrs.) Nancy Langhorne Astor,
Taplow, Bucks, England.

— *Sentinel,* Vol. 22, p. 114 (October 11, 1919).

THE RUSSIAN ATTACK on East Prussia left me without a home and without any means. My parents had previously passed on; and when my two oldest brothers fell in the war, I was disconsolate and without any support. In addition, I was physically very ill. In that condition Christian Science found me. It taught me to live, to love, and to be grateful; and for this I am deeply grateful to Mrs. Eddy. According to the doctors I was suffering from an hereditary, incurable, herpetic eruption. I asked a Christian Science practitioner for absent treatment, which was given me most lovingly. When my thoughts had become clearer and purer, when false thinking had given place to right thinking, then also my body was made clean.

Before I knew Christian Science I underwent an operation for appendicitis; and I was told that later on I should have to be operated on again for other things, being too weak at that time to stand the strain. After some time all the symptoms appeared which mortal law said would necessitate the predicted operation. I confidently asked the kind practitioner for help. On the third day the pain became so severe that I had to lie down. In the afternoon the pain ceased; and then something wonderful happened: parts in my body changed their position without causing me pain. With surprise, but also with relief, I perceived the divine operation. Nothing is impossible to God. He is Life. After three days I was again about my daily duties. The fact that I had to alter my clothes because my figure had changed, and that I never had any more pain, was proof to me that I was healed.

(Miss) *Marta Gehring, Nienburg a. d. Weser, Germany.*

— *Herald,* German edition, Vol. 22,
pp. 80–81 (March, 1924).

SINCE I WAS healed of consumption of the lungs simply by reading the Christian Science textbook, *Science and Health* by Mary Baker Eddy, without ever seeing or speaking to a practitioner, it is my great hope that this testimony will encourage those who seem unable to get help from others to realize that through the study of the textbook alone they can gain their freedom from sickness and sin.

Over twenty years ago I was a physical and mental wreck. I was suffering from consumption. On the advice of a medical specialist I went to live in sanatoriums in England and in Switzerland in search of health, but I did not improve. Being a soldier, at the end of one year I had to go before a medical board who would decide whether I should remain in the army or be retired. The specialist in Switzerland under whose care I was, gave me no hope. His verdict was that I must leave the army, and that if I lived in the open air I might exist for two or three years. Six weeks before I was due to go before the medical board, a friend lent me *Science and Health* and asked me to read it. I knew nothing about Christian Science, but I had not read much of this book before I realized that it was something for which I had been searching all my life, namely a reasonable and logical Christianity. As I read, I began to understand something of what the Bible means, something of what Jesus means, something of his teaching and of his works, and this filled me with a peace and joy which I had never known before.

I was so absorbed and interested in this book that I ceased to think about my body or the disease. I had found a God whom I could understand. My one desire was to know more about this God, and I could scarcely stop reading *Science and Health* day or night. At the end of six weeks, just before my medical board examination, I went to see the medical specialist who originally had sent me to live in sanatoriums. To his amazement and mine, he could find nothing wrong with me. I had been healed simply by reading the book, and as proof of that healing I was passed by the medical board, returned to duty, and within a few years went out to the war in France and remained there from 1914 to 1918 without being wounded, sick, or sorry.

My healing was a wonderful experience, because I realized that if God could heal anything at all, then obviously God could heal everything. If the realization of the truth about God and man could heal an individual, then this same truth could heal the relations between capital and labor, could solve the problems of supply and unemployment, and all the troubles, both national and international, with which the world is confronted today; and finally I realized that the brotherhood of man, which I had always regarded as a pious hope, was and is a practical proposition.

General Spencer E. Hollond, London, England.

— Sentinel, Vol. 39, p. 434
(January 30, 1937).

AT THE AGE of fifteen I was stricken with diphtheria, followed by a complete paralysis of my body, which necessitated my being artificially fed for nine months. I was nursed at New Cross Fever Hospital in London for a full year, and was never expected to recover.

I managed to pull through however, sufficiently at least to be taken home to recuperate, the doctors telling me that I had an enlarged heart and must on no account over-strain it. I lived an outdoor life on a farm for a while and at the age of eighteen I emigrated to Rhodesia where I shared a cattle ranch with another man. When the 1914–18 war broke out, I was again far from well, but like other farmers, I downed tools to join the Rhodesian Forces. While undergoing the necessary medical examination the doctor exclaimed, "Look here, young man, you've got pericarditis, you're not fit for the Army, you should be in bed. I will get you into King Edward Hospital." During my stay there I suffered several heart attacks and was finally invalided back to England.

I improved somewhat but when compulsory enlistment was enforced, as men were badly needed, I was obliged to attend another medical board. I told the doctors nothing of my previous medical history, and anxiously awaited their verdict. To my horror, and yet somewhat to my satisfaction from another point of view, I was accepted for military service. For nine months I struggled along with light duties, until one day, while on guard, I fell unconscious and was taken to the camp hospital.

They could do nothing for me there and sent me to the Heart Hospital in London, where I was told that in addition to heart trouble I also had consumption of both lungs. I was given an immediate discharge from the Army with a disability pension. I went rapidly from bad to worse, and as they could not keep me long, I was literally carried home to die. It was at this point, that I prayed to God, whatever and wherever He might be, to let me have another chance to live, and do some good in the world. The very next day, a Christian Scientist came to lunch with my stepmother, who told her of my condition. She asked to see me and was shown to my room.

Up till that moment, the many kind doctors who'd attended me had gone to my body and done what they could for that, but had paid no attention to my thought, which directly controlled my body. Now the Christian Scientist did exactly the reverse: she took no notice of my body but went straight to my thought and set that right with the truth of being as taught in Christian Science — that is, the truth that God made man perfect, in His own spiritual image and likeness, and that as I realized I was that image and likeness, I would lose the sense of disease and be free from it. She quickly convinced me of the fact that disease is primarily a false mental state, a disturbed condition of thought that has become manifested upon the body through fear, ignorance, or sin. She pointed out that in proportion as this erroneous consciousness is forsaken and thought established in accord with God's ever-present law of truth, health, and harmony, which Christian Science reveals, the body returns to normality and freedom.

Never shall I forget the joyous atmosphere of love, health, and life abundant she brought to my suffering sense, nor how gently and firmly she administered this stimulating medicine of Mind. I quickly realized that God was not a person but the divine Principle of being: and that heaven was not a place but a state of harmonious consciousness which destroys sin and sickness; and thus it was that I lost my fear of their outcome, death.

I was given a copy of the Christian Science textbook, *Science and Health,* by Mrs. Eddy, to read, and was told that the reading of this book alone had healed hundreds of cases of inveterate disease, including all those mentioned in the final chapter on "Fruitage." I was so weak that I could hardly hold the book, but it seemed to reveal an entirely new language. Here and there I found statements and passages that gave me fresh hope and encouragement, especially where it says (p. 22): "Waking to Christ's demand, mortals experience suffering. This causes them, even as drowning men, to make vigorous efforts to save themselves; and through Christ's precious love these efforts are crowned with success."

Then and there I decided that I, too, would make vigorous efforts to save myself by turning resolutely away from fear, self-pity, and the distressing symptoms of disease, and holding my thoughts to this new and enlightened sense of God and man, which was being presented to me in Christian Science.

With the loving help of the practitioner, to whom I shall ever be grateful, I was up and about in two days. When I went to thank the cook and other members of the household for all that they had done, it necessitated my descending and ascending several flights of stairs, which I accomplished without disaster; and this gave me such confidence in good that I was able to make a further demonstration by attending a Christian Science service on the following day.

One by one the ailments left me, and I knew that I was healed. The fact that I was restored to soundness was later confirmed by an Army Medical Board. On that occasion, when the doctors were about to examine me, one of them turned to me and said, "Well, young man, what is the matter with you?" I replied, "Nothing, sir, so far as I know!" "Then what is all this written up on your medical history sheet?" I answered, "That was my condition, but I don't think you will find it so now!" After a thorough check up, they proceeded to write "Nil" against all the symptoms from which I had suffered, and said, "You are a very fortunate young fellow; there will be no more pension for you!"

I did not mind about the pension; I had found the "pearl of great price," the truth that Jesus said would make us free. I left that room rejoicing, thanking God for His goodness to the sons of men. From that time onward, for forty-nine years, through my understanding of Christian Science, which has been increasing all along, I've never again needed the help of a Christian Science practitioner, and have never been away from work for one hour on account of ill health. In fact, I've had a wonderful, happy, and hard-working life.

Richard Knox Lee, London, England
Radio/TV series, "How Christian Science Heals," 1963.

The testimonies that follow are representative of hundreds of others from outside the United States during the 1920's:

I GIVE MY TESTIMONY with gratitude to God for His unfailing love and protection through all our human experiences. I began to read and study Christian Science about fourteen years ago, not because I felt the need of physical healing, but because I wanted a practical religion, a religion that would help one to be good. I married soon afterwards and came out to Egypt. My first child was stillborn and my sufferings were very great. My husband sent a cable to England asking for Christian Science treatment for me, and, but for that, I believe I should have passed away. As it was, I felt that Science had failed me, and I returned to England for an operation.

Later I learned that Christian Science is the true knowledge of God and can never fail, and that what seemed to be failure was simply my own lack of understanding. I went to a nursing home and underwent the operation, which proved an utter failure. I was in despair. My mother, a student of Christian Science, was with me at the time, and feeling in need of help and comfort, she went into the Christian Science Reading Room close by where she met a lady who returned with her to see me. I told my mother that Christian Science had failed me and that I did not want to hear any more of it. This loving visitor so renewed my hope, however, that before she left I asked her to help me. In about a month I was completely healed and returned to Egypt.

83

My last two children were born without medical assistance and with practically no suffering whatever, and I was up and about within a few days. I have three children, and they are fine, healthy boys. We have been able to overcome all climatic conditions by remembering that, in the words of one of our hymns (No. 81): —

> In atmosphere of love divine,
> We live, and move, and breathe.

In all these years we have not had a doctor and have not touched a drop of medicine. Divine Love has met our every need. We have found the truth available during sea voyages, in finding a house to live in, and in sickness. We have been able to overcome dysentery, whooping cough, influenza, typhoid fever, and many other ailments, sometimes through our own understanding of the truth and sometimes through absent treatment. There is a great deal more that I could tell, but all I will say now is that I do not know how I could live without Christian Science, and my heart goes out in love and gratitude to our dear Leader, Mrs. Eddy, for her noble life work. I must not close without also expressing sincere gratitude for all of our periodicals. Whatever one's need of the moment, there is always something in them that answers that need. "By their fruits ye shall know them."

(Mrs.) Kate I. MacLaren, Sidi Gaber, Egypt.

— Sentinel, Vol. 23, pp. 726–727
(May 21, 1921).

W<small>HEN</small> I first heard of Christian Science I had been a confirmed drunkard and smoker for nearly twenty years; and incredible as it may seem, I had not been sober for two years. I had often tried to conquer the craving for strong drink, but had failed utterly, and had become such a slave to it that I almost lived on it, taking very little else. Fear that I might sometime be unable to obtain drink has frequently caused me to hide bottles of beer in the ash bin. My habits had reduced me to a physical wreck, but even this was only part of my misery.

For years our home had been a habitation of discord. My husband was a drunkard, and had frequently caused me very serious injuries when under the influence of drink. Finally he found it impossible to live with me, and left me, saying he would never return. This caused me to be penniless, and at the time of which I write my only possessions were a pot of beer and the rags in which I was clad. My bed, furniture, and clothing had been sold or pawned to buy drink. The house in which I lived was empty, and although it was winter time I had neither food nor fire. My relatives and neighbors shunned me; and my loneliness and misery were such that I had tried to end my life, but had been prevented.

That was my condition when a lady, who I afterwards found was a Christian Science practitioner, knocked at my door to make some inquiry. She did not know me, and knew nothing of my plight, but at once saw that I was ill; and her comforting remarks caused me to tell her my tale of woe, which I concluded by saying that no one cared for me. My visitor instantly replied: "But God cares for you, and I care for you. God is your Father and your Mother, and He loves you just as He loves us all. He supplies all your needs, and gives you health and happiness." At that moment all craving for drink left me, and I was healed physically and morally. I was conscious of a sense of love and peace and hope that I had never known before. The lady asked if I would pour out the pot of beer; and I immediately did so, having no desire for it. She then purchased a supply of food and clothing for me, and left me until the following day, when my husband returned home. He told me that on the previous day, when about to enter a beer house, he felt that he could not go in, and found that all desire for drink had left him, and he suddenly longed to return home. He was astonished to find me changed into a happy woman, healed of all my sickness as well as of the drink and tobacco habits. Neither of us has ever touched drink from that day to this, and it is now six and a half years since we were healed. Though my husband was twenty miles away, he was healed at the same time and as quickly as I myself, and his character was also instantly reformed. I am now a well woman, leading a normal and happy life. My husband, relatives, and friends are all restored to me, and our home is now one of peace, harmony, and love.

> (Mrs.) *Sarah Ellen Walker,*
> *Todmorden, Yorkshire, England.*

> — *Sentinel,* Vol. 30, pp. 595–596
> (March 24, 1928).

WHEN I WAS about ten years old I began to suffer from attacks of bilious headaches which occurred every three or four months, each lasting four or five days. My father, who was a physician, tried for a long time to cure me through his skill. Not succeeding in his endeavors, he turned to other methods of treating the sick available in this country. Although these other methods were tried, one after the other, all of them failed. Hygienic precautions and very strict dieting also gave no relief. I came at last to the sad conclusion, "What cannot be cured must be endured." I then gave up the use of all material methods. I was about fifty years of age when the attacks of headaches began to occur at shorter intervals. Because the pains were almost intolerable I had recourse to morphia injections once or twice daily till the paroxysm came to an end. At the Chicago Exhibition in 1893, I got several books and leaflets on Christian Science from a Christian Science Reading Room in the exhibition which I visited two or three times. I was too busy to read them, however, until I returned to India, and then found them highly interesting. But not meeting any Christian Scientists here to talk with on the subject, I did not continue to study it. My headaches went on unabated.

The question of sin and disease had long occupied my thought. They both appeared to me the great scourge of humanity. I searched long for means to prevent and cure these evils. I studied various healing arts, including modern rational allopathic medicine and the homeopathic and electric systems. But their practical employment failed to meet our needs. I studied various religions also, although the Scriptures pointed to God as all-sufficient. Yet nothing less than the demonstration of Truth could satisfy me. My curiosity, however, finally led me to the study of *Science and Health with Key to the Scriptures* by Mary Baker Eddy in conjunction with the Bible. From the beginning of 1920 I read these books two or three hours regularly every morning. In four or five months I was very agreeably surprised to note that during this period of time I had been perfectly free from the terrible attacks of the bilious headaches which had previously made the greatest part of my life miserable. And from the start of these studies a sense of spiritual uplift within me had been giving me great satisfaction.

The chief object of my giving this testimony is to draw the attention of those who stand in need of spiritual help to the infinite love of God, who is "our refuge and strength, a very present help in trouble." "All things work together for good to them that love God," says the Apostle Paul. *"And Love is reflected in love,"* says Mary Baker Eddy, on page 17 of *Science and Health.* So we ought to love God supremely in return for His infinite love.

Dr. Sadig Ali, Kapurthala, Punjab, India.

— *Sentinel,* Vol. 30, p. 874
(June 30, 1928).

Aʙᴏᴜᴛ ᴀ ʏᴇᴀʀ before I retired from the Indian Forest Service, the Government of Bombay was kind enough to select me to report on the Gir Forests of the Junagahr State, in the Province of Kathiawar. This forest area is about one thousand square miles in extent and is very inaccessibly situated and practically uninhabited. I was able to give myself only two months in which to submit my professional opinion, and there was no time to be lost, owing to the advent of the hot weather and the consequent difficulty in securing drinking water.

I had moved my camp, in stages, to the southern extremity of this large block of forests, and the same evening I rode a distance of three or four miles in order to fish in a small stream. It was while I was making a cast with my rod and line that I slipped and fell heavily between two large boulders, with the result that I at first thought I had broken my right ankle. I immediately turned to divine Love and tried to realize the truth in the manner we are taught in Christian Science. Though in considerable pain I rode back to my camp and settled down to read the Bible and *Science and Health with Key to the Scriptures* by Mary Baker Eddy. Meanwhile my right ankle and leg had swollen to alarming proportions, and for two days and two nights I was unable to leave my tent, though holding on to the truth to the best of my ability. There was no Christian Science practitioner in India in those days; and even if there had been, the fact that I was some thirty miles from the nearest telegraph office and my post was being brought to me with some difficulty by horse and camel riders, would have rendered communication unsatisfactory. I had therefore to depend on God and do my own work.

On the third evening the thought came to me that some step would have to be taken, otherwise my men would be obliged to carry me to the coast line, and from thence the state would have me sent by steamer to the European General Hospital in Bombay. As a Government servant I had no alternative whatever in these matters. The state had already incurred heavy expenses getting me into the Gir Forests and I was being paid a liberal fee for my advice. It was clearly not right that error should dominate my affairs, doing me harm and causing heavy loss to others.

Turning, therefore, yet more completely to divine Principle, I took the necessary human footsteps and managed, with the aid of two sticks, to hobble into the little village close to my camp. While in this village, amongst the half-naked men, women, and children, who are required to live very hard lives in a climate said to be one of the worst and most unhealthy in India, an overpowering sense of compassion and pity for them came over me. In other words, the flood light of Love entered my consciousness, seeking to the very joints and marrow. In that very moment I was instantly healed of all pain. I threw my sticks away and, to the consternation of the staff in my camp, walked back — whole. This beautiful demonstration was a final lesson to me. It showed me that if only we will reflect enough unselfed love, however adverse the material conditions, however isolated we may appear to be, our healing is absolutely certain.

Captain William Arnold Wallinger, Geneva, Switzerland.

— *Sentinel,* Vol. 30, p. 854
(June 23, 1928).

[Original testimony in Swedish]

For many years I suffered from a disease in my feet, accompanied by excruciating pain. It seemed necessary to amputate part of the left foot; but after the foot was somewhat healed, after the operation, the disease broke out in three of the toes on the right foot. The specialists from whom I sought help were unable at first to understand my case; and after experimenting to the best of their ability, one after the other gave it up. Lastly, a skin specialist believed he had correctly diagnosed the disease; but even he found himself unable to cope with it, and after a time told my wife that he considered my case hopeless, as according to his experience the disease was incurable. He begged her to break the news as gently as possible to me, letting me understand that my future as an actor was at an end, and suggesting the contemplation of some kind of work which could be carried on while sitting down.

Such was the desperate and sorry condition of things when Christian Science was brought to my notice by a fellow actor who could not help telling me where I could both seek and get help in my great need. A loving practitioner was recommended, and I turned to her for help. The healing was very slow at first, owing to my inability and unwillingness to read on account of the terrible suffering I was undergoing; but through the patient work of the practitioner, the pain gradually stopped; and after several months the healing of my foot began to take place, and continued with phenomenal speed.

About the time the healing was almost complete I met a doctor who had heard of my much discussed case, and he succeeded in persuading me to let him see the phenomenon. The practitioner was abroad. I evidently could not declare the truth sufficiently strongly, and my faith was apparently very weak. I felt troubled, and fear got the upper hand. The doctor was very much interested, and expressed his desire to help me. I visited him a few times, with the result that the sore, which when first shown to him was the size of a cent, became as big as a dollar. He explained to me that it was a scientific impossibility that the foot could be healed without an operation.

Then it was that I wakened up to the understanding that I already knew of the greatest Science of all sciences and the greatest Physician, God, in whose care I could safely leave myself. After fourteen days of faithful dependence on God, the sore was healed.

I ought also to mention that in order to get some temporary relief from pain I had become a slave to narcotics and morphine, but within a very short time I was entirely freed from them through the work of the Christian Science practitioner. I also had great difficulty in learning to walk again, but by degrees this too was overcome.

For three years I have filled all my engagements, playing one important rôle after another in full vigor and without the slightest difficulty.

Sture Baude, Stockholm, Sweden.

— *Sentinel*, Vol. 30, pp. 754–755
(May 19, 1928).

[Original testimony in French]

Not being able to admit that God would permit evil, and on the other hand not being willing to believe in a God of limited power, I was without hope and without a guide in the world when, in the spring of 1917, I found on the officers' table, where I was taking a meal, a pamphlet entitled, "Christian Science, its Principle and Method." I read it with interest, and through this reading acquired the certainty that I had found the way which would lead me to the understanding of God. I immediately procured a Bible, the Christian Science textbook, *Science and Health with Key to the Scriptures* by Mary Baker Eddy, subscribed to *Le Héraut,* and began to study the Lesson-Sermons in the *Christian Science Quarterly,* endeavoring to put into practice what I acquired of the truth.

Through spiritual understanding, confidence has replaced fear and doubt, excessive timidity has practically disappeared, anger and impulsiveness are more and more giving way to kindness; and a knowledge of God, which is daily increasing, facilitates my work in every way. In short, the "old man" is giving place to the "new man."

I may say that this transformation is going on far from Christian Science churches, and I have only rarely had the pleasure of being among Scientists. I have generally received by correspondence the counsel and help which I have sometimes asked from practitioners, who have never saved themselves time or trouble. Accordingly I express my gratitude to them.

I hope that my testimony will be helpful, especially for isolated students who may have the tendency to believe themselves alone and without help, forgetting, perhaps, that they can avail themselves of God as "a very present help in trouble." The Psalmist says: "If I ascend up into heaven, thou art there: if I make my bed in hell, behold, thou art there. If I take the wings of the morning, and dwell in the uttermost parts of the sea; even there shall thy hand lead me, and thy right hand shall hold me."

Octavien Antoni, Sarrebrück, Sarre.

— *Herald,* French edition, Vol. 12, pp. 341–342 (November, 1929).

[Original testimony in German]

IN MY WORK in a coal mine, where I am daily and hourly surrounded by danger, I have often been able to apply the healing power of Christian Science successfully. I should especially like to mention an experience I had some time ago. As I was about to bore a hole in the coal, water flowed from it. I filled the hole with powder and requested my comrades to move away from the place. But as the surroundings were damp from the water, the blast failed and there was no explosion. In a few moments I went to see if it were necessary to bore another hole. The drilling machine, however, would not work and fell out of my hand. An inward voice said: "The powder is burning, do not remain in this place any longer." I obeyed. I had hardly gone more than a few yards when I stumbled over a rail and fell with my face to the ground. I could not get up immediately. At this moment the powder exploded, and the pieces of coal flew beyond my body without harming me in the least. As I fell I immediately realized the truth, that nothing could ever injure me, for I was always secure in divine Love, and "accidents are unknown to God," as Mrs. Eddy says in the textbook, *Science and Health with Key to the Scriptures* (p. 424). My comrades were very anxious about me when the powder exploded; for they knew I was still near the place. But how surprised they were to find me, surrounded by the pieces of coal, safe and sound!

I thank divine Love with all my heart for warning me in time at a moment of greatest danger, and for preserving and protecting me from all danger and for healing me. I also thank our beloved Leader, Mrs. Eddy, for the wonderful textbook, which enables us at all times and in all places to apply Christian Science successfully.

Wilhelm Bergel, Weisstein, Kr. Waldenburg,
Silesia, Germany.

— Herald, German edition, Vol. 27,
pp. 374–375 (December, 1929).

[Original testimony in German]

FIVE AND A HALF YEARS AGO I was a broken-down individual, mentally and physically. According to physicians, I was suffering from tuberculosis; and they gave me only a short time to live. As the fall approached I grew constantly worse, my temperature usually being 101.5 degrees, but often higher. Besides this, I was sore and torn internally. I had recently passed through inexpressibly trying experiences which weighed heavily on me. I was surrounded at that time by dark impenetrable night, as it seemed to me, and death was awaiting me. And I did so want to live! In such an hour of despair it suddenly came to me, like a ray of light, that I had once heard something about Christian Science. I did not know anything about its teaching, but I had heard that it would heal every kind of sickness. I must admit I did not have any faith in this, but, as a drowning man catches at a straw, I decided at least to try Christian Science; it was my last hope.

As nothing was known about Christian Science at that time in Dorpat, I went to Riga, where I immediately received loving treatment from a Christian Science practitioner. After three treatments the cough left me, and after eight I was healed. This healing took place quite suddenly. I was walking along the street when it became tangibly clear to me that I, as God's perfect likeness, must reflect health, and that I lived, moved, and had my being in Him; and all at once it seemed as if something fell from me, I felt so light and happy — and I knew and felt I was well.

There is no language in the world with which I could express what I felt at that time. I could, in my overflowing joy, have exclaimed to everybody, Rejoice with me, for I am well! My heart was filled with exultation, and it seemed as if everything in me was singing and ringing. Besides being physically healed, I was also healed mentally.

(Mrs.) Ellen Hendel, Dorpat, Esthonia.

— *Herald,* German edition, Vol. 27,
pp. 87–88 (March, 1929).

During these years when Christian Science was spreading throughout the world, it was reaching an increasing number of people in the United States in a wide variety

of circumstances. More and more it was coming to be
seen not just as a method of healing but as a way of life.

HAVING SPENT the greater part of my life from 1902 to 1913
behind prison bars, I feel that I have a message of interest to my
fellow men. In 1902 I was sentenced to serve three months in the
county jail of a large western city, and the day of my release I was
rearrested, and sentenced to serve two years in the state peniten-
tiary. Leaving this institution at the expiration of my term, broken
in health through having had bronchitis, typhoid pneumonia, and
other ailments, I was seemingly driven again to resort to swindling,
or what is legally known as "obtaining money under false pretenses,"
the charge on which I had already been sentenced twice.

Finally, in 1913, while I was in the hospital ward of the Utah
State Prison, being confined for forgery, some one called my attention to the Christian Science literature so kindly placed there by
the distribution workers of Salt Lake City, advising me to read it.
I read the selected articles, and they seemed so sincere and fair in
their statements that I determined to learn more of the religious
beliefs of the people who could write such articles. I already possessed a Bible and was furnished a copy of *Science and Health
with Key to the Scriptures* by Mrs. Eddy, through the kindness
of a gentleman doing the work of reader at the Christian Science
services in the prison. I read this volume six times and also studied
the Lesson-Sermons, read the *Sentinel, Journal,* and *Monitor,* as
well as every pamphlet and book on the subject that was printed
or sold by The Christian Science Publishing Society. About six
hours daily were spent in this way, just because I enjoyed it all and
could not seem to get enough of it. I had no idea that I would be
healed or helped by this study, but I was pardoned when my term
was about half over, in spite of the fact that I was thousands of
miles from home and seemingly had no one to help me. I know
that "the sunlight . . . glances into the prison-cell," also that
"Love is the liberator" (*Science and Health,* pp. 516, 225), as
Mrs. Eddy tells us.

The Tide of Healing

For the past few years I have not been tempted to resort to the old methods of getting money, but all my financial needs are being met just to the extent that I apply the rules of right thinking and living, as outlined in the Bible and the Christian Science textbook, and have availed myself of the articles printed in the periodicals. Instead of being troubled by high altitudes and damp climate, or having difficulty in eating certain foods, I have made several trips from coast to coast of the United States without suffering any inconvenience whatsoever, in spite of the doctor's statement as far back as 1911 that the left lung was badly affected and the right lung slightly affected, and that it would be advisable for me to live in California, if I wished to get well. The above-mentioned results were all obtained without the aid of a practitioner, but through the diligent study of the Bible and *Science and Health* with the aid of the Lesson-Sermons.

Charles P. Gough, Denver, Col.

— *Sentinel*, Vol. 20, p. 794
(June 1, 1918).

FIVE YEARS AGO, I had just spent my last dollar on a bottle of medicine for my wife, when an angel of God's presence caused me to tell a friend my tale of woe. He was a student of Christian Science, about which I had never heard. I told him I was about at the end of my row, as I had been spending all I could rake and scrape up for medicine for my wife, and the doctors had said she could not be healed of pellagra, which she had had for years. My friend told me to have no fear, but have my wife read the *Sentinel* which he gave me. Inside of a week or two she was well and out in the field helping me, completely healed.

A few years afterwards my baby boy had infantile paralysis; and nine doctors passed the death sentence. Two of the doctors, after taking an X-ray picture, confirmed the sentence. I had help from a Christian Science practitioner, and the baby was healed at once. When I went to pay the doctor for taking the X-ray picture, he said,

"I am awfully sorry for you, George; I know the child is dead."
I told him that Christian Science had healed him, and that he was
playing around, happy as a lark.

Since then my wife has had a painless childbirth. We have had
many more demonstrations, which cause us to be very grateful to
Mrs. Eddy for founding Christian Science to bless and heal the
world.

George Watson, Rome, Georgia.

— *Sentinel,* Vol. 25, p. 314
(December 16, 1922).

A s ONE who has had the mental companionship of Christian Science through the years of adolescence and has used it through five
years of college student life, I am happy to be able to testify of what
this religion of divine Principle can mean to a young man during
these formative periods.

Something of the manner in which my parents and I groped for
a solid footing in the understanding of Life is hinted in the fact
that before I was fourteen years old I had been under the teachings
of four divergent churches or sects. If one is inclined to wonder
what the universe is and for what purpose he is in it, his early years,
under any system of thinking less comprehensive than Christian
Science, are likely to be mentally discomforting. It was, therefore,
as a philosophy which could explain all existence from the consistent and rational basis of spiritual reasoning that this Science
appealed to me. The sense of satisfaction, comfort, and security
I have had in feeling thus firmly established in a system broad
enough to answer all my needs has more than rewarded, and still
rewards, the time I have spent in its study. Some of these rewards
have been in the shape of physical healing. Through Christian Science I have been freed of sick headaches, which were becoming
chronic, and have been healed of earache and influenza.

Christian Science has also helped me to settle the choice of a
vocation through the assurance that my profession, whatever it

might be, — and it is now journalism, — would be the expression of divine activity, and could only lead into the place God would have me fill. The fact that my college grades were among the highest in my classes is attributable, I know, to the aid of Christian Science in reflecting divine intelligence. Participation in college activities and appreciation of contact with my fellow-students were made easier for me by the understanding in Science that all are the sons and daughters of God, and endued, in reality, with His qualities. For the very fact that I have completed a university course I am grateful to Christian Science, since my schooling was made possible only through a series of demonstrations over disease and lack.

I am grateful, too, for the heritage which Mrs. Eddy has left to the youth of the land, in setting forth an understanding of God by which each one can look forward with certainty to a success not measured in the sharpness of his competition with fellow-mortals, but comprised in a life-purpose simply to be and enjoy the untrammeled reflection of good.

Tully Nettleton, Oklahoma City, Okla.

— *Sentinel*, Vol. 26, pp. 254–255
(November 24, 1923).

Rejected as physically unfit for war service, my vocation as a contractor demoralized because of war emergency, I enlisted my services in the Hog Island shipyards, placing myself at the disposal of the employment department. I was placed in the riveting school to serve as apprentice for two weeks; then was assigned to duty on construction work on one of the ships. We were admonished by our foreman to use only white-hot rivets in the riveting of a fuel tank in the hold of a ship. While we were working under the high pressure of the keen necessity for ships for troops and supplies, often to the disregard of safety precautions, one day my foot slipped, due to insufficient scaffolding in the tank, causing me to release the heavy piece of steel used to hold against the head of the rivet while the riveter drives or flattens the hot steel on the opposite side.

The release of this bar permitted the rivet to be driven without an instant's warning from its proper place, with seemingly great force, directly into my left eye, which was less than eighteen inches away, the full force of the blow, in addition to the white heat of the rivet, making contact with the unprotected eyeball. Instantly the fear of loss of vision, accompanied with excruciating pain, came into my consciousness, together with all the false laws which I had been taught as a child. The "still small voice" of the Christ, Truth, however, flooded my consciousness with the true sense of vision and the truth about God and man in His image and likeness. The audible declaration of the "scientific statement of being," as given on page 468 of *Science and Health with Key to the Scriptures* by Mary Baker Eddy, with the conviction of its truth, quieted all fear; and with the overcoming of fear the pain subsided and I received an instantaneous healing of the belief that I had been painfully injured or burned. From the time of the accident to the realization of the truth that makes free and my healing, less than fifteen minutes elapsed.

The Labor Compensation Act was in force in the yard, and as this required all injured workmen to be taken to the hospital for medical attention I obediently complied. I was examined by the eye specialist and a life sentence of destroyed vision was pronounced. It was also asserted that I would suffer severe pain that night and for several nights; that crushed ice packs must be kept on my eye to alleviate suffering, and many other disturbing assertions were made. These suggestions had no effect other than to increase my convictions of Truth; and no attention was paid to the specialist's admonitions. After listening to my wife reading to me from *Science and Health* for two hours, I went to sleep and slept soundly all night, with never a suggestion of pain; neither has there been, even to this time, eight years after the experience. The accident occurred on a Friday. I worked on Saturday, attended services on Sunday, and read the *Christian Science Sentinel* in the afternoon with no discomfort or impaired vision. I was rejoicing through all this false thinking and manifestation in that I knew of the efficacy of Christian Science, that I had been a witness to the presence of the healing power of the Christ, Truth, which had annulled one of the so-called strong laws of matter the instant it was applied, and that the Bible truths are applicable to our every human need and are demonstrable — "God with us."

Robert H. Shannon, Summerland, California.

— *Sentinel*, Vol. 29, p. 174
(October 30, 1926).

ONE MORNING I found that there was a breaking out on one of my fingers. I tied it up and tried to forget it, but it would not be forgotten. I treated it in Christian Science, but it did not yield. The condition spread, and I asked for help; but the difficulty stubbornly refused to abate. A doctor informed me that the trouble was diabetes, from which I had previously suffered, but which I supposed had been overcome. He said that it was practically impossible for me to recover from the attack; that my only chance was to go to a hospital and have insulin treatment. He doubted, however, whether that could save me, and told my sister that gangrene had set in and I should probably lose my hand. The doctor knew that I was a Christian Scientist, and that I had met the previous difficulty through Truth. He said that I might try what my faith could do, but he did not think it would help me.

I thank God that my husband and my sisters made no opposition to my decision to rely on Truth and Truth alone. And their faith, and the faith of the practitioner, were a tower of strength to me. But, in spite of this, instead of improving I grew steadily worse. The dear practitioner, knowing how many years I had been in Christian Science, exhorted me to pray and work unceasingly; and I obeyed her.

At last, however, it seemed as if error were going to master me; for I became confused, unable to work clearly, or to pray. I struggled and struggled to clear my thinking, but I could not. One night I became so weary with the incessant fighting, so hopeless and tired, that I felt I could do no more. The battle was too much for me, and I gave it up — conquered. After an interval I became aware of a voice calling me by name, and crying: "God is your Life! God is your Life!" I heard it, but it meant nothing to me. The voice persisted: "God is your Life! God is your Life!" It still conveyed no meaning; I wished I could be let alone, I was so tired. Again the voice kept up its message, and then I knew what the message was. I began to struggle mentally to throw off the apathy into which I had apparently been sinking. I opened my eyes, and the faithful practitioner was leaning over me, and around my bed were standing my dear ones. The victory had been won. I had been called back to life.

Several years have passed, and I am here to bear witness to the fact that God is my Life. What can I say that can express my gratitude for this marvelous demonstration? I thank God for His goodness in sending us Mary Baker Eddy, the Discoverer and Founder of Christian Science; and may He aid all of us who are realizing the truth of her discovery to live the Christ-life, and to obey the Master's injunction to go out into all the world, preach the good news, and heal the sick.

(Mrs.) Genie H. Rosenfeld, New York, New York.

I nursed my sister, Mrs. Rosenfeld, through her illness, and was present when she was called back from death to life. I had been alone with her, and she had seemed no worse; then she moaned, and I went to her bedside. She said to me: "It is all over; this is the end. Good-by." I ran to the telephone and summoned the practitioner, who arrived in what seemed an incredibly short time. From the distance she had to come, however, the time which must have elapsed was from half to three quarters of an hour. I summoned my other sister at the same time; and she, my brother-in-law, and I stood beside the bed, and can testify to the truth of every word in the above testimony.

(Miss) Dorothy H. G. Johnson, New York, New York.

— *Sentinel*, Vol. 33, p. 734
(May 16, 1931).

The Tide of Healing

Over the years a number of testimonies have borne
witness to the applicability of spiritual law to ranching
and farm problems, as the following excerpts illustrate:

I FIND THAT ANIMALS respond quickly to Truth. In a few treatments given to horses, I have seen the distemper knot and fistula
disappear, and there has been no return.

George Fox, Pilot View, Ky.

— *Sentinel,* Vol. 3, p. 754
(July 25, 1901).

My SLIGHT UNDERSTANDING of Christian Science enabled me
to pasture two thousand sheep on a range infested with poisonous
weeds, with no bad results whatever.

Charles N. Hayden, Concord, California.

— *Journal,* Vol. 43, pp. 154-155
(June, 1925).

LIVING ON A RANCH we have long been seeking the truth that
meets the special problems which come to us as country people.

The question of strength was the first thing I solved when confronted with tasks that seemed beyond my city muscles. The thought
that strength is spiritual and available as a quality of God has sustained me in many exceedingly arduous tasks. The extremes of
weather, of heat, storm, and in winter of cold (sometimes thirty
degrees below zero), have been met for the children's protection
with the thought that God's ideas are surrounded by divine Love

and that mortal extremes of temperature cannot disturb this harmony. The crop is being protected with the truth that evil is not of God's creation. Back of all is the great truth that life is spiritual, that supply is spiritual, not dependent on so-called matter, but on God, whose infinite supply mortal thought cannot hinder flowing towards us when we look for it with spiritual understanding, knowing that God is All and God is good.

(Mrs.) Eva Langley Jacobs,
De Winton, Alberta, Canada.

— *Sentinel*, Vol. 30, p. 934
(July 21, 1928).

AT THE TIME of which I write we were sheep-farming about fifty miles from Bloemfontein, in the Orange Free State, and had to meet many difficulties, among which were stock diseases, drought, and the locust pest. My sister, seeing the effect of Christian Science on me, also became an earnest student, and from then on we began to use the little understanding we had to meet our difficulties. During two periods of drought our stock were kept alive by the realization of God's power to maintain His ideas. Some neighbors lost many sheep, even though they moved their flocks to what seemed better pasture, while our flocks remained on our farms. We ceased to dose our sheep as a preventive against disease, and our losses were negligible as compared with the death rate on neighboring farms, where continual dosing was practiced. Sheep, horses, and cattle treated in Christian Science recovered from diseases that, from a material point of view, were considered fatal.

Further, we were privileged to witness a most convincing proof of the power of Truth to heal even those who have no understanding of divine Principle. A native, who for months had complained of severe pain, was sent to a doctor, who diagnosed his malady as a severe case of sciatica, which could be cured only by a three months' course of injections. This case was completely healed by Christian Science in a week. In due course other native servants asked for help, and later, when we sold our farms, all the natives living on them had ceased to use medicine.

When I look back on the past seven years with its trials and triumphs for Truth, I can only say with the Psalmist, "Thy righteousness is like the great mountains; thy judgments are a great deep: O Lord, thou preservest man and beast."

Hubert T. Back, Rosebank, Cape Province, South Africa.

— *Sentinel*, Vol. 33, p. 974
(August 8, 1931).

During the depression years of the 1930's many testimonies had to do with the healing of lack and unemployment. Christian Science does not attempt to "use" God for human purposes, promising material prosperity as the result of certain mental techniques, but neither does it regard poverty and deprivation as signs of spiritual grace. It finds the key to this question in the words of Jesus when he was speaking of the things that seem necessary and useful in human experience: "Seek ye first the kingdom of God, and his righteousness; and all these things shall be added unto you" (Matt. 6:33).

The great problems of economic depression, mass poverty and unemployment, famine and exploitation — still present in many parts of the world today — need the wise and compassionate efforts of society toward their solution, or amelioration. But Christian Science holds that the final solution to every problem must be spiritual; it must involve that discovery and demonstration of the kingdom of God which brings the "added things." Jesus did not present this kingdom as a far-off Utopia or as a reward beyond the grave but as a present possibility within the reach of the spiritually awakened individual.

In the kingdom of God — the realm of the spiritually real and eternal — there can be no lack of good for any of God's children; but this good is necessarily spiritual. St. Paul describes the fruit of the Spirit in such terms as love, joy, peace, longsuffering, gentleness, goodness, faith, meekness, and temperance.

To a radically Christian faith the individual need never

be a helpless cipher at the mercy of ruthless economic forces beyond the control of divine Love. He need never wait until society has engineered a better set of circumstances for him. He can turn, wherever he is, to the divine fact that the kingdom of God is already and everywhere present and thus begin to discover the abundant spiritual riches God has bestowed on him. This inevitably brings a greater measure of intelligent purpose, opportunity, activity, and right reward into his human experience.

The two depression experiences given here were related some years later on the radio series "How Christian Science Heals":

AT ONE TIME, during the depression, I found myself penniless in a strange city.

I'd gone to this city with a group of sales people I'd made a connection with. But we'd only been there a day when these men began to talk about leaving town without paying the hotel bill. I couldn't go along with anything like that, so, I separated myself from them.

But I was penniless so I went to the manager, and told him I didn't have the means to pay the bill, but that I would have. Then I went to the Christian Science Reading Room to study and pray. I knew this was the only way I could possibly solve the problem. As I prayed for direction and guidance, the thought came very strongly to give. But I thought, "I don't have anything to give." That happened several times as I sat there and prayed. Finally the thought of service began to come to me. Well, I turned that over in my mind until finally I saw how I could be of service.

At one time I'd sold a piece of equipment used by hotels, restaurants, and stores — a meat slicing machine. It consisted of over 1000 parts and I knew every one of them. In fact, I had a set of servicing tools right in my car. These machines were in common use everywhere, but in these depression times the merchants weren't prepared to ship them back to the factory for repairs.

So here was my answer. I decided to make some calls and offer to service these machines. And I was received with open arms. Between three and five that afternoon, I'd lined up enough work for two weeks. And for two years after that I made a living in this way, covering six states. And perhaps I might mention another way in which this understanding helped me. It was a physical healing that came about entirely through prayer and reliance on God. I'd had attacks of neuritis and also arthritis over a number of years, and finally this trouble appeared in a very alarming form. My hands and arms were incapacitated. I had to hold my head in a rigid position and the slightest move brought excruciating pain.

I had help from a Christian Science practitioner, and from my own study and prayer I realized that once again it was a question of spiritualizing my thinking. So I prayed earnestly to get a clearer understanding of man's spiritual nature in the likeness of God. As I did this, I saw I had to get rid of some hatred and resentment that had been smouldering in my thoughts.

When the healing finally came, it came suddenly — about five o'clock one morning. It was complete, it was final. I was back at work in two days.

But, you know, it's the over-all picture that really means so much to me. There's just no comparison between the poverty of my earlier thinking, and the wealth of spiritual understanding that has come to me since.

Arthur McNamara, Chicago, Illinois
Radio/TV series, "How Christian Science Heals," 1960.

As a young woman I was left alone with five young children to raise. Christian Science taught me how I could rely on God every step of the way.

Times were hard but in spite of that, we were able to have enough to make a happy home. When I was first left with my youngsters, I went to work as a power sewing machine operator. About two weeks before Christmas, we were all paid off, and told we wouldn't be called again until the end of January. This was during the depression. It was just a small amount of cash I'd received, but I thought to myself, I'll budget it, and make it do until I'm called back to work. But when I got home, I had no purse — I'd lost it on my way home.

We talked about it, the youngsters and I. They didn't question that this need would be taken care of by relying on God. We held steadfastly to the fact that it is the outpouring of good from God, divine Love, that supplies our needs. And what comes from God can't be intercepted or withheld.

Well, I'd lost my purse on a Friday, and by the following Wednesday, we were practically out of everything. I took the last of what I had in the house — a potato, a handful of rice, and a few little things, and made some soup. Nobody went hungry, but that was the last I could give them. But I wasn't disturbed, because the Bible tells us the righteous shall not be forsaken, nor their children have to beg for bread. That very day, there was a letter from someone who'd found my purse, telling me where I could get it. But that wasn't all. The next day I got a call to go back to work, so I wasn't even laid off. And we had a very happy Christmas.

I could go on and on, telling how the understanding of God has supplied all our needs through the years. If all you have left in the house is the understanding that God is Love, and you use that, your needs will be taken care of.

(Mrs.) Ruth D. Coone, Seattle, Washington
Radio/TV series, "How Christian Science Heals," 1959.

Many testimonies in the Christian Science periodicals relate to the healing of children. Examples of such healings are included in each of the accounts in the following group. It is worth noting that children themselves grasp the basic truths of Christian Science readily and find no difficulty in demonstrating them through healing. In many cases it is a healing of or by a child that has brought other members of a family to the study of Christian Science.

SOME YEARS AGO my first baby was born with water on the brain, and the bones on the top of the head were closed. The doctor said that the child could not possibly live more than two weeks. He called in another doctor and the verdict was the same. The child was removed to a private hospital, where the spine was to be punctured to remove some of the water and relieve the pressure on the brain, but with no hope of healing the child. The evening before the operation my sister came to me, and, although I knew nothing of Christian Science, she at once let a Christian Science practitioner know of the child's hopeless condition. When the doctors arrived next morning to perform the operation they found the nurses in a great state of excitement, for during the night the child had been perfectly healed.

During the three months that followed the child lost all trace of malnutrition and the bones on the top of the head separated in a normal way. The doctor could not believe it possible, so I took the baby for him to see. He said that I must have changed the child, as he had never seen or heard of a recovery from a similar condition. Some time afterwards the child's photograph took the prize for the most beautiful child-study in Australia.

(Mrs.) Gladys Field,
Subiaco, Western Australia.

— *Sentinel,* Vol. 34, p. 234
(November 21, 1931).

[Original testimony in Swedish]

IN SPITE OF my honest and serious efforts during nine years before I came to Christian Science, my business was in a hopeless condition, its existence seemingly filling no need. A belief in overproduction and overpowering competition was dominant and constantly disappointed my hopes of success. In our home we were on the verge of ruin on account of economic depression, sickness, and despair. Through the patient and loving guidance of a Christian Science practitioner the business soon became sound and successful. And still more, by a very simple alteration in the manufacturing, it was proved that the goods filled a great need without any competition in the market.

A Century of Christian Science Healing

Shortly afterwards my wife also, after some opposition, went to the Christian Science services; and many illnesses disappeared. The children attended the Sunday school, and our home was thus brought into complete harmony. When, later on, my wife gave birth to a child it was proved that the application of Christian Science dispels all opposing beliefs such as the physician's very pessimistic forebodings about the outcome. Under Christian Science treatment the birth was perfectly normal, but the child was so weak that death was predicted. It could not retain any food, and its temperature was below normal. After three weeks it seemed as if the prophecy about the child had been fulfilled. I got a message from the hospital advising me that all functioning had stopped and that tests with two thermometers had failed to show any sign of life. I then tried to realize that everything in God's kingdom is always right, and that there is no discord in the ever-presence of divine Mind; and I asked a practitioner for help. After two hours I was told, "The child lives, eats and retains food, and the temperature is normal." This child is now well, strong, and intelligent.

These demonstrations took place in 1928. We are exceedingly grateful to God and to all Christian Scientists for carrying on their work of establishing the victory of Truth.

Hesekiel Carlsson, Sundbyberg, Sweden.

— *Journal*, Vol. 50, pp. 739–740
(March, 1933).

THE DISCOVERY OF *The Christian Science Monitor* was an important, progressive step in my experience. For over three years, while resident in the United States of America, the *Monitor* was available for me to read. But I was so prejudiced against what I thought Christian Science to be that I declined to peruse it. However, on my arrival in India, one of the first things to greet me away up here in the Himalayas was the *Monitor*. This time I read it. Inquiry as to who subscribed for it led me to a loyal student of Chris-

The Tide of Healing

tian Science, to whom I shall ever be grateful. This student lent me a copy of the textbook, *Science and Health with Key to the Scriptures,* by Mary Baker Eddy.

I had not read the textbook very long before chronic constipation and indigestion, for which material remedies had been used in vain for over twenty years, were completely healed.

Our infant son passed on with dysentery, for, despite the healing just mentioned, we were not ready to put full trust in Christian Science and its help was not sought on his behalf. The day after he passed on our young daughter showed signs of the same disease. We were now ready to trust Christian Science, and with the help of a Christian Science practitioner she was instantaneously healed.

At exactly the same age as our first son when he passed on, our second son became ill with a severe ear trouble. He was removed to the hospital of the institution where I am employed. My wife and I resolved that if an operation was suggested we would not permit it, for we were knowing that the operation of divine Love was all he needed. A Christian Science practitioner was called at once. The day after his admission to the hospital, the doctors pronounced him seriously ill, and said that nothing more could be done for him. I again telephoned to the practitioner, three hundred and fifty miles away, and that night our son was healed. Predictions about the ear taking a long time to heal and his hearing being affected proved false. The healing was complete. How can we ever thank the loyal practitioners who so lovingly help us in our times of great need?

Hugh C. Kelly, Kalimpong, Bengal, India.

I gladly verify my husband's testimony.

The harmonious births of our three children have proved to me beyond question that with the understanding which Christian Science gives of God's law, this experience holds only joy for the mother and pain has no place in it.

(Mrs.) Alfreda E. Kelly.

— *Sentinel*, Vol. 40, pp. 575–576
(March 19, 1938).

A Century of Christian Science Healing

I AM fourteen years of age and a pupil in a Christian Science Sunday School. While at the beach during the summer of 1936 I had an opportunity to know just how much the training in the Sunday School means to me.

My three younger cousins, a little friend, and I started out to take a canoe ride. We often did this, as my little cousins were trained to keep very still. As we were passing the pier, a little boy whom we knew called to us and asked to be allowed to go with us. I hesitated at first, but decided to take him as he was so eager to go.

All went well for a while. We sang as we paddled along, having such a fine time. All at once the little boy whom we had taken in at the pier stood up and leaned over the side of the canoe. Over it went, and all of us with it. The water was twenty-five feet deep, and we were about three miles from shore.

The little four-year-old girl came up under the canoe, so I went under to get her. The little boy who caused the upset went down twice. As he came up the last time I pushed the canoe toward him and told him to come toward me, which he did. Then, with five children hanging to the canoe, my cousin, who is ten years old, suggested that we know the truth. I had seen a fisherman's boat go by a little while before, so I told the children to hang onto the canoe while I went for help. As I swam away I could hear their voices getting fainter and fainter in the distance. Some of them were repeating "the scientific statement of being" (*Science and Health* by Mrs. Eddy, p. 468). The smaller ones were saying the prayer by our Leader, written for little children (*Miscellaneous Writings*, p. 400). I knew that we could not at any time be separated from God. As I went along I thought of all that I had learned in the Sunday School. I shed my clothes piece by piece. I got tired and cold at times, and once I almost went to sleep, but some phrase of Truth would come to me to spur me on. At last I saw the fisherman's boat, so I kept swimming and soon reached it and told my story. The fisherman pulled me in and turned the boat in the direction of the children. As we neared them I saw four of the children still hanging onto the canoe, but could not see the small four-year-old. Real-

izing that God is the only power, I looked again and saw her float-
ing on the water. We soon reached them and took them all in, every
child safe and sound. We were a happy crowd going home.

The fisherman said that I swam a distance of about four miles.
I know that without the understanding of Christian Science which
I have gained in the Sunday School I could never have swum this
distance, as I have never in my life done any long-distance swimming. It was two hours from the time I left the children until I
returned. The ten-year-old cousin did his bit keeping up the children's courage, so I think his work was just as important as mine.

The folks on shore looked upon this as a miracle, but to me it
will always be a wonderful demonstration of God's power and
presence.

After we were all settled at home, the little four-year-old was
asked what she had thought all the long while she was waiting
for me to return, and she said, "Well, I knew that the water was
over father's head and I knew that it was over mother's head, but
I knew that it wasn't over God's head."

Samuel H. Meeks, Alexandria, Virginia.

— *Sentinel*, Vol. 40, pp. 495–496
(February 19, 1938).

SEVERAL years ago, in the office where I was employed, a group
of women who were friendly toward Christian Science asked me if
I had ever known of the healing in Christian Science of harelip.
I was particularly interested in the question, for I had spent months
of mental agony prior to the birth of my first baby, fearing that he
would inherit the condition of cleft palate, which had appeared in
two members of my husband's immediate family, and, according
to general belief, having skipped a generation, was due to manifest
itself in his offspring.

Work was begun by a Christian Science practitioner as soon as
I realized the baby was coming, but I had little understanding and
my fear was great. When the child arrived, not only normal but

very pretty, my gratitude was boundless, and I wondered then how I could have doubted God's power.

I was not troubled further by this error until about the fifth month of my next pregnancy. Then suddenly one morning the mental suggestion became so strong that I was almost overcome with terror. I left my work and rushed for my copy of *Science and Health* by Mrs. Eddy. The book opened to a page showing the falsity of the belief of heredity. It was as if God had spoken to comfort me, and there was no further anxiety. The child was normal.

When he entered kindergarten, much fuss was made because he still spoke in "baby talk," and seemed unable to pronounce certain consonants. I was asked to let him join a special speech class. Only one other child in the school was given this highly specialized training. I realized that my boy must be considered much retarded, and visited the class to see what was being done with the youngster. While explaining to me what she felt was the difficulty, the teacher suggested: "Let me look at his throat. Sometimes the formation of that is responsible for speech problems." The boy opened his mouth wide for her inspection. She looked surprised, and asked, "Have you ever had surgical work done on him for a cleft palate?" I replied that we had not. "That is queer," she said. "There is an indication here that the palate has been cleft at some time but has grown together again. It must have been during the embryonic stages." She knew nothing of the child's family or history. No such operation could have been performed without my knowledge, for the baby had never been away from me. For a moment my sense of standing on holy ground was so overwhelming that I could not answer her. I can never be grateful enough that this instance of the protective power of Christian Science was revealed to me. The boy had only three or four sessions in the special class. In a few months he was enunciating distinctly.

(Mrs.) R. Louise Emery,
San Pedro, California.

— Journal, Vol. 60, pp. 180–181
(June, 1942).

The Tide of Healing

WHEN I was just a boy, I developed a severe earache. Finally my mother took me to a prominent physician in Brooklyn. He told her I had double mastoiditis and both ears would have to be operated on immediately.

We had just begun to study Christian Science and my mother still didn't know too much about it. She was rather hesitant to depend upon it in a case like this, but she felt impelled to postpone the operation. So she said she would like to think it over. The doctor said there wasn't time. He must call an ambulance at once and get me to a hospital. Otherwise he would have to drop responsibility for my life.

In spite of this bad news my mother did not become fearful. In fact, she decided to take me home. She had found Christian Science just after my dad passed on. There were four children, and our funds were very limited. She was ill and just about desperate. But Christian Science healed her of the grief, the illness — and the whole situation straightened out in a wonderful way. I think this gave her the courage she needed when I became ill.

On the way home she asked me what *I* wanted — Christian Science treatment or go to the hospital — and I told her I wanted to be healed in Christian Science. So she called a Christian Science practitioner, who gave me treatment daily and came to our home periodically. During the next few weeks some undesirable traits of character such as wilfulness and selfishness had to be replaced in my thinking. Also, my mother had to give up her belief that I had inherited certain physical weaknesses from my dad.

The turning point in the healing work came one afternoon when I myself took a radical stand for the truth. My mother was reading the 91st Psalm to me and came to the verse:

> Because he hath set his love upon me, therefore will I deliver him: I will set him on high, because he hath known my name.

I asked her to leave the room. I then sat up in bed and ordered error out as a liar, claiming my unity with God. I knew He would heal me, and soon I was entirely well.

In order to get a certificate to re-enter school, I had to go back to the same doctor. He was surprised to see me alive. In fact, he told my mother he had watched the obituary columns every evening for my name. He then re-examined my ears and said I was perfectly healed.

I might add that during World War II, I passed several rigid physical examinations, Also, I flew frequently at high altitudes and never had the slightest trouble with my ears.

George L. Aghamalian, New York, New York
Radio/TV series, "How Christian Science Heals," 1955.

As the world drew closer to war, testimonies continued to show the diversity of backgrounds, problems, and interests which had characterized Christian Science healing for many decades.

WHILE WORKING at night on a road construction job, I was caught in between a gas shovel and a truck in such a way that the truck, loaded with five yards of rock, ran over my legs and stomach with the rear wheels. Voicing what I knew of the truth, I did not feel any pain until workmen put me in a truck to take me to the hospital. I was met at the hospital by my mother, and while talking with her I felt my hip slip back in place. X-ray pictures showed a broken pelvis bone and three broken vertebrae.

A Christian Science practitioner in an out-of-state city took the case, and after twelve days I was out in a wheel chair and left the hospital the sixteenth day, walking out on crutches. No bones were set nor casts put on me. In less than six weeks I was walking without crutches or cane. Two months to the day I drove with my mother on an automobile trip covering a distance of about seventeen hundred miles. Before the end of six months I was working as a lineman for a power company.

The Tide of Healing

I have since been examined and X-rayed by doctors and found to be in perfect physical condition. I do not feel any ill effects from the experience, and know that only the power of Truth could bring about such a remarkable healing.

This was all done by absent treatment, and I did not meet the practitioner for more than a year after the healing.

This is but one of the many healings I have experienced, and I am very grateful for Christian Science, to the practitioners, and to Mrs. Eddy, who gave us the truth.

L. Hall Thompson, Nome, Alaska.

— Sentinel, Vol. 40, p. 96
(October 2, 1937).

[Original testimony in French]

IN 1935 our life was very difficult. My husband and I were both in poor health, which made our dispositions very trying. The doctors whom I consulted said that my nervousness was due to a fibroid tumor and phlebitis, which kept me almost constantly nervous and disquieted. I also suffered from the effects of otitis. From then on our life seemed hopeless.

It was then we found Christian Science. A woman whose husband had been healed by Christian Science told me about it. At the time I was incredulous; I could not be persuaded that God really exists. In my ignorance I laughed, shrugging my shoulders, when this woman told me that God would help us. But I was willing to go and see a practitioner, drawn by curiosity to learn more about Christian Science. In that first visit I was touched by the friendliness of the practitioner and I felt encouraged to read *Science and Health.* When I left this lady's office I already felt relieved and it seemed to me that life was sweeter. Even then I had begun to forget my desire to end my life. From that time my health so improved that now I am entirely well.

All the troubles diagnosed by the doctors have vanished into nothingness. But my gratitude overflows when I think of the veritable revelation I had one unforgettable July day. This revelation lifted me out of darkness. I was reading *Science and Health*, and as if a veil had been torn from my eyes, I suddenly understood that Truth is God, that there is only one Mind, God, Life, Spirit, intelligence, substance. From that moment I read with a heart of love that I might understand God better, and then only I appreciated fully the practitioner's help and consecration which had sustained me all along the way.

I must add that a problem involving our business was solved almost miraculously. It seems to me that since I have known of Christian Science all my hopes have been realized. I am infinitely grateful.

(Mrs.) Ernesta Ravinale, Paris, France.

— *Herald,* French edition, Vol. 22, pp. 58–59
(February, 1939).

I wish to express my deepest gratitude for the great help which I have received from the study of Christian Science, and I give this testimony with the hope that it may encourage others to partake of what is truly their birthright.

My first awakening to the truth of being came in the form of a direct appeal to God for help, during a trying experience in the war, when my knowledge of Christian Science was very limited indeed. On looking back, I am convinced that the fact that this call was answered instantaneously in a very wonderful way, laid the foundations for the desire, which came later, to learn more about Truth and how it operates in human affairs. It taught me first and foremost that God is ever present and available under all circumstances, and that if we turn to divine Principle with all our heart, our need will be met at once and to our complete satisfaction.

Since that first experience I have received many physical healings. A broken bone in my leg was completely healed without any material means, such as splints and so forth, being used at all. This was a case of absent treatment, information being given to the prac-

The Tide of Healing

titioner, first by telephone between Switzerland and London, and a few days later by means of wireless on board ship between England and the West Indies. An X-ray picture, taken on my return, showed the break, but the bone was reported as being perfectly set and healed. I have had gangrene from shot wounds arrested through Christian Science help. Though much fear that I might lose my leg was expressed, an extremely quick recovery was made.

We have witnessed many healings in my family: three children have been born with Christian Science aid alone, severe bladder trouble has been healed, and double pneumonia, contracted by one of the children during measles, was completely destroyed overnight.

In public life, inestimable help has been received in countless ways. The knowledge, as gained in Christian Science, that there is only one Mind, and that man in the image and likeness of God reflects that Mind, has again and again brought harmony to many difficult situations.

At times the way has appeared to be dark and obscure, but I have learned from experience that there is no tunnel which does not have an ending, and that when one does emerge, it is into the light. For this and for all the physical healings that I have witnessed; for the kindly counsel from those who are farther along the road; for the patient, loving help of several practitioners, and above all for the selfless labor of our beloved Leader, Mary Baker Eddy, who gave us this "pearl of great price," I can never be sufficiently grateful.

David, Earl of Airlie, Cortachy, Scotland.

— *Sentinel*, Vol. 42, pp. 815–816
(June 8, 1940).

AFTER MANY YEARS of preparation, I was ordained by an orthodox church council to preach. During my ministry my faith received a severe shock. An epidemic seized the town in which I was preaching. Being a pastor I was called to help relieve the suffering which, to me, was heartbreaking. I would be asked to pray that God would spare their lives to their loved ones. I did pray, but my faith, being without understanding, was giving way. I doubted the truth of my theology.

I turned to the Gospels, and read, "God so loved the world, that he gave his only begotten Son, that whosoever believeth in him should not perish, but have everlasting life." But in the face of my present experience, this did not seem to me to be true. I became an agnostic, and finally was deposed. For a period of thirty years I sought the meaning of life. I longed for the peace that was mine when I had a simple, childlike faith.

Things grew worse; I became morose, cynical, and held all religion in contempt. In 1929 more trouble came to me through the so-called depression. Then my wife, the dearest friend I had on earth, passed on. I too wanted to die and, as I then believed, end it all. While in this state of mind I was induced much against my will by my younger daughter, a student of Christian Science, to go to church with her on a Wednesday evening. I was full of hatred and prejudice, and the service was a blank to me. After the service she introduced me to an advanced student of Christian Science. He gave me a cordial greeting and then began to ask me about myself. I started to tell him what I thought of the whole religious system. To my surprise he was very patient, forbearing, kind, and even loving. Then he spoke to me of the God whom I had sought thirty years before, God, good, who knows no evil, sin, disease, or death; the divine Principle of all being, Mind, Soul, Life, Truth, Love. He revealed to me my real self as the reflection of God, His very image and likeness, not a poor lost sinner, without hope, but a blessed child of God.

I was lifted out of the dungeon of despair into the sunlight of divine Love. My daughter lent me a copy of *Miscellaneous Writings* by Mary Baker Eddy. I read until the small hours of the morning; I was astounded to find such wonderful literature. I was like a dry sponge drinking in water. I obtained Mrs. Eddy's great work, *Science and Health with Key to the Scriptures*. The first sentence was as a glow of heavenly light to me (Pref., p. vii): "To those leaning on the sustaining infinite, to-day is big with blessings."

The Tide of Healing

I caught a glimpse of the spirit of the writer and thanked God for the revelation. The second paragraph furnished me with food for thought, in the words, "The time for thinkers has come;" and, "Ignorance of God is no longer the stepping-stone to faith." The light of Truth was fast driving out of my consciousness theological errors.

While reading the chapter on Prayer, I became aware that I had not smoked for some time and had no desire to do so. I also lost the taste for liquor, and a habit of using foul language. This wonderful chapter taught me how to pray and what to pray for.

Months have rolled into years since I started to study this wonderful book, the "key" that has opened the Scriptures and made the Bible, to me, a new revelation.

My one desire now is to have more love, a better understanding of divine Principle, and to prove my understanding increasingly by demonstration; to be more Christlike, and to be worthy to bear the name "Christian Scientist."

John J. Spouse, Detroit, Michigan.

— *Sentinel,* Vol. 43, pp. 454-455
(February 8, 1941).

I SHALL ever be especially grateful for one exalting healing. By birth a Jew, as a child I was given some instruction in Hebrew and the Old Testament. One day in Malaya I read some of the New Testament for the first time. I was so amazed and attracted by the life of Jesus that I spent three nights reading the Gospels. I commenced to go to church irregularly, but as a Jew felt uncomfortable and self-conscious. About three years later, I went with a friend to the Protestant cathedral in Singapore and there heard a sermon on the crucifixion. It seemed in one moment every hope had been dashed to the ground, that I was one of a race responsible for having robbed the world of its greatest teacher, and could not dare nurture that hope so attractive to me. Unable to restrain myself I sobbed in great distress, for I so wanted what I then believed I could never get. From that time I did not again go to a church until I became interested in Science.

One day soon after coming to Science I was working with my books when I felt a great sense of God's presence. My questions which had not been put into words were answered, and I was shown at that moment that the world had never been robbed of its greatest teacher, that the lesson of the crucifixion was uninterrupted life. I saw that no one was a Christian merely by subscribing to a creed, but only those who emulated the Master and demonstrated his teaching; as he himself said, "If ye continue in my word, then are ye my disciples indeed." Never since have I been self-conscious as a Jew.

Since the outbreak of war I have completed over thirteen hundred hours' flying as a pilot, without a scratch or bruise for myself or crews.

I have learned to know Mrs. Eddy, the Discoverer and Founder of Christian Science, as she would wish, through her works, and to love and honor her leadership.

(*Lieut.-Commander "A"*) *Edward K. Lee, R.N.V.R.,*
Trinidad, British West Indies.

— *Sentinel*, Vol. 45, pp. 1781–1783
(October 16, 1943).

When Mrs. Eddy founded *The Christian Science Monitor* in 1908 she announced its object as being "to injure no man, but to bless all mankind" (*The First Church of Christ, Scientist, and Miscellany*, p. 353). A month later a writer in the *Christian Science Sentinel* (Vol. 11, p. 324) commented on the paper's challenge in this way: "The first conspicuous effect of this wonderful gift to ourselves and to the world has been to lift one's eyes to an horizon far beyond one's own doorstep. The call to help in the world's thinking is no longer something that can pass unheeded, it is an imperative duty. Things we did not like to look at nor think of, problems we did not feel able to cope with, must now be faced manfully, and correct thinking concerning the world's doings cultivated and maintained."

The Tide of Healing

Large numbers of Christian Scientists found this borne in on them by the events of this period. World War II brought bombings, uprooting, persecution, imprisonment, hunger, danger, loss of home and loved ones to many of them, and to others all the challenges of active service in the armed forces of various countries. Christian Science was banned in Germany and in Nazi-occupied lands, as well as in the Far East, and many of its practitioners were imprisoned at one time or another; but it carried on underground and actually grew and prospered through the war years.

Something of the spiritual saga of those years is recorded in *The Story of Christian Science Wartime Activities, 1939–1946* (The Christian Science Publishing Society, 1947). The large-scale relief activities of The Mother Church, camp welfare activities, ministrations to Christian Scientists in the various armed services, aid to refugees, methods of underground organization — all these are described in the book, and numbers of individual and group experiences are cited from the letters of gratitude which came to The Mother Church during and after the war.

A few random examples of wartime experiences follow. The first few are from letters quoted, along with many others, in the aforementioned book as illustrations of the ways in which men and women in the armed services learned to know God better during the war years.

THE BIG BREAK-THROUGH came and we were rushed to the front right after Christmas. What happened in the days and nights to follow would be beyond human capabilities to describe — the fight with the enemy and the even worse battle with the bitter cold. Few people know the suffering and the sacrifices made up there. It is impossible to describe the shell fire, the long nights cramped in a foxhole with the Krauts only a few yards ahead, the terror that overcomes one when he sees his friends screaming and pleading for help, right before his eyes!

You will never know what Christian Science meant to me. Though half dazed most of the time, I had a strange sense of peace and freedom from fear, and I was able to help many of my friends gain renewed courage and faith. At all times I kept the fundamentals of what I have learned foremost in my thought, and under the most desperate circumstances I held fast to Principle. In the daytime I read — sometimes aloud to my foxhole buddy, whoever it happened to be, cramped there in the bitter cold. At night I prayed while standing watch. I did not pray selfishly, either, nor for myself, but just for freedom from this world of materiality for all of us.

(pp. 403, 404).

At Munda, on New Georgia, during more than two weeks of almost incessant fighting, I was cared for and saved from fear. We had been fighting for a number of days and were out of water. Many were being wounded, and many others were going off the front carrying the wounded. Few men were left to hold ground. Our nearest source of drinking water was nearly five miles behind us, from which we had been cut off. The jungles were steaming hot; we had been without water for hours and faced going without it all night.

This was a human need and all realized it. Each turned to God in his own way. Indeed, all men pray under circumstances like this. I stepped off the trail and sat down to pray. It was up to God, and I just let it be up to Him. Soon afterward, an artillery shell of our own, intended to blast the enemy ahead of us, fell short and hit on the trail, hurting no one. Water gushed out of the hole! Our need was met. We were all grateful and praised God, one to another. We didn't feel that any miracle had occurred; this was just natural.

As I left the front a day or so later, I found a small Bible on the trail. Having lost my own, I picked it up eagerly. The water incident had been continually in my thought since it occurred. I opened the Bible at random and my eyes fell on the 35th verse of Psalm 107, "He turneth the wilderness into a standing water, and dry ground into watersprings."

(p. 409).

Although I did my work daily while in Stalag III at Luckenwalde, there arose among us an epidemic of diphtheria. The doctors considered me as one of the most critical cases and rushed me to the hospital, but within twenty-four hours I was healed as a result of my constant study of Christian Science. The doctor at the hospital did not examine me until I had been there between thirty and thirty-six hours, and he was amazed to find me in nearly perfect health.

I was also reading to two of my fellow patients, one being a diphtheria case, not able to speak, and the other suffering loss of sight in one eye as a result of having been hit with a grenade. As the latter patient had seemed to be in such agony of pain up until that time and I had succeeded in calming him, the doctor asked me to stay in the ward, not as a patient but as a ward boy. I spent as much time as I could with these two boys. After three or four days, the one with diphtheria was able to speak, and he asked to borrow my books whenever I was not using them.

The problem of the other patient seemed a little harder to meet, and it took nearly two weeks before he could read for himself, and then his recovery came remarkably fast. My books received a maximum amount of use during the time I spent at the hospital. Several doctors in the prison camp, as well as other patients, were continually borrowing them, and it was somewhat of a problem to get to use them myself at times.

(Pages 346–347).

For twenty years I had been the victim of depraved appetites. I had tried many so-called cures but none gave me any permanent relief, and I became worse. After being stationed in Iran about a year, I reached the point where I could not keep going, and I searched in desperation for some help.

There was a young man in our outfit who had attracted me. He did not indulge in tobacco, whisky, or gambling, and yet he seemed happier than any of us. I learned that he was a Christian Scientist. I had been introduced to Christian Science about seven years before but wouldn't live up to any of the rules; therefore, I failed to receive any benefit from Science, and dropped it. When I questioned the boy, he loaned me a *Christian Science Sentinel* and offered to help me in any way he could. Through Camp Welfare I was supplied with a Bible, *Science and Health*, and *Quarterly*.

However, it took me several months of suffering at my own hands and from my own wrong thinking before I was ready to accept Truth wholeheartedly and abide by the rules laid down.

So, in a smoke-filled barracks, where gambling games were going on in one end and all kinds of drinking bouts in the other end, I set out to find the truth that would liberate me. I read constantly for two days and nights, and the third night I slept like a baby, something which I had not done in years. The next morning when I awoke, I looked at the cigarettes on my table and I did not have the slightest desire for one. I was the happiest person alive. And the most beautiful and wonderful thing about the experience was my healing of the desire for whisky and narcotics, which had tormented me so many years. From that day my regeneration began and I can truthfully say that I am a new man. The blessings which have come to me since that morning have been too numerous to mention.

My regeneration was so outstanding that the men in my outfit wanted to know what caused such a happening, and through my healing, fifteen other men began to study the Bible and *Science and Health*. The books were ordered and came from the United States, Egypt, and India to these men, who consisted of Americans, Hindus, Moslems, and Indian Roman Catholics. One Indian sergeant made a beautiful demonstration over a cigarette habit of fourteen years' duration. He has since become a very consecrated student of Science and has done excellent healing work for himself and others.

(Pages 406–407).

The manifold ways in which the power of God can be proved in time of war are illustrated by the three entirely different experiences which follow, all of them from the Pacific theater of war:

AT THE OUTBREAK of the recent conflict with the Japanese I was on duty in the United States Navy Yard at Cavite, Philippine Islands. I served throughout the Philippine defense campaign and was led safely from that theater of war to our forces in Australia. This deliverance was the culmination of so many proofs of God's care that they cannot be told here in detail.

Briefly, I was included in a small party sent away from Corregidor on a certain mission shortly before the fall of that fortress in 1942. When I arrived at my new station it was possible to cable my teacher for help in recovering from the effects of malaria and of diarrhea contracted on Bataan. The results were immediate, and the healing has been permanent. Although a long convalescence had been predicted, I was restored to health and full vigor, and was assigned to duty in about ten days after asking for treatment.

When the enemy overran this new station, I was directed to evacuate my command and myself. Just before this occurred I sensed that some change was in the making. I therefore cabled my teacher once more, making the simple request that work for guidance be done once a week until I was heard from again. With four companions I made my way from this place, a point well inside the Philippine Archipelago, to a group of islands lying southwest of New Guinea, in all about fifteen hundred miles, through enemy-infested waters.

Our vessel was so primitive, with navigational adjuncts so elementary, that only the guidance of the one ever-present Mind can explain the fact that on one leg of the journey we crossed about eight hundred miles of open sea unmolested in weather well suited to our needs, and made a perfect landfall. We had neither charts nor sailing guides, only a page from an atlas.

After three months of adventurous travel replete with instances of protection, supply, and guidance, we arrived at a tiny harbor in the group of islands mentioned above. At various times we met natives with whom it was not possible to hold any spoken communication, yet these friendly people contrived to aid us in many ways and to contribute materially to our safety.

On the morning following our arrival and just five hours before our scheduled time of departure, an Allied vessel entered the harbor. I therefore visited the commanding officer of this new arrival in the hope that I might obtain information against which to check the validity of the plans that had been made for the remainder of our journey to Australia. When this officer learned our destination, he informed me that outrigger vessels such as ours could not be sailed in the waters that lay before us. He then offered us passage, which I accepted gratefully. When we reached the open sea beyond these islands all of us felt a deep thankfulness, for it seemed very probable that our simple craft with only sails for its motive power would have foundered in the rough seas that characterized this region.

It is noteworthy that we were three months sailing to this meeting point; that because of the near presence of the enemy and the imminence of his advance in our direction we had resolved to remain only twenty-four hours; that for the same reasons our rescuer had orders to depart the same day he arrived, and that no Allied vessel had been in this vicinity for several months. It should be noted also that the projected visits of our two vessels to this out-of-the-way place overlapped by just five hours. Thus, divine guidance and protection were again manifested.

Throughout this experience the one whom I had asked for help followed the text to be found on page 132 of *The First Church of Christ, Scientist, and Miscellany* by Mary Baker Eddy, which reads, "The Christian Scientist knows that spiritual faith and understanding pass through the waters of Meribah here — bitter waters; but he also knows they embark for infinity and anchor in omnipotence."

One of my shipmates remarked to me recently on the extraordinary nature of our voyage and asked whether I realized "that no one was ever sick during our trip." Another, a then self-styled atheist, convinced of a material universe functioning strictly by chance, declared about our experience afterward, "Too many things worked out just right to be the result of chance; there had to be a law of some kind at work." He had indeed witnessed the operation of divine Principle.

(Comdr.) Alexander R. Slimmon, U.S.N.R.,
Manila, Philippine Islands.

— *Sentinel,* Vol. 47, pp. 1989–1991
(December 15, 1945).

The Tide of Healing

I was living in Hong Kong when the Pacific War broke out, and I was an electrical engineer in the Public Works Department. So I was one of about two thousand five hundred Europeans interned by the Japanese Army in January, 1942. We had a sudden switch from foods we had been eating all our lives to a diet that lacked the food elements that a European is used to. Twice a day we had a small soup bowl of rice, sometimes combined with chrysanthemum leaves or a thin-leafed water spinach. As a result, the camp was continually full of cases of nutritional diseases, such as beriberi and pellagra or wounds that wouldn't heal.

But through what knowledge I had of Christian Science I knew enough about scientific prayer so that I was able to overcome the problem of an insufficient and unbalanced diet. Never once during the whole three years and eight months of internment did I suffer any of the symptoms of the various malnutritional diseases, or any disease at all. In spite of the thin diet, I was not weakened, nor did I lose any weight during the period, and we worked very hard each day. Other Christian Scientists in our group also had similar protection.

We prayed earnestly and regularly to God to supply our everyday needs, and we made a daily study of the Bible and Mary Baker Eddy's book, *Science and Health with Key to the Scriptures*. We knew that God supplies daily needs through spiritual ideas and that a grateful frame of mind is an open door for adequate supply. So we made it a practice to be grateful for every little thing, and we quietly voiced this gratitude aloud. I remember someone speaking of being grateful even to have water coming out of a tap or faucet in camp. We held to this plan of continuous gratitude and found it was very effective, although an American columnist who was also interned with us said one day in a rather puzzled way, "You people find the strangest things to be grateful for." And as a result of the frequent expression of gratitude, we found many little ways to improve the lot of the whole camp and supplement the meager diet. One of the problems of an imperfect diet was the loss of memory, and many of the people in camp complained of this. In fact, it was not at all uncommon to find that people couldn't re-member the simplest things. But I'm grateful to say that my appli-cation of Christian Science not only preserved my physical condi-tion, but my mental faculties. During the period of internment I gave lectures on electrical engineering to a group of fellow internees twice a week for three months, although I had never previously lec-tured or taught in any way and had no proper textbooks. I had to rely almost entirely on memory.

Final proof of the power of divine Truth to sustain man, no matter how difficult the circumstances, came at the end of our period of internment as the camp was disbanding. The man who was in charge of the repatriation was asked by one of our group when our turn to be shipped out would come. He said that the Christian Scientists in the camp would be the last to leave because they were the healthiest people there.

James Connell Brown, Ferndown, Dorset, England
Radio/TV series, "How Christian Science Heals," 1954.

THE WAR years were ones of great depression and mental struggle for me. It was Christian Science that finally pulled me through, because it is so logical, a Science that one can reason out for one-self, without having to depend on others. During this period of wavering and doubt, I found these words by Mary Baker Eddy par-ticularly helpful (*Science and Health with Key to the Scriptures,* p. 393): "Rise in the strength of Spirit to resist all that is unlike good. God has made man capable of this, and nothing can vitiate the ability and power divinely bestowed on man."

One of my chief problems was a great repugnance to entering the Army. From as early as I can remember, the prospect of having to enter the Army had been hanging over my head like the sword of Damocles. It was not so much the physical hardships as the terrific mental pressure which I dreaded, because I felt I might not be able to stand this pressure. However, the problem was beau-tifully worked out through the prayers of my family, and I found that as the day of my induction drew nearer I became calmer and calmer instead of more and more agitated. My brief term of service was filled with opportunities for the application of what I had learned, and altogether was a valuable experience of growth in spiritual understanding.

Another big problem, in fact the biggest problem of my life so far, was a false sense of nationalism, which is always an obstacle to clear and unprejudiced thinking. The first step in my healing came a few days after I had been demobilized, when I heard of a testimony which a Japanese friend had given in America shortly after the outbreak of war. In it she said: "I do not have to think American thoughts. I do not have to think Japanese thoughts. I have only to think God's thoughts." These words came to me as a great shock. For the first time I realized how blind I had been. I had been so busy thinking of myself as a Japanese that I had had no time to think of myself as God's child. I saw clearly that what was needed was to see things in the light of divine Principle and not of nationality. Since then, every time a narrow and limited concept of man has presented itself I have tried to correct it with the truth that man is God's idea. I rejoice to acknowledge that as I have done so I have been able to see things in their true light, with a clear and unobstructed vision.

Takashi Oka, Tokyo, Japan.

— *Sentinel*, Vol. 48, pp. 1396–1397
(August 10, 1946).

While many testimonies tell of striking instances of protection in war, there were other cases where lives were lost and where Christian Science brought a healing of grief to the families. Sometimes this was instantaneous; sometimes, as in the following example, it took growth in spiritual understanding to accomplish the healing:

WHEN THE WAR started my son was under 20 but he volunteered for service with the Royal Air Force. He was assigned to duties as a wireless operator and posted to Coastal Command which took him out to the West African coast.

After about a year he unexpectedly arrived home. He had a short leave and then left to return to Africa by way of Gibraltar. The large flying boat never reached Gibraltar, and we received word that he was reported "missing."

I was in service myself and away from home so the initial shock of the news was very great. I had been a student of Christian Science for more than 15 years and I had come to know God as divine Life and infinite Love. I knew of God's tender love for His creation, and I prayerfully clung to the thought that no matter what had happened, my son was always in God's care and keeping and therefore safe.

At this time I was greatly comforted and helped by my study of the Bible and the Christian Science textbook. Something Mary Baker Eddy writes in *Science and Health* was particularly helpful. It deals with the sorrow of Christ Jesus' disciples at the Passover meal just before the Saviour's crucifixion, and it shows the spiritual significance of the bread. This is what we read (p. 33): "Their bread indeed came down from heaven. It was the great truth of spiritual being, healing the sick and casting out error." And further on we read: "They had borne this bread from house to house, *breaking* (explaining) it to others, and now it comforted themselves." I saw that in my case the "truth of spiritual being" was the truth of God as divine Life and man's relationship to God. And I can assure you that this truth comforted me.

The message finally came from the Air Ministry that they couldn't hold out any further hope. Now I realized I had to prove whether I really understood what I had been studying or whether I merely believed it.

I had to see clearly that man is actually spiritual, indestructible, deathless, made in the image and likeness of God. Since God is infinite Life, He must be man's true Life. I realized it isn't possible for the good in a young and promising life to be cut off since God is Life. Just because I couldn't actually see my son, talk to him, or be with him humanly wouldn't alter his real life one bit.

When these facts were absolutely clear to me and I was certain that in reality there couldn't be any death — or any separation, then I was all right. My grief and distress vanished and they've never returned. I can talk of my son — things that happened when he was a boy or experiences we had together — and there's no feeling of depression but just the joyous freedom that has come through my study of Christian Science. I might add that the final healing came in just a few weeks so it wasn't time that healed me. It was the understanding that God is divine Life — and knowing man's unbroken relationship to that Life.

Ernest Dutton, Belfast, Northern Ireland
"How Christian Science Heals," Radio Program No. 141.

When the destructive forces of hatred and despair are loosed in war, the Christian is imperatively summoned to prove the healing power of love. At such a time he is challenged also to find that spiritual joy which the Saviour, on the eve of his crucifixion, promised should never be taken away from his followers. The final testimonies in this section give hints of the way in which peace can be demonstrated in the very midst of war, and Love be found as the universal victor:

DURING the Second World War, after the Conscription Act had been passed in Britain, the Royal Navy found it necessary to establish Naval Detention Quarters to deal with some of the men who were being drafted into the service. I was appointed as captain in charge of one of these establishments during the last two years of the war.

One day we received a message from the depot that a very difficult case was being sent to us and that extra care should be taken that he injure no one; he was under court-martial sentence as a habitual deserter. He was not long with us before he ran foul of all forms of authority, smashed everything in his cell including the window and the light, tore his uniform to pieces and ripped up his boots; he then tried to strike the staff if he saw an opportunity and entirely refused to co-operate. He was antisocial and a rebel against all forms of discipline. He was punished according to the regulations, but to no effect. The chaplain had several talks with him; then the medical officer, who was a psychiatrist, tried to reason with him, and the schoolmaster also tried to help him. I had several interviews alone with him in his cell, but all to no avail. We then asked his foster parents to visit him, but they had to admit after a long interview that they had failed to make an impression.

During the dogwatch and after working hours, I went into his cell and tried again to reason with him, promising him that if he would only give me his word to behave, he would be treated as a man; but he just lay on the floor and would not say a word.

All material methods had failed; both human kindness and strict discipline were of no avail, and the whole prison was watching this contest. Returning to my house I prayed for some three hours, as a student of Christian Science, for guidance. I was led to go back to the prison, feeling that I was going with the power of the Spirit, yet not knowing what to do. Just before midnight I called the warder to unlock the cell, and then sent him on his rounds. Upon going in, I saw the man still on the floor, motionless. I went over to him in the dim light and stood over him. Then the thought came to me, Right there is the son of God. I held this thought to the best of my ability for fifteen minutes; neither of us said a word. I then went out and called the warder to go in and release him, give him a wash, some fresh clothes, and his bed, and turn him in.

The next morning the chaplain visited the man in his cell, and these were his words to the padre: "When the captain came into my cell last night about midnight and stood over me, I felt like the meanest man on earth and wished the floor could have opened up and let me through." That was the end of the trouble; he was friendly and obedient to regulations, and I had several long talks with him before he left us to stand trial again for the injury he had done to another man before he came to us. He was given two years in a civil prison. Some six months later I visited him there and found him as happy as a man can be in prison; he was given a good report by the prison authorities. Not long after that I received a letter from him thanking us for what we had done for him and asking that I give his kind regards to the staff. This man came to us breathing out hatred and injury to one and all, but left us with his kind regards.

I am grateful for the teachings of Christian Science, which make practical to this age the counsel of the Apostle Paul, "Overcome evil with good" (Rom. 12:21).

Captain Arthur G. Curtis, Sturry, Kent, England.

— *Sentinel*, Vol. 53, pp. 1540–1541
(September 1, 1951).

WHILST I WAS nursing in a military hospital during the war, under the heading of "doing my bit," it came my turn for night duty. I found myself with three wards and approximately seventy men to care for, including four serious pneumonia cases and one bronchial case. Most workers had a great deal to do, but as a Christian Scientist I wanted very much to bring a sense of harmony into the work. It had been my habit to spend at least fifteen minutes during the day realizing the presence of God, and I found on night duty that I could best do this at midnight. The bronchial case was a man who so resented hospital life that he expressed himself in the most awful profanity. For three nights he was the most disturbing element, and on the fourth night I found myself much upset and distressed; so, as soon as I was able, I shut myself in the duty room to realize the harmony of God's presence. Suddenly I saw that whereas I was willing to give extra care to the very sick patients, this condition demanded much more and I must be obedient to Jesus' command (Matt. 5:41), "Whosoever shall compel thee to go a mile, go with him twain." I knew that that patient could never resent divine Love.

Very early the following morning, while attending to another patient, I saw that this man was out of bed, so I called to him to come and hold the pillows while I helped the patient. Swearing, he came, and whilst he was assisting me, the patient looked up and asked if he might inquire what I did every night quietly in the middle of the ward for about fifteen minutes. Seeing that the man was sincere, I told him I tried to realize a sense of harmony in the ward, the presence of God, that a better sense of health might be established. As I left the bedside, the man who had been swearing followed me and stumblingly said, "If I swear again, please know it is a mistake." In a few days his bronchotomy operation was canceled, and he was classed as an "up-patient." He became so helpful in the ward, and so reliable, that I was able to give much more time to the four pneumonia cases, with the result that the medical officer in charge said these cases had recovered much quicker than he had expected. The matron commented on the peace and quiet of these wards at that particular time.

A year later I was myself attacked with pneumonia, but with the help of a practitioner it was quickly overcome, and duties were resumed within a week. For the quick response of the practitioner and for the kindness of the medical officer, who knew I was a Christian Scientist and left me free after examination, relying on my word that immediate help would be received, I am most grateful.

(Miss) Grace Mary Frith,
Isleworth, Middlesex, England.

— Sentinel, Vol. 51, pp. 1981–1983
(November 5, 1949).

DURING my first winter as a prisoner during the Second World War, I suffered from sinusitis. I worked prayerfully as best I could, but without obtaining any relief at all. Then I examined my consciousness to see what there might be in it which could be delaying the healing. I discovered I had a deep hatred for my country's so-called enemies and a deep resentment at being a prisoner. Each day, in order to fight these arguments of personal sense, I read and pondered the Sermon on the Mount.

Little by little my thoughts were transformed and permeated with the wonderful light which shines forth from these words of Christ Jesus. After several months of such work I was finally able to pray sincerely for all those around me, including the so-called enemies, and to express gratitude to God for the way in which I had been guided and protected up to that time. A little later I found to my great joy that I was no longer suffering from the sinusitis.

Roger Pantet, Saint-Germain-en-Laye,
Seine-et-Oise, France.

— *Journal*, Vol. 81, p. 48
(January, 1963).

Wᴴᴵʟᴇ ᴀɴ ɪɴᴛᴇʀɴᴇᴇ in a concentration camp during World War II the writer fell ill, and sores appeared on his hands and feet. Fellow internees said these sores could not heal because of malnutrition. This opinion had the happy effect of making him intensify his study of Christian Science and rely more and more on God.

The sores began to heal, and in about three weeks all except a large and deep one on the sole of each foot had closed, and for this progress he was very grateful. Then came a desert experience when, no matter how hard he worked in Christian Science, there was no improvement whatsoever. When he earnestly asked God to show him what more to do, he clearly saw that he must love and not hate. To love those who were meting out cruel treatment under the most appalling conditions prevalent in this camp seemed something impossible of achievement. However, the clear instructions to love could not be ignored; so he set about separating all evil from his thought of man, and slowly there dawned in his consciousness the truth of being — that man as the son of God is lovable.

As he persistently worked with this truth and denied mortal sense testimony, the stubborn sores began to close; and when he reached the stage where he could see that man is always loving, he was completely healed. This lesson on love given to him by Love has been of inestimable value ever since.

Charles Robert Rodÿk, London, England.

— "O Dreamer, Leave Thy Dreams,"
Sentinel, Vol. 55, p. 1243
(July 18, 1953).

Many wartime experiences have never been told except to close friends, and others cannot be published because they contain information of too personal or sometimes too political a nature. The final testimony in this group is a tape-recorded account of a testimony which has been given verbally but never before in print. It is given here in its full, unedited detail and conversational informality as an example of the many individual experiences not formally recorded.

I WAS LIVING in Austria, it was the year 1942. At the time I was in Stalag 17A. It was a prisoner of war camp on the Hungarian border. There were also young people there like myself whose parents were known to have worked in the underground.

Because I had very poor eyesight I was given two weeks of absence to seek the services of an eye specialist in Wiesbaden. The gentleman was quite a prominent doctor. I had corresponded with him and asked if I could come and see him. When he first examined me, he told me that he couldn't do anything for me, that what I needed was faith in God.

My answer was "How can I have faith in God? Do you want me to take it out of the air?" And he said, no, that he would give me a book to read, and that if I could understand God I could have faith. So he gave me the Christian Science textbook, *Science and Health with Key to the Scriptures* by Mrs. Eddy, which was in German and in English.

I didn't read it. I wasn't interested in religion. I didn't want to know anything about God. But every day, every time I came to see him, he asked me if I had started reading the book. Finally, I started reading it. And I think the two things that startled me, that made me think that this was something tremendous, were, first of all, the definition of God. I thought that if a God existed, He would have to be the way Mrs. Eddy defined Him in the beginning of the chapter of Recapitulation. And the second thing was the idea that good had more power than evil, and that we could prove this in our lives. To me this was tremendous because we seemed to be surrounded by the power of evil and nothing else at all.

So when I had to return to the camp, I wanted to take the book with me. At first the doctor didn't want to give me the book, since you couldn't buy books at that time. He offered to send me quotations, but I wanted the book. So he gave it to me, and also a Christian Science *Herald,* a German *Herald.*

I returned to my camp, and just the little bit of reading I had done — about a week of reading — was enough so that the expression on my face had changed so much that some of the people in the camp didn't recognize me. I also picked up a Bible on the way to the camp, and when I got back, I started studying day and night. It just absorbed all my thoughts. I sat in this one room that we had — twelve women in one room — with one light bulb on the ceiling. I sat on the floor and just spent every minute studying that I possibly could.

I first received the book in September of 1942, and sometime in January, 1943, I was studying and all of a sudden I caught a glimpse of what man is: the spiritual image and likeness of God. It was just as if a fog had been let open and I saw that man — as he really is — cannot be detained in a prison, he cannot be confined in a camp, but he is as unlimited and unbounded as God. It practically seemed ridiculous to think that you could keep man behind barbed wires, or confined within anything.

So I picked up the Bible, *Science and Health*, my German *Herald,* and a few personal things, and I walked out of this camp by broad daylight. I didn't try to hide anything. I just walked out the one street — there was only one road out of the camp. There were watch towers, there were continually soldiers on duty, and they had trucks and armed vehicles. But I went down on foot for about two hours and a half to the closest railroad station, and I took a train to Vienna. No one came after me; no one even saw me walk out.

My motive, my only desire was to learn more, to understand more of this teaching. It seemed to me that I couldn't understand the explanations about God. I couldn't understand the explanations about spiritual existence, because all I had ever known was material existence — what we can see and feel and hear with our five senses.

So I tried to find my father, who at that time was working in the underground against Hitler, and I got hold of him for half an hour in a street. I told him very quickly that I had found this teaching and I thought it was tremendous. I had a terrific urge to find out more, and I absolutely needed some money from him to go and find people that could explain this to me. He thought that it was something to beware of, but he did give me the money I asked for. It was the last time I saw my father.

I took this money and put it in a little postal book, which you can take to any post office and draw out what you need. And with the German *Herald* in hand, I systematically tried to find a Christian Scientist somewhere that would help me. I started with Vienna, and I couldn't find anyone except Mrs. ——— who at that time was living with Princess ——— in her palace as her companion. She was willing to see me.

She told me that the Christian Science movement was not permitted — that they were not permitted to practice or speak about Christian Science in the Third Reich; and that there were churches and they were closed, there were Reading Rooms and they were closed. She thought that the best thing I could do was to study and listen and ponder. She assured me that what *Science and Health* contained was the truth, and for me just to go ahead and study quietly and not talk about it. She said she couldn't see me any more.

I still felt such a need to speak to somebody that I decided to go north to East Germany and find some of the people that were listed in the German *Herald*. I went eventually to Breslau.

I should say, too, that after leaving camp I didn't have any identity card. It was absolutely necessary in the Third Reich to have an identity card, because you were continuously checked on the trains, in the street cars, on the streets. But I was never checked. No one ever seemed to ask where I came from or what I was doing, although I really was of an age where people either had to work or they had to be in some form of effort to win the war. I also never had a food ration card, because you could only get the food ration cards by having an identity card. But I always had a meal when I needed it. Not having an identity card also meant that I couldn't go to a hotel, I couldn't go to boarding houses. But at that time the station had quite adequate deck chairs, because everyone was on the move. There were many soldiers coming from the front, there were people who had lost their homes through air raids, and there was a continual movement of people who didn't have homes, so it was quite normal to spend the night in a railroad station and wait for another train. No one ever questioned me.

By this time through reading the Christian Science textbook I had received a conviction that God exists; also that He is very willing to take care of us, and that we can ask Him for advice and guidance and that we would get the answers. I found that I would get very direct answers and very apropos.

I remember in Breslau I had no idea where I was going to go . . . I didn't know what to do. So I just turned to God and said: What do I do now? And the thought came to me that I should go to Berlin. That was in 1943, when the air raids were quite frequent. But I followed the inner voice. I got a ticket for the night train. It was all blacked out because of the air raids, and the person standing closest to me was a soldier who had just returned from the Russian front. The train moved, and as we stood there hour after hour, he started pouring out all the experiences that he had had at the front.

This sort of intimate communication from the heart prompted me to tell him about Christian Science, to tell him that somehow I felt it was a tremendous thing, but that I couldn't find anyone to explain anything to me; and yet that I had had proofs, and so I thought it must be true. It was such a wonderful thing if it were true, I said, and if I could only find someone to talk to, to find out if people actually lived this teaching.

And he said, "Christian Science! I've heard of it somewhere. You know I think I have an aunt and she has a friend, and I think that friend is a Christian Scientist, and her name is Miss ——— and she lives in Rostock. Go and see her. I think she's a Christian Scientist."

So after having spent one day in Berlin in different air raid shelters I went back to the station and made my way to Rostock, which is northeast of Lubeck, in northern Germany, a very small town.

I found the lady. She lived at the address that was given to me. She was in her eighties at the time. She was a lovely person. She was not afraid. She was a Christian Scientist. They had a small informal group in Rostock. They were never molested and their books were never taken away. They didn't hold any meetings at that time, but they did have all the literature. She said I could come, and I could talk to her, and she would give me any of the books that I might want.

I learned about the Christian Science movement from her. She tried to answer all my questions, and when I think about her — it was the erectness and the love she expressed which really impressed me, and the complete lack of fear. She did what was right, what she felt was right, in spite of threats — she didn't receive any personal threats, but I mean it was well known that you just didn't talk about Christian Science.

She couldn't house me because she was living with a sister in a small apartment, but she told me that I could come and talk to her any time I wanted. So I thought it was important that I find living quarters close to her, but I couldn't live in any hotel or boarding house or anything like that.

So as had become my habit, I stood in the street and I asked God what I should do.

The thought came to me to go to this hardware store and buy something very small. As I entered the door, I greeted the storekeeper in my Austrian way of greeting. Two gentlemen leaving the store stopped short. They had recognized my Austrian accent, and asked me if I was Austrian. I said, yes. They told me they were, also, and that they were working up there in the war effort. They were both Nazis, and they also had a car. They asked if they could do anything for me because I was a fellow countryman of theirs and up in northern Germany was sort of far away from Austria. And I told them very frankly that I needed living quarters.

They thought they could find them and they took me to Warnemuende which is a resort on the North Sea. It was filled with boarding houses and hotels. They all stood empty, because everyone had been evacuated. It was a war zone up there, for fear that the British might land any minute. So they thought that I could just take any boarding house that I wanted and live there. However, as we drove there — to me it was just the working out of Love again — they talked to each other and they thought it really wouldn't be too good if I just lived alone in a boarding house. And they thought of an elderly lady that owned one of these boarding houses that had refused to leave. She just wanted to stay where she had always lived, and the police left her there. She was about the only inhabitant of Warnemuende at the time. So they took me to her and asked her if she could put me up. She was delighted to have a boarder, and she gave me the best room she had, on the first floor with a view over the canals and the ocean and a big, nice chair to sit in and think, and a nice comfortable bed. I stayed with her until August of 1943, going three or four times a week to Rostock, talking to Miss ———, getting new books from her and taking long walks along the ocean to read them.

During that time I always had a meal, although I had no food ration card. And sometimes I got a meal in a rather strange fashion. One day somebody gave me a bread card for a whole month — just gave it to me, and I never saw the person again. And another time a policeman stopped and asked me if I already — it was a Sunday, and I was going along the ocean with my book — and he asked me if I already had eaten, and I told him I hadn't. He told me about a lovely place where they served gorgeous meals. Meals were sort of important at that time, because you didn't get to eat too often with food ration cards — I mean good things. So I thanked him for the information and he left. I knew I couldn't go there. But then he came back on his bicycle and said: "I thought perhaps you didn't have the necessary tickets." And he just gave me exactly enough for the meal. He tore it off his meat card and his bread card, and card where you get butter and that sort of thing — just enough for that one meal. I never forgot this, because here I was without an identity card and he could have arrested me; but instead he gave me enough tickets to buy a meal with.

It was a very fruitful time up there. I think I gained a great deal. I think the ocean and the wideness and the peace and quiet helped me greatly to understand the greatness and the wideness of God.

A Century of Christian Science Healing

Towards the end of July I noticed the two young men who had brought me there. They were living there in a different place and sometimes I met them in the street. It seemed that they asked me an awful lot of questions and they looked at me in a strange way. I had a feeling that perhaps I had better leave. I didn't feel completely welcome or safe up there any more, so I took leave from my landlady and I thanked Miss ——— for the many hours she had spent with me explaining Christian Science.

When I left Rostock, I went to Hamburg. I arrived in Hamburg toward the end of July of 1943. That night a week-long air raid started. I think the British came by day and the Americans by night, or the other way around. They came continuously for one week until the whole city was razed to the ground. The suffering was abominable. Everything was burning.

This was the first time that I could really prove the efficacy of Christian Science. I was led to the 91st Psalm. Later I found out that the 91st Psalm is the Psalm of protection. I didn't know it at the time, and yet this is where my Bible opened. With this 91st Psalm, not only I was comforted and protected; also the other people around me were comforted and protected. I read it to them in one of these air raid shelters — it wasn't really a shelter, it was just a basement, and they were very peaceful and quiet. But then the house collapsed on top of us, and we had to leave that shelter, too.

It must have been the next morning, which was Sunday morning (the smoke was so thick that we never saw the daylight). The suffering being so extreme, I felt that I must go and help. I found a crew of young people, which was something like Boy Scouts except it was an organization formed by the Nazi youth. They were going into the cellars trying to dig out people, and they laid them out on the street. Anyone who was willing to help was put into service. It was like nursing really. What you were supposed to do was to see if these people were living. If they were living, wash their eyes and their nose — wash the dirt off so they could breathe and open their eyes. And if they were dead, just go on to the next one. We were very short of water. I only had one canteen with water.

I had been studying so much and I was so sure of God's presence and His help and His love, I guess death didn't really enter my thought. I knelt down by the first one and I talked to him about God, that He was Life, and that they reflected this Life. I just knelt there and talked to them until they opened their eyes. Then I washed their eyes and their nose and I went on to the next one.

Now there was another crew of people working, and they took the people who had opened their eyes and that were obviously alive, and they put them on a truck. Then the truck took them outside of Hamburg into the surrounding villages, where the people had all opened their houses and took in these people from Hamburg and fed them and let them come to.

I remember well that long line of people in the middle of the street, and there were two rows of burning houses. I just knelt down beside each one and told them about God and about Life and it was so natural, the whole thing. They opened their eyes, and then I washed their eyes and went on to the next one. I don't know how long this went on . . . maybe a day, maybe two days . . . and by that time it was about Tuesday and someone took me and put me in a truck, too, and said: "You've had enough."

The truck took us outside, and I, myself, was taken to a small village. There were some people who took me in, and they fed me juices to drink. We all had very thick lips from all the smoke, and swollen ankles, but otherwise I was fine.

I slept for the night, and the next morning I woke up and I wanted to help, I wanted to do something. So I went to the Red Cross and asked them if I could help and they said, yes, I could. They put me into a school house that was converted into a hospital. There were just rows of people, lying on the floor, mostly with wounds of burning, and there was a doctor, two nurses and myself. We had 140 people to look after — 70 on each floor.

My experiences at this time in being able to comfort, help, and heal, slowly showed me that the truth did work. I could practice it, I could prove it.

Well, this is practically the end. I returned to Vienna towards the end of the year. I was in my early twenties then. I was married by that time, and my husband was at the front.

In the spring of 1945 the Russians came to conquer Vienna. They had conquered Budapest, had fought in Budapest for two months. It was rather a ghastly fight with a lot of cruelty and bar-barism. The radio was full of all the things they had done and that everyone should try to get out of their reach before they came. Also, there were a lot of word-of-mouth stories, because many of the Hun-garians had come west and had brought their horror stories with them.

Now I denied those stories simply on the ground that I felt that whatever was true was true about everybody regardless of national-ity or friends or enemies. I was not willing to accept anything I knew was not the truth from the point of view of God's perfect creation.

But I would have liked to leave Vienna, naturally, and one morn-ing a friend of my husband's came with a truck and he said: "Quickly, quickly, pack something. I'm going to take you over the border. I'm going to take you away from Austria, if possible, over the border into Switzerland."

It seemed wonderful at first, because I had been brought up in Switzerland and it was a free country, and no war; it just seemed like a dream. And I ran back into the house to get some things together and thought this was the answer to my prayers. But I had constantly been confronted with such big decisions. I was so used to turning to God before anything I ever did, that I stopped in the hallway and said spontaneously: "What shall I do?" And the an-swer came as fast as the question had been asked: "Whom are you running away from? There are no enemies." I saw that in God's creation there are no enemies, and there is no need to run.

So I went back to this young man, and I told him that I wouldn't be going with him, that I was going to stay right here. He tried to persuade me. Naturally he thought he had an obligation towards my husband, who was his friend, to take me to safety, and he thought I was just being very foolish, stupid. But I stayed, and I felt quite sure that this was it. By that time I knew that if I heard God's voice, I would obey it, and I stayed. By staying I gave a home to a cousin of mine who had lost hers, and to some others, also.

I didn't have much food. No one had any food at that time. But at the corner of my street only a few houses away, there was a grocery. And the grocer was a very heavy, big man who would come to my apartment for peace and quiet, and rest. It was rather amusing because he was twice my size and twice my age, and he would come and say: "This is like an oasis." And every time he came, he brought something — a loaf of bread or something else. Other people that came, too, would say: "There is so much peace here." And everyone brought something. You know, I always had enough food for the people that I had to feed, including myself.

There was a lot of fighting in the streets when the Russians came. Most of them were Asiatic Russians, who have customs that date back to the Middle Ages. When they come to a city, for three days they have complete freedom to plunder, to loot, and to do anything they want to. Even their commandant couldn't do anything about it, and told the population of Vienna that the only thing we could do would be to shut ourselves into our houses. And there were lots of Russians that came to my house, and I was completely without fear. I was so convinced of the truth that there is only one man, the man made in God's image.

They might have come to steal, but they finished up with one of those Russian dances to amuse my cousin and myself and they left slapping us on the shoulder and calling us "Mamuschka." So actually it was complete protection. And they brought food, too, so we had enough to eat. Some of the people on my street noticed and said: "You and your house, you are the blind spot in the eye of every Russian."

I still kept reading the textbook from cover to cover (that was about the fourth time by then). My desire to know more about Christian Science made me feel that as soon as I could I'd like to go to England. As soon as I had the opportunity, I went to England and, of course, the English people had had wonderful steadfastness and staunchness. They stood on the truth they had learned — the English Christian Scientists. The testimonies in the English churches after the war were just absolutely wonderful, and I was sure that this was it. So then I joined a church in London, and very soon after became a member of The Mother Church, and had class instruction. And that's it.

(Mrs.) L. Adrienne Vinciguerra,
Santee, California.

A Century of Christian Science Healing

1945-1965

It has been pointed out that for each testimony included in this book scores or even hundreds of similar accounts may have appeared over the past century. Yet each is a wholly individual experience. The kingdom of God, or revelation of reality, comes to men individually, not *en masse*.

If one should take a thousand cases of the healing of cancer by Christian Science, one would find a thousand different lives touched by the Christ-power, a thousand different ways in which the transforming vision of the absolute Principle of being had entered into the relative circumstances of a human life, even though the Principle and Science of the healing were in each case the same. In the scale of Christian values it is not statistics but the quality of individual experience that counts, and the mere massiveness of Christian Science healing through the past century is of far less importance than the spiritual light which in varying degree shines through each experience of God's healing power.

In 1953 a weekly radio series entitled "How Christian Science Heals" was instituted by The Mother Church and later was supplemented by a regular television series with the same name. Many of the testifiers who appeared on these programs had already had testimonies published in one or another of the Christian Science periodicals, but the format of the programs permitted the background circumstances of the healing as well as the thinking involved in it to be developed more fully.

Each person was therefore interviewed at length before the selection of his testimony and further information pertinent to his healing was obtained, as well as additional verifications. This was done in order to establish as fully as possible not only the *fact* of his healing but also the *how*, including the mental processes and the moral and spiritual regeneration involved.

For this reason a number of testimonies from the programs have been included in the present section. While it is not the purpose of this book to explain the metaphysics of Christian Science or to discuss in detail the nature of Christian Science treatment, the more extended testimonies in this section indirectly convey a good deal of both the basis and the method of Christian Science healing. A thoughtful reading of these accounts will show that in Christian Science spiritual healing means not merely a changing of the physical evidence but a step-by-step bringing to light of the true nature of God's creation, a demonstration of the presence of the kingdom of God here and now.

Some of the testimonies from programs given over the air have been abridged to make their inclusion possible, but others have been expanded with material from the preliminary interviews which was excluded from the broadcasts because of time limitations. In each case, however, the testimony is entirely in the testifier's own words and is used with his permission.

The testimonies in the group immediately following include several accounts of healings which took years for their completion — years of spiritual, moral, and mental growth, years of exploration, dedication, and regeneration. Even an instantaneous healing is only the beginning of such a transformation of the human by the divine, or else it is a sudden forward step in a regenerative process already begun.

A NUMBER of years ago I very suddenly lost my sight. My husband took me to all the local specialists and they pronounced me beyond help. Then I was taken to a large clinic in Chicago. I stayed there for 6 weeks under the observation of 20 eye specialists. They told me I couldn't possibly regain my vision because the sight film had been destroyed. The eye difficulty was attributed to a condition I had before our second child was born, and I was advised not to have any more children. Also, they reported evidence of tuberculosis and I was told I'd better return home for treatment. They gave me only two years, at the most, to live.

A Century of Christian Science Healing

I might say here that I was brought up by devout Christian parents who were both students of the Bible. It was through my love of the Bible that I found the way out of my troubles. Things seemed to be as bad as they could be. I was totally blind and growing weaker. We were in desperate circumstances. My husband had spent all his earnings to help me and the firm he was with had gone bankrupt and he was out of a job. He went to another state to look for work. The children and I went to stay with my mother, and later on we went to my sister's. I prayed frequently but I usually finished by thinking that ours surely was a lost cause.

One day my sister was reading the Bible to me and she came to the verse in Matthew, "And all things, whatsoever ye shall ask in prayer, believing, ye shall receive" (21:22). I asked my sister to read this passage over again two or three times. This was an awakening to me for I saw that I had been denying that this statement was true every time I finished praying. Now something changed in me and I began praying with confidence.

My husband had been out of work for three months. But just a few days later he found a job. When he wrote me this I knew my prayer had been answered.

Then a wonderful thing happened. My husband found a nice apartment for us and sent for us on Easter Sunday. It was in the home of a college professor whose entire family were Christian Scientists. I have never known such kindness and consideration as these people expressed to us. As a result of this, the prejudice and resentment which I'd had for years towards Christian Science disappeared. I finally decided to try this religion. I soon had two proofs that I could be helped. One was the solving of a very serious business problem and the other was the healing of an intestinal condition that had bothered me since I was 16 years old.

My husband and daughter read to me from *Science and Health with Key to the Scriptures* and Mary Baker Eddy's other writings and from the Christian Science periodicals. I also had regular help from a Christian Science practitioner.

The first indication that my sight was returning came when I began to recognize the difference between dark and light. I didn't tell anyone for fear this was just an illusion. But then I gradually began to see forms. Of course, we were all overjoyed at this progress. This continued for about a year when I began to make out some letters on billboards along the highways — then full sentences. For the next three years progress was slow and gradual, but steady.

There were many changes in my thinking that had to take place. Through Christian Science I got rid of fear, shame, resentment, condemnation, criticism, hatred, and a sense of inferiority.

I learned that God is good and that He loves all His creation and that we must love each other. I learned that God's law is the only true law and entirely good, and I learned to be obedient to it. I learned gratitude. I learned patience, and to think constructively in my opinions of man and the universe. And most of all I learned that man, spiritual man — the man of God's creation — is complete and perfect now. You might say I had to reconstruct my concept of what man is, including myself. I learned most of all that sight or vision is spiritual and cannot be lost, decayed, carried away, or dimmed.

My sight kept on improving and later I was able to read. For many years now, I have been able to see very well and I do all that I want to do, even to driving a car at night with perfect ease. Being able to see, after four years of total blindness, is indeed quite wonderful to me. The tuberculosis disappeared years ago along with the blindness. And you remember, I told you that I was advised not to have another child, but since then I have had two more lovely children without any ill effects.

> (Mrs.) Bernice Lewsader, Lansing, Michigan
> Radio/TV series, "How Christian Science Heals," 1956.

At the time I was introduced to Christian Science, I was suffering from a heart condition I'd had from birth. I'd gone to many doctors, including some of the finest in Europe, but they could do nothing for me and pronounced my condition incurable.

Later on, after I was married, I injured my spine in a fall and was bedridden for seven months. The heart condition was aggravated to such an extent that my husband feared for my life. He spoke about me to a friend who'd been healed in Christian Science, and this friend assured us that I could be healed too.

At the time, I had a very wrong idea about Christian Science. But after listening to this friend, I consented to have a Christian Science practitioner come to see me. The practitioner spoke to me of the loving goodness of God and of His great love for man — that God is Love.

And with this new understanding a wonderful feeling of peace came over me, a peace that I had never, never known before. Within a week's time, I was perfectly healed.

Some time afterward I had occasion to have a physical examination, and the doctor said, "There's one sure thing — you have a perfect heart!"

This healing gave me courage to rely on God when it was found some years later that I had cancer. My husband insisted that I have a medical examination and was greatly concerned when a physician told him the condition was too far along to be operated on. But I assured my husband that if God could heal the heart trouble, then He could heal this too, for "with God all thing are possible."

As I turned to God in prayer, I suddenly found myself thinking of Mary Baker Eddy's experience — how she was instantaneously healed of severe injuries from an accident when she turned to the Bible for help. And so I immediately began a deep study of the Bible myself. The trouble had reached the stage where I could no longer take care of my home; so I had the whole day for study.

As I studied the Bible in connection with the Christian Science textbook, *Science and Health with Key to the Scriptures* by Mrs. Eddy, I found I was gaining a clearer and clearer insight into the spiritual meaning of the Scriptures. I found new significance in the New Testament account of Jesus' disciples. Not only the spiritual qualities of thought that each of the disciples represented, but the human failings each had to overcome.

For instance, Peter, who denied Jesus three times. And as I searched my own thoughts, I saw that I'd sometimes denied the Christ too. Saying that I was sick was denying the Christ, Truth, which Jesus expressed in his healing work and which is always available.

The Tide of Healing

And the two disciples who wanted to sit, one at the right hand and the other at the left hand of Jesus. They reminded me that I had thoughts of pride and vainglory to overcome.

But when it came to Judas, I said to myself, "Well, there's one thing sure, I've never been like Judas." But then I thought, "His main problem was jealousy." I bowed my head. I knew I'd been jealous at times. I'd long been jealous of a member of my family. Here was the root of the problem, and I saw that the solution lay in a better understanding of divine Love.

Then I thought of John, the beloved disciple. He expressed Love always; and Love can never be destroyed! And just as Jesus lovingly washed the feet of his disciples after the Passover supper, the understanding of the truth and love he taught could cleanse my thought of jealousy, doubt, pride, apathy — everything standing in the way of my healing.

And such was the case. It took a number of years, but these were fruitful years. There was a wonderful mental purging going on during that time, and it led to a complete healing. I was entirely healed and healthier and stronger than I'd ever been in my life. That was thirty years ago.

I'll always be grateful for the way Christian Science led me step by step to a spiritual understanding of the Bible.

(Mrs.) Adelina Werner, San Francisco, California
Radio/TV series, "How Christian Science Heals," 1958.

LATE in 1929 my family physician rushed me to the hospital and called in six or seven physicians and surgeons, specialists in malignant diseases. After a thorough examination, the doctors declared that I had a quick-growing cancer, and that my time was short. I begged for an operation, but I was told that I didn't have one chance in a thousand of surviving it, that I was too far gone for treatment. I remember my family physician wept, so you can imagine how I, the patient, felt. He loved the family and felt so sorry. He told me to be sure to put my affairs in order because I was dying. Since no more could be done for me, I was taken home.

At this point I called a very close friend and asked him if he would take care of my family — my wife and two young sons, for I didn't want them to become charity cases after I died. I was traveling on the road then as a salesman and he was a fellow traveling salesman. He was not a Christian Scientist himself, but he knew friends who had been healed in Christian Science and urged me to try it. He used to call on me every day. We were great friends. "You love your family," he said, "and you'll do anything for them. Why don't you try Christian Science?"

But I had lost interest in religion, so I didn't pay much attention. I was brought up to believe in a God who knew and performed good and evil. Sickness, suffering, lack and deprivations were the accepted facts of existence in our family, and were attributed to God. I didn't want to have anything to do with this kind of God, so I turned away from religion.

Then a friend of my fellow salesman, whom he had told about me, offered to loan me a little book on Christian Science entitled *Miscellaneous Writings* by Mary Baker Eddy. I took it, but to be truthful, I felt sure it wouldn't help me. Two weeks later this friend telephoned desiring to visit me. So I began to read the Preface to this book, in order not to appear ignorant or ungrateful. In the opening paragraph my eyes fell on the words: "The noblest charity is to prevent a man from accepting charity; and the best alms are to show and to enable a man to dispense with alms." So I thought, Christian Science might be this noblest charity. As I read on and on the pages were positively illumined. It just gave me a feeling of hope and joy I cannot describe in words.

I read *Miscellaneous Writings* all that night and I decided to buy the textbook, *Science and Health,* the first thing in the morning. And so I got out of my bed the following morning, after having been confined several weeks. I walked eight blocks to a Christian Science Reading Room, purchased a copy of *Science and Health*, and walked back to my home. My wife was amazed.

The very next day I went to a Christian Science practitioner for help in understanding the book. I had to unlearn that God was a stern, severe Deity. The new impression I began to receive was that God is Love and can do nothing but love His creation, and that God actually is loving me. This made me feel very good.

In a most reassuring manner, the practitioner told me that man, being the image and likeness of God, could not really have disease, because God is the creator of all, and God never made disease. He explained that since God is Love and fills all space there actually could be no cancer or any other evil. I asked the practitioner to tell me more of this God who is Love. I began to see that this God that the practitioner was talking about was the cause of all existence — the cause of my existence; and because God is Love and perfect, He could not make anything unloving or imperfect.

And for the first time I began to see the real meaning of the Christ, that it's much more than just a name associated with our dear Master, Christ Jesus. I saw that the Christ is the Truth which Jesus taught and demonstrated — the divine Truth which is present in every age to heal and help. I was impressed, for instance, with the statement appearing on page 332 of *Science and Health*: "Christ is the true idea voicing good, the divine message from God to men speaking to the human consciousness."

I pondered these things over a period of months, and I grew continually stronger. When finally after some weeks I walked into a Christian Science church I heard them singing as I walked in — "His arm encircles me, and mine, and all." I actually felt that it was God's arm, divine Love's arm, that was holding me. Not only did the cancer disappear, but one by one headaches, stomach trouble, and a long list of other ailments left me.

I held a highly paid position as a representative of a very fine firm, but I began to see that I couldn't go on with the job because it required entertaining my buyers with liquor, tobacco and other means which were not in accord with Christian Science. So I resigned my position, and trusted in God who I began to see was my real and only support.

I used to have various grudges against certain ones. I started to reverse every unloving thought I had about people and things. I was pressed to the understanding that to be the image of Love, I had to love. I had to see through the eyes of God. I had to change my thought. I had to see that the other fellow was also the image of Love. I had to reject the suggestion that any evil can be done in a universe filled with Love, filled with infinite good. One friend in particular I had to see as in the presence of Love. And suddenly, after two or three months, this man whom I had most hated came in with his wife and offered to help me to go in business. It amazed me. Besides monetary help, he offered me a line of credit and advice to set me up in a wholesale candy business, which led me eventually to own a wholesale grocery business with five branches in towns near Los Angeles.

My healing took place over 35 years ago, and I feel much better now than I have ever felt in my life. About eight or nine months after I had been healed, my family and I were having dinner in a restaurant when my old family physician came in. He told me he couldn't believe it, he had forgotten all about it, and thought that I was dead and gone. He wanted to know what it was that healed me. I said that it was Christian Science.

It was such a change in my life that it is difficult to describe in words just what the feeling was in me and in my family. I became a better husband, a better father to my children, a better neighbor, and a better citizen.

J. Henry Ball, Los Angeles, California
Radio/TV series, "How Christian Science Heals," 1956.

FOR MANY YEARS I had been a medical nurse. As I read the textbook, *Science and Health with Key to the Scriptures* by Mary Baker Eddy, dark images of disease were removed from thought, and the glorious light of the freedom of the sons of God replaced the false theological belief that God was testing me. I had been taught this from childhood.

At a time when my husband and I had sold some property, a very dishonest situation arose. I took no part in the unhappy affair, and I was very pleased with myself for keeping still. I learned, however, that this was not the way that Christ Jesus held his peace. Some time later I tripped, falling backward and striking my head. As I fell, I quickly turned to God, and these words came to my thought: "Ye stiffnecked people." When I regained consciousness, I was able, by holding my head in a certain position, to get up and go into the house.

Again I lost consciousness. My husband called a doctor. He diagnosed it as a broken neck. The doctor said he would get the necessary things with which to put me in a cast, for he did not dare to move me. But my husband, knowing I was a student of Christian Science, said he would let him know whether or not he was to return.

Later, when I regained consciousness, I asked my daughter to telephone to the woman who had asked me to read the textbook and to tell her I was suffering from self-righteousness. I had thus interpreted "stiffnecked," which had come to my thought. I had taken no part in the audible discussion, but I had accepted the belief that one of my fellow men was guilty. I had failed to impersonalize evil and to apply the truth that God's man is never dishonest, selfish, or tempted by evil. This would have healed the situation.

It came to me that Christ Jesus held his peace by reversing and rejecting sense testimony, and I recalled the import of the meaning of "A Rule for Motives and Acts," given in the *Manual of The Mother Church* by Mrs. Eddy (Art. VIII, Sect. 1).

Having seen the error for what it was, I was healed in a very short time. That afternoon, about three hours after the doctor's visit, I went to do some shopping and met the doctor on the street. He could hardly believe it and commented that he had left me with what he considered to be a broken neck.

(Mrs.) Hazel Teresa Cook, Blackfoot, Idaho.

I should like to verify my wife's testimony. Christian Science has indeed blessed our home, not only in my wife's healings but in many other ways. I have had healings of physical difficulties. I am not a member of the Christian Science movement, but I deeply appreciate the truth of its teachings.

Ray Cook.

— *Journal*, Vol. 78, pp. 326–327
(June, 1960).

The next testimony and the poem which accompanies
it throw light on the way in which healing may come in
the face of even the most stubborn evidence of physical
disability:

I HAVE EXPERIENCED quick healings in Christian Science, but I
have also learned that, even if a healing does not come at once, it
will still certainly come if the truth is persistently and correctly
applied. About twenty years ago I began to lose the use of my legs.
I sought help in Christian Science, but the condition grew worse
until I was no longer able to attend to my professional work.

At the time I held an established post in the British Home Civil
Service, and when my regulation sick leave was exhausted I was
required to have a full medical examination in order that the authorities might decide on their next step. I agreed to the examination,
but explained that I was relying on Christian Science for healing and
did not desire any material treatment. An ambulance took me to
a service hospital, where I spent a week under thorough medical
examination. The surgeon in charge then told me that I was suffering from some form of paralysis for which there was little likeli-
hood of cure. He also told my wife that I could not be cared for
at home, as among other things bedsores would soon develop. I did
not see his written report to my department, but the outcome was
my being invalided from the service.

I returned home and was effectively cared for there without any
special nursing attention. When bedsores began to develop, they
were quickly healed by Christian Science. However, for almost ten
years I was unable to stand or walk; I could only sit up for a short
time each day, not always that. The difficulty in moving spread, and
other complications developed. Several times it appeared that I
was about to pass on. I could eat little and slept poorly. Our home,
an upper flat in central London, was for four of these years under
air attack. Financial supply had to be found, too.

The Tide of Healing

But all the time spiritual growth was going on through Christian Science. Sometimes I studied alone. Sometimes I had treatment from a steadfast practitioner, who brought me great inspiration. Always I had the unfailing support of my wife. When too weak to turn the pages of *Science and Health* I started to learn it by heart so as to grasp every detail. I learned more than half the book by heart. Its teachings were food and rest to me.

As I studied and received treatment, great spiritual joy filled me — joy that God governed and nothing could interfere with His purpose of present perfection and satisfaction for all. And with the joy came an ever keener sense of spiritual innocence, a perception that man, being the individual expression of divine Mind, could never have entertained at any moment any incorrect thinking which could have caused or could justify suffering. The recognition of good's allness and evil's nothingness followed and irresistibly took charge of the physical condition. In the tenth year improvement began. I started to walk again, and sleep and appetite returned to normal. There were setbacks, and certain readjustments were not easy, but step by step the healing was finally established.

Along with the physical healing, successive new opportunties for interesting work opened up. Sometimes these made demands which seemed beyond my strength at the moment; but as I went forward in God's strength, the demands were met. At last I found myself leading a fully active life again, occupied more satisfactorily than ever before. All the good of those years has remained with me; all the loss and evil are as though they had never been.

Peter J. Henniker-Heaton,
Cambridge, Massachusetts.

— *Journal*, Vol. 73, pp. 214–215
(April, 1955).

At a time when his physical condition seemed to be at its worst, the writer of the preceding testimony expressed his conviction of spiritual perfection in a poem which was later published in the *Christian Science Sentinel*. The

poem is reprinted here for its evidence of the kind of understanding faith in God that moves mountains. The words
Truth, Life, and Love are used in Christian Science as
synonyms for God.

O Thou Unchanging Truth

PETER J. HENNIKER-HEATON

O THOU unchanging Truth, whose facts eternal
give us the courage to outface the storm,
to rise against the senses' swift alarm
and stand unmoved at Spirit's high tribunal,
Thy Word acquits us and Thy Word is final.

O Thou abundant Life, whose freshness daily
admits no common round, no dull routine,
this is our joy and this our discipline,
to take Thy gift of life and use it fully;
this is our highest task, to spend it freely.

O boundless Love, forever undiminished,
how far and little seems the lie of pain.
We were with Thee, before the world began,
and shall be with Thee, when the world has vanished;
Thy work is perfect and Thy work is finished.

— *Sentinel*, Vol. 44, p. 2179
(December 12, 1942).

A Christian Science practitioner's diagnosis of the mental
and moral factors in a case that may need healing is
wholly spiritual, and it is not normal for Christian
Scientists to seek medical diagnosis. Thus a large number of diseased conditions which are healed in Christian
Science cannot have a medical name attached to them
with any certainty. However, many individuals turn to
Christian Science for help after first employing medical
aid; in some cases they have been under prolonged medical

The Tide of Healing

observation, often with consultation among several doctors. Testimonies frequently refer to medical diagnoses and prognoses which have been made under such circumstances. In other cases healings have been medically confirmed when the patient submitted to a physical examination because required to do so by an employer, an insurance company, school authorities, the Armed Services, etc.

A writer in the *American Journal of Sociology* in 1954, after examining 500 testimonies from four volumes of *The Christian Science Journal*, made the statement — based, as he wrote, "upon impressions rather than upon objective analysis" — that the "number of cancers, tumors, broken bones, and cases of pneumonia and acute appendicitis which were self-diagnosed by the writers seemed large." This seemed highly doubtful, since Christian Scientists as a rule do not attach a name to a disease on their own authority, and in any case it left out of account the large number of healings in which there indubitably had been medical diagnosis. A subsequent careful examination of the same four volumes of the *Journal* showed that there had definitely been such diagnosis in 4 cases of cancer, 8 of tumor, 21 of broken bones, 7 of pneumonia, 7 of appendicitis, 22 of heart disease, 21 of tuberculosis, 6 of asthma, and 3 or less of diphtheria, blindness, peritonitis, scarlet fever, arthritis, spinal meningitis, diabetes, gallstones, epilepsy, tetanus, polio, uremic poisoning, pelvic ovaritis, smallpox, pyorrhea, hernia, deafness, curvature of the spine, jaundice, dropsy, bronchial catarrh, abscessed teeth, ulcerated eyes, paralytic stroke, etc.*

This partial list, drawn from the same 500 testimonies examined by the writer of the article, omitted the large number of similar cases in which the context of the testimony implied medical diagnosis but did not explicitly state it. It left out such things as unspecified "growths," or "organic troubles" for which operations had previously been prescribed by physicians or unsuccessfully undertaken (in several cases repeatedly) and dubious cases (e.g., a knee condition diagnosed by one doctor as a tubercular joint and by another as a loose cartilage).

The bare enumeration of diseases healed omitted such features as their instantaneous cure in some instances,

* See letter by Will B. Davis in *American Journal of Sociology*, LX, pp. 184, 185 (September, 1954).

including one of the cancer cases; the number which physicians or surgeons declared beyond remedying by operations or any other means, in several cases giving the patient only a few more hours or days to live; and, above all, the transformation of thinking which accompanied and explained the physical changes. A mere catalogue of the healings in the New Testament would do similar injustice to the spiritual purpose and power they reveal.

When a person who has been classified as a terminal case in a hospital is restored to long years of health, freedom, and activity he does not need medical corroboration to assure him of his healing. Nevertheless, when doubting Thomas demanded physical proof that Jesus had indeed risen from the grave, it was given him, and the testimonies immediately following indicate the sort of corroborative evidence which Christian Scientists frequently mention in their testimonies:

IT IS with great joy and happiness that I share the wonderful blessings that have come to me and mine. Through Christian Science the darkest and most fearful hour I have ever experienced was changed to one of joy, confidence, and faith.

Some years ago our only son was taken ill with an acute attack of rheumatic fever. He grew steadily worse and was removed to one of the largest medical institutions in the United States. After some weeks we were told by the chief surgeon that there was nothing more his staff could do. They would give him no more medication, as he was too far gone. He said that the youngster was beyond their help and was in God's hands, and he added that we should go home and pray. I replied that I did not know how to pray, that I was considered totally and permanently disabled, and that my prayers had not helped me. The doctor told me to hurry home and telephone our minister for spiritual assistance.

Upon reaching home I tried to telephone the minister, but his line was busy. During one of the moments when I was waiting to call again, our telephone rang. A woman we had recently met was calling in reference to a business matter. She discerned my anxiety and asked what the trouble was. I told her, and she inquired whether we had ever considered trying Christian Science. I replied, "What could we do with that now?" She very lovingly stated that she could be at our home in ten minutes and discuss the situation, if we would be interested.

Upon her arrival she read a few statements from *Science and Health with Key to the Scriptures* by Mary Baker Eddy which were so appealing that I inquired what to do next. She recommended that I call a practitioner, and I did. After talking with him for ten or twelve minutes, I returned to the living room, free, happy, and assured. My first words were: "There is nothing more to worry about. The boy is in God's hands." After eating my first full meal in weeks, I began to study the chapter on Prayer in the copy of *Science and Health* which the woman had left with me. My custom had been to visit the youngster three times each day during all those weeks when he was in the hospital, but on this particular evening I did not even consider going to him, and I positively knew he was in God's care. I spent the evening in complete peace.

The next day I visited the practitioner. Afterward I went to the hospital, where I was told by the authorities that something very wonderful had happened to our boy within an hour after my leaving the day before, and that he was now doing exceptionally well. When I reached his room he was sitting up in bed smiling at me. Several days later he was discharged from the hospital completely well. After spending an active summer on his grandmother's farm, he returned to school. It was necessary that he have a doctor's certificate, and after he had been thoroughly examined by the hospital staff, the chief surgeon said: "This is the most unusual case in our files. No human hand could ever have performed what has been done for this boy. You have found your God. Now, never give Him up."

So great was my gratitude for our son's healing that I attended a Wednesday evening testimony meeting. There I gave an expression of my deep and sincere appreciation of Christ Jesus and of Christian Science. At this time I realized for the first time that I too had been completely healed. I had worn a cast for several years for a spinal condition and suffered from ulcers, throat infection, a chest condition, and other difficulties. I was so completely free that a few months later I was accepted by one of the large insurance companies for a sizable life insurance policy, even though it was known that there were court records of my having been judged totally and permanently disabled. The following year I passed a military examination and went through rigorous training. I have been completely free and well ever since.

Burt B. Wolf, Detroit, Michigan.

— *Journal*, Vol. 73, pp. 270–271
(May, 1955).

I SHOULD LIKE to express my gratitude for my son's healing. When the war in Poland had come to a stop, he was ordered to a garrison in our home town, and there I believed him to be safe. But a few weeks later I was called up from a hospital and asked to come to Berlin by the next train. My son had had an accident, and his life was in danger. I immediately denied the reality of the accident and went to the hospital. I found three doctors standing beside my son's bed. They told me that they had already made two heart injections in order that I should find my son alive on my arrival. They further told me that now their ability to help him had come to an end.

I told them, "I place my son's life in the hands of God. May I let him have Christian Science treatment?" Two of the doctors requested that a room be made available so I could be alone with my son. I asked a practitioner to assist me. Each second day the doctors visited my son; nearly all the doctors and professors from the hospital were present then. Sometimes there were sixteen to eighteen doctors at my son's bedside. My Bible, the Christian Science textbook, *Science and Health,* and other writings by Mrs. Eddy were always lying there openly, even when the doctors came in. My son was unconscious. After ten days a nurse was about to inject artificial food, but I forbade it. She then complained about it to the head nurse, who recognized in some measure that my son was receiving spiritual food which was meeting his need.

The Tide of Healing

A fortnight later my son for the first time opened his eyes. I rejoiced, but the doctors said: "Do not rejoice too early. His broken leg is going to be five centimeters short, his arm will remain stiff, and his jawbone and nose are broken. Your son has a fracture of the skull and a very serious concussion of the brain. We are anxious with regard to the mind of your son. If he does not regain it within six months, then you will have a son who is insane, and there will be no joy for you."

Again I had to be very firm and to realize clearly God's presence and to know that man reflects divine intelligence, for he is the perfect expression of God's being. A few weeks later, on Christmas Eve, my son recognized me. My joy and gratitude to our Father-Mother God were very great indeed. After three months my son was able to walk on crutches. The first doctor who attended him told him, "Only the faith of your mother made you whole, for our human ability had come to an end."

After eighteen months my son again went to war. His leg is not shortened, his arm is not stiff, his mind is as clear as it was before the accident. He is married, and he and his family are faithful followers of Christian Science.

(Mrs.) *Ida Klettke, Potsdam.*
Babelsberg, Germany.

— *Sentinel*, Vol. 52, pp. 84–85
(January 14, 1950).

M Y CONDITION was diagnosed as cancer of the esophagus. The doctor said I would live only a few months, and told me how sorry he was they could do no more for me.

After the second visit with a Christian Science practitioner, I felt so full of joy and happiness I couldn't go to sleep. At 4 a.m. I realized I was no longer in pain. Then I slept soundly, and the next day was able to eat whatever I wanted — I hadn't done that in four years. In just one week, I was back at work.

For over a year I studied every day to understand more fully the nature of man as a spiritual idea, the likeness of God, Love. I gradually saw that God's man is not subject to disease. Finally the pain quit coming back, and I was completely well.

Several years later, I applied for an insurance policy and had a physical examination, from which I received a perfect bill of health. The doctor checked my hospital records and gave me a very thorough examination, because the healing seemed so incredible to him.

(Mrs.) Orion C. Hadden, Albany, Georgia
Radio/TV series, "How Christian Science Heals," 1960.

The following dialogue is from an interview with Lewis E. Perkins and Mrs. Frances Perkins of Englewood, Colorado, in the radio/TV series, "How Christian Science Heals":

MRS. PERKINS:

When Jim, our oldest boy, was ten, he was thrown to the pavement while getting off a streetcar. He landed with great force on his elbow. Nobody knew he was hurt, so he got up by himself and went on to the YMCA. He said he repeated the Lord's Prayer every step of the way. The people at the Y phoned me, and just as soon as I heard he was injured, I called a Christian Science practitioner.

MR. PERKINS:

Then she called me and I brought our son home.

MRS. PERKINS:

When we looked at the arm, it was plain that it was broken. We had to make a decision as to what to do, and we remembered a statement in *Science and Health* where Mrs. Eddy refers to this very problem. It's on page 401:

"Until the advancing age admits the efficacy and supremacy of Mind, it is better for Christian Scientists to leave surgery and the adjustment of broken bones and dislocations to the fingers of a

164

surgeon, while the mental healer confines himself chiefly to mental reconstruction and to the prevention of inflammation."

As we thought it over we felt the thing for us to do in this case was to call a surgeon.

MR. PERKINS:

A neighbor of ours was a surgeon, so we called him. He felt he had to take Jim to the hospital for X-rays, and after he'd studied the X-rays he said, "The arm is injured so badly, the boy will never again have complete use of it." He added that the elbow joint was shattered, with six breaks there and one above it.

MRS. PERKINS:

Yes, and as the surgeon talked to us, I thought, "Well, your concept of the boy is different from ours, because you're thinking of him as mortal and material, but man is actually a spiritual idea, the child of God." And I saw clearly that no accident could ever happen to a spiritual idea. My fear subsided and from that moment I had no doubt whatsoever that the arm would be completely normal again.

Because of the swelling, the surgeon had to wait three days before he could even attempt to set the bones. Then, even though he was a surgeon with many years' experience, he called in two specialists for consultation because he felt the case was so serious. He looked through the fluoroscope at the arm and was just astounded, because every particle of bone was exactly in place where it belonged. He had these specialists who were standing by look at it, too, and they all marveled because the bones were completely in place.

MR. PERKINS:

So all they had to do was put a cast on it to hold it in place.

MRS. PERKINS:

Yes. That was all they did.

MR. PERKINS:

Before the cast was removed, we decided we ask the streetcar company to pay the expenses we had incurred — since it was the result of the carelessness of their operator. Because the boy was a minor, a judge had to approve the settlement. The boy, of course, appeared in court and his arm was still in a cast. When the judge heard the evidence in the case, he said, "I think you folks are making a mistake. This boy may be crippled for life and he's entitled to damages from the ——— Company." We said that we thought the boy's arm would be healed and all we wanted was expenses. So the judge called the surgeon back to the stand and said, "Have you ever known an arm broken as badly as this one was to recover completely?" And the surgeon said, "No, I never have." And then he surprised us by saying, "But this arm will. This boy is going to have complete use of his arm again, because I know the boy and I know what's in back of the case."

The surgeon had known from the time we had called him that the child was having help from a Christian Science practitioner. Well, the judge agreed that the expenses should be paid by the company and he dismissed the case.

MRS. PERKINS:

The boy's healing went on rapidly. He was out of the cast in just a few weeks. The doctor was very happy when the boy could first touch his shoulder with his fingers to show that the arm was supple again. About a year later, the doctor made a visit to our house because he was attending me at the time our next child was born. And he called the boy in from the yard where he was playing, and looked at the arm. He patted the boy on the back and said, "This is remarkable. This is remarkable."

The injury had happened in the fall, and that very winter Jim was out playing with the boys again on the playground — hanging from the horizontal bars and doing everything a 10-year-old boy would do, and there was no trouble with the arm. In high school he was a member of the basketball team, and he served as an officer in the Navy in World War II.

MR. PERKINS:

There was an interesting sequel to this. It happened about fifteen years later. One of our daughters — Pat, she was about fourteen at the time — was ice skating when she fell and injured her arm. There happened to be a doctor standing nearby and he went to the child and examined her arm and said both bones in the wrist were broken.

MRS. PERKINS:

When Pat was brought home we turned to *Science and Health* again — to that same reference I mentioned earlier but this time we noticed especially the part on the next page that says: "Christian Science is always the most skilful surgeon, but surgery is the branch of its healing which will be last acknowledged. However, it is but just to say that the author has already in her possession well-authenticated records of the cure, by herself and her students through mental surgery alone, of broken bones, dislocated joints, and spinal vertebrae."

We were ready to say that Christian Science is the most skilful surgeon. We'd certainly had a beautiful proof of that. Our boy's arm had been set through Christian Science help and then healed through Christian Science treatment. And then we thought, "Well, we don't want anything for our daughter but the most skilful surgeon." So we called a Christian Science practitioner and left the case completely in the hands of the practitioner. This time we decided to rely entirely on God for the adjusting and healing of the bones. We let Pat go to school in a day or two with her arm in a sling, to support the weight of it. Within a week or so the pain and discoloration were gone. In about six weeks she was able to use the arm again. It took a few weeks more and then the arm was completely normal in appearance and in her use of it.

MR. PERKINS:

She's very athletic. In fact, she was hanging from rafters and things within six weeks after. She's played basketball in school, but swimming is her chief sport, and she's been on the swimming team.

MRS. PERKINS:

A few months later our eight-year-old son, Ed, fell from his bike and broke his arm about half way between the elbow and wrist. It seems ridiculous that such a thing should happen again, but there was a wonderful lesson in it.

This time we had no fear whatsoever, because we knew that

167

although the accident looked real to the physical senses, it never had happened to the child of God.

We called a practitioner, and within just a few hours the pain was gone. We had the boy carry his arm in a sling, but found on the third day he'd thrown the sling away because he got tired of carrying it around. In a week he was using the arm normally and naturally.

Lewis E. and (Mrs.) Frances Perkins, Englewood, Colorado
Radio/TV series, "How Christian Science Heals," 1957.

In Appendix B of *Christian Science: Its Encounter with American Culture* by Robert Peel (Holt, 1958) evidence regarding several aspects of Christian Science healing is examined. The following excerpt is from that appendix:

(On Feb. 4, 1955, a testimony by Dr. Ernest H. Lyons, Jr., professor of chemistry at Principia College, Illinois, was presented on the regular weekly radio broadcast, "How Christian Science Heals." The relevant part of that broadcast follows.)

I WAS PREPARING a compound and I had to start with potassium cyanide. . . . To start the work I melted the potassium cyanide in an iron dish over a powerful burner. I set the iron stirring rod on the edge of the dish and turned away briefly. When I reached for the iron rod again I picked it up by the hot end. I dropped it immediately, but not before my hand was severely burned, and I could see crystals of the poison dislodged from the rod in the wound. But I was not frightened of poisoning for I was conscious of the presence of infinite Life, God, overruling the picture of accident and possible death. I washed my hand in water and wrapped it in a towel, and I was able to go ahead and complete the preparation. Within three days scarcely a scar remained and in less than a week all effects disappeared. Later I talked to an expert on cyanide poisoning and he told me that such an experience would ordinarily prove fatal in a few minutes.

The Tide of Healing

(This testimony was later repeated on the television series of the same title. Following this telecast Dr. Lyons received a letter from a woman in California informing him that a consulting chemical engineer who roomed at her home had seen the program, had ridiculed the testimony as stating an evident impossibility, and had implied that the whole thing was fraudulent. The woman, who was a Christian Scientist, asked Dr. Lyons if he could give her a few facts that would indicate his standing as a chemist and a reliable witness. He replied by stating his professional background: B.S., Massachusetts Institute of Technology, 1931; M.S., California Institute of Technology, 1933; Chief Chemist, The Meaker Company, Chicago, Ill., 1934–46; Professor, Department of Chemistry, Principia College, 1946, to date; Ph.D., University of Illinois, 1953; Summer Lecturer in Chemistry, University of Illinois, 1955; author of numerous papers on electrodeposition and contributor to technical publications. In reply he received from his original critic the letter which follows.)

DEAR DR. LYONS:

Some weeks ago as I was watching the T.V. I saw the program conducted by the Christian Science church in which you appeared and gave a testimonial regarding a healing experience you once had with a burn from a hot, poisonous substance, potassium cyanide, as I recall. Mrs. ———, who is my landlady when I am in ——— has been kind enuf to write you and has shown me your letter in reply. She did this because she is a devout Christian Scientist and was disturbed by my remarks about the unscientific nature of the evidence you presented.

Now it seems to me that as a chemist, you should be loath to give such testimony and make such statements as you did when you have no way of determining the amount of cyanide absorbed into your system at the time of the accident. Many of us in chemistry handle violent poisons, sometimes with our bare hands, and we do not suffer from them if we handle them intelligently. I do not need to remind you that H_2S is a violent poison, even rated above HCN, yet it is commonly used by chemists and even by students in analysis. I am sure you would not take a recognized lethal dose of cyanide by mouth or by injection and expect such a miraculous recovery.

Personally, I feel you have done the profession of chemistry a disservice by making the inaccurate and unverifiable statements you did. Such statements can be easily overlooked by us chemists but can have injurious effects on the layman who does not understand that chemical reactions proceed according to definite laws and not according to the wishful thinking of the individual — a fact that has taken our predecessors hundreds of years to establish.

(In reply, Dr. Lyons wrote the letter which follows.)

DEAR MR. ———:

I can readily understand your reaction to my statements on the TV program, because I questioned the incident myself until I was forced to the conclusion which I presented there. Obviously, it was impossible to give a detailed account on the program.

The accident occurred when I was preparing potassium cyanate in order to carry out the Wohler synthesis of urea. The wound, which extended across my right palm, exposed the tendons. There appeared to be several masses of white crystals in the fluids and burned tissues, but naturally I did not take time for an extended inspection. The wound was so deep that for some days my hand was drawn together.

There appear to be five possible explanations for my survival:

1. The material was not potassium cyanide. An old sample might be completely hydrolyzed to the carbonate. In this event it would have been impossible to obtain urea. I obtained 10.8 g., whereas Coben's laboratory manual specifies 15 g. There is no reason to expect decomposition of the cyanide on the stirring rod.

2. The shock, pain, and fright might have led me to imagine crystals in the wound, or to mistake pieces of skin for crystals. Since the end of the stirring rod was heavily coated with crystals, it is virtually inconceivable that some were not dislodged and entered the wound, whether I saw them or not. After the first shock, I was surprisingly calm, and I doubt that hysteria influenced my observation.

3. The amount of potassium cyanide absorbed was below the

lethal level. This level is so low that such an occurrence is highly improbable. Furthermore, even a much smaller absorption leads to milder symptoms, none of which were observed.

4. The cyanide was washed out of the wound without being absorbed. In the opinion of a safety expert from duPont, sent to check the safety practices of my former employers, who use cyanide in ton lots, this is impossible under the circumstances described. A workman who fell into a relatively dilute cyanide solution in a plating machine my employers had installed in the Cadillac plant, was lifted promptly from the three foot deep tank, sprayed with a hose while his clothes were removed, and thoroughly washed until his death in about ten minutes, reportedly due to absorption of cyanide through the skin, although only the lower portions of his body were affected. This without a break in the skin.

5. Cyanide was absorbed but rendered harmless by the higher law of life. Although this may sound incredible, such instances are not uncommon to Christian Scientists. There is ample evidence, meeting both legal and scientific standards, that Christian Science healings have occurred which contravene material laws. In many instances, competent medical diagnoses were made before and afterwards.

The existence of a higher law, which can save life and relieve suffering in even the most hopeless circumstances, is so important that I am constrained to bring my experience to public notice. I cannot see that this will be any disservice to my profession; rather, the contrary.

As to taking another dose of cyanide, of course I would not do so voluntarily, nor would any other Christian Scientist. The reasoning on which this is based is explained in the Christian Science textbook. In reply to a similar question, Christ Jesus said, "It is written, thou shalt not tempt the Lord thy God." However, should I be exposed accidentally, my life could again be protected.

The exceedingly stringent demands made by Christian Science frequently lead me to examine and re-examine my reasons for accepting it, one of which is the experience recounted, but each time I have been forced to recognize that here is the science of sciences, the rational explanation of Jesus' healings, the answer

to every need of humanity. I feel my protection was in direct ful-
fillment of Jesus' promise, "If they drink any deadly thing, it will
not hurt them."

Very properly you will have your own interpretation of my experience, and it may not agree with mine. There is no need for
controversy over this, but I hope that this account will show you
that my statements are not based on wishful thinking, nor entirely
unscientific evidence, nor unthinking enthusiasm, but in sincere
acknowledgment of what seems to me to be the Christ.

Yours very truly,
Ernest H. Lyons, Jr.
Head, Department of Chemistry

> People first turn to Christian Science for many different
> reasons. In a book entitled *The Christian Science Way of
> Life* by DeWitt John with *A Christian Scientist's Life* by
> Erwin D. Canham (Prentice-Hall, Inc., 1962), the two
> authors discuss this matter along with others — the one in
> general terms, the other in terms of autobiography.

In THE eighty-odd years since the Church of Christ, Scientist
was founded by Mrs. Eddy, it has spread to all the continents and
to most of the countries of the free world. What has largely blazed
the trail and given the movement its momentum is the healing
work — even though, as indicated earlier, physical healing is only a
token of the power of Truth. If one studies the early histories of
individual Christian Science churches in a given country he finds
that in a majority of cases, remarkable healings led to the holding
of services and this in turn brought the establishment of a church.
In some instances the healings came about when a copy of *Science
and Health* somehow found its way into unfamiliar hands; in other
cases it was when a student or perhaps a practitioner came to a
new area to live.

In more recent years many of the new churches have grown up

in suburban areas near cities where Christian Science is already well established. But in modern times, too, it is the healing work which has often provided the foundation.

To cite an example, there is a small town in Oklahoma which had no church group until a few years ago. The events that led to its establishment began one day when a woman I know found a discarded magazine in her yard. Evidently someone had tossed it away. Painfully she bent over to pick it up, for she was becoming a cripple. She wore a special steel corset, and braces in her shoes. She also suffered from anemia and heart trouble.

The magazine proved to be a copy of the *Christian Science Sentinel,* a publication she had never heard of. The woman's condition had been called incurable, and it had been expected that in time she would be confined to a wheelchair. But she began the study of Christian Science — which to her brought a new interpretation of the nature of God. In a few months' time she was completely healed.

Being a long-time resident of the town, she was well known and the word of her healing spread. From time to time others, braving the strong religious tradition and bias of the town, came to her with their problems. Over a period of several years the number of those studying Christian Science grew until today there is a Christian Science Society — the forerunner of a full-fledged church — in the town. The woman herself finally gave up a highly successful career as a music teacher to devote her time to the practice of Christian Science healing.

DeWitt John, *The Christian Science Way of Life,*
pp. 65, 66.

The woman mentioned above was Mrs. J. J. Kaiser, of Clinton, Oklahoma, who related her healing on the radio-TV series, "How Christian Science Heals," reprinted in the *Christian Science Sentinel* of July 29, 1961.

THEN CAME the moment of threatening tragedy. My mother was suddenly afflicted with growths in her throat, some kind of ulcerous condition. The kind family doctor and friend could do nothing for her. His diagnosis was that she could not live through the day unless the obstruction broke. At this time my mother remembered a copy of *Science and Health with Key to the Scriptures,* by Mary Baker Eddy, which had been left in our home two or three years before by a woman who had done housework for us. She had glanced at it, and Christian Science had made an impact on her thought, but she had not looked into it carefully. She also remembered a Christian Scientist in Sanford. This friend gave us the name of a Christian Science practitioner living some seventy-five miles away in Boston. Thereupon the Christian Scientist friend telephoned the practitioner and asked him to give my mother Christian Science treatment. Within a few hours the growths broke and ran harmlessly away, and my mother fell asleep, fully healed.

It was as if sunlight had burst into our lives for the first time. The swift, miraculous nature of the healing bespoke a truth new and powerful to us. My mother was radiant with joy. She began an intensive study of Christian Science, and so did my father and I. We entered and became active in the Christian Science church in Sanford. There was a little local turmoil, since one of my father's leading backers in the newspaper was the physician who had been unable to help my mother, but this wise man realized, I believe, that a power greater than his medical knowledge had been at work. We had the joy, the freedom of persons released from bondage.

From that day forward, my life experience — and that of my parents — was one of unfoldment. Within a year my mother had made such swift strides in the study of Christian Science that she was able to take what is called class instruction: a course of careful, organized study with an experienced teacher of Christian Science, so that she could engage in healing work professionally. For the rest of her human life, she was deeply and joyfully engaged in bringing this liberating, curative, regenerative truth to others. Her patients were numerous, and the marvelous, seemingly miraculous cures that came about, were the source of unending challenge and gratitude. Though my mother passed on a decade ago, after forty years of healing service, I frequently meet and am deeply touched by persons who express to me their gratitude to her for having helped them through trials and into the sunshine.

Erwin D. Canham, *A Christian Scientist's Life,*
pp. 198, 199.

The first Tenet to which all Christian Scientists subscribe (found on page 15 of the Church Manual by Mrs. Eddy) reads: "As adherents of Truth, we take the inspired Word of the Bible as our sufficient guide to eternal Life." Christian Scientists assiduously study the Bible every day. The present weekly radio series, successor to "How Christian Science Heals," is entitled "The Bible Speaks to You."

In a book entitled *Why I Am a Christian Scientist* (Thomas Nelson & Sons, 1958) Thomas L. Leishman, an author of several books on the Bible, tells how he was led to become a Christian Scientist through its interpretation of the Scriptures. The following excerpts are from the first chapter of that book:

I WAS REARED in a country manse, situated in the lowlands of Scotland, within sight of the Cheviot Hills. My father was a well-known Presbyterian minister, a scholar and writer of deep and sincere convictions. His father and grandfather were also ministers, each of whom served in his day as Moderator of the General Assembly of the Church of Scotland. . . .

My mother's father was a consulting obstetrician, Professor of Midwifery and Dean of the Faculty of Medicine at Glasgow University. Her brother, Lieut.-General Sir William B. Leishman, K.C.B., K.C.M.G., F.R.S., LL.D. was Director General of the (British) Army Medical Service in the twenties. Among his many assignments he was an Honorary Physician to King George V, and is still widely remembered in medical circles for his bacteriological researches and discoveries. . . .

As school was followed by college, it is not surprising that I felt drawn to study for the ministry of the Church of Scotland, and in due course was licensed to preach by the Presbytery of which my father's parish formed a part. . . .

After I had graduated M.A. and B.D. at Edinburgh University. . . . I came to New York, on a fellowship granted for one year by Union Theological Seminary, and later renewed by the Seminary for a further year. . . .

One of my closest friends in New York proved to be a Christian Scientist, one who lived what she believed and who, in the midst of all the fun and varied activities in which our student group took part, attended regularly the services and meetings of that denomination, not only on Sundays, but also on week days. . . .

Some months later, while on my way to take charge of a summer Mission in western South Dakota, a copy of the Christian Science textbook was loaned to me, and I was told of some outstanding instances of healing experienced by friends whom I had grown to respect and admire. I learned that these cures, including healings of infantile paralysis and tuberculosis and of a broken arm and leg, had taken place as a result of conscientious study of this amazing book and practical application of its teachings. As I was soon to discover for myself, these teachings are based directly on the Bible, which they confirm and explain. . . .

My first contact with this outstanding and beautifully written book proved to be the basic turning point of my life. The more I studied it, the more clear it became that so far from being a modern or newfangled treatise with scanty references to the Bible, here was a book directly and obviously based upon it — a book which took seriously the Master's explicit command that his followers in all ages should heal the sick, as well as overcome sin and preach the gospel.

My immediate and vital interest in this volume of over 700 pages is perhaps best shown by the fact that during the next few weeks — from July 1st to September 8th, as my diary shows — I read it through five times from cover to cover, gaining new inspiration and enlightenment at each reading. I preached every Sunday, but spent most of each week studying *Science and Health*.

The Tide of Healing

On my return to New York that autumn, I continued to study the Christian Science textbook concurrently with my theological work. Before many months had passed I had reached the unescapable conclusion that Christian Science was the faith which I must accept at all costs. . . .

It is often said that one of the most virulent scourges of our day is mental disease, and everything from drugs to shock treatment to psychoanalysis is marshaled to combat it. Christian Science teaches that man's true selfhood cannot be alienated from the Mind that is God, from the creative Love that formed the universe, and this truth comes to the rescue of the individual who is classified as either physically or mentally ill, psychotic or neurotic. The command to "cast out demons" by the power of Christ has relevance to an age that no longer believes in literal demons but is haunted by a thousand fears and aberrations. A single example illustrates many such modern healings:

HAVING fruitlessly sought health in various nerve and mental hospitals for several years, when I entered another mental hospital in the year 1955, I settled down hopelessly to its dreary routine. Shortly after my arrival, the chief medical superintendent underlined his comment that I could not last five minutes outside by having me certified as insane and in need of care and protection. Though I was convinced of the injustice of this, the stigma of this additional emotional wound was quite sufficient to worsen my condition.

I consoled myself by practicing Braille-writing in the company of an inmate who was losing his sight and by scouring the dusty ward bookcases in search of reading matter. The bookcases yielded two books that were to have an incredible influence on my life; one was the Christian Science textbook, *Science and Health with*

Key to the Scriptures by Mary Baker Eddy, and the other was a book about the Canary Islands.

There were between one and two thousand patients in the hospital, but I had no rival claimant for these two books, which I read almost continually in the seemingly endless time available. The effect of the first book was that it brought bright, new hopes; the second brought a yearning to be free to live in the beautiful, sunny Canary Islands.

After more than two years I escaped from the hospital, and I arrived penniless, ragged, unshaven, and very ill in a large city. Having neither money nor introductions, I was obliged to sleep on the ground in a public park, and the bitter cold added to hunger drove me to seek a warm refuge in the city. It was with this idea of temporary comfort, and with no idea of healing, that I entered a Christian Science Reading Room.

On the third day of subsequent daily visits, the librarian recommended that I see a practitioner, who would, she felt sure, alleviate my all-too-obvious suffering. Though my previous tentative interest in Christian Science had benefited me, it had not convinced me; but it seemed both wise and polite to agree to her recommendation.

On my way to the practitioner, I jotted down penciled notes of my thoughts as a guide to the state of mind which the doctors at the hospital had considered to be one of insanity. I hoped these notes might be of some use to the practitioner in his efforts to help me. I recall that they ended with the words, "I want to go where the oranges grow." (Three years later I was able to send the practitioner a beautiful orange grown in my Tenerife garden.)

When he had read the self-revealing notes I had made, and I had replied to a few brief questions, he said: "The oranges you are seeking are the fruits of Love, and I am going to show you how to find them. For a start, I love you. I love you for your truthfulness and honesty, and on these spiritual qualities we will build an entirely new, strong, moral character, which can resist the mental malpractice to which you appear to have been subjected."

Accompanying his words with actions, he washed, reclothed, and fed me, so that even if I bore little resemblance to the British radio star that I had once been, I certainly differed in aspect from an escaped lunatic. Step by step, ridding me of the temptation to succumb to earlier vices, both guiding me and teaching me Christian Science at the same time, this kind practitioner sustained me as I legally established my sanity, reestablished my musical career, and wrote a Braille instruction book for use by blind musicians.

A new blow came in the news of my mother's sudden death. But the practitioner's work was well done. Every move was made in accordance with divine Principle and every doubt dissolved by reference to the works of Mrs. Eddy, so that I found myself surrounded by loving friends, whose many kindnesses demanded so much gratitude that there was no time for grief.

The trembling, unshaven, yellow-skinned wreck who had first confronted the practitioner was by now transformed into an enthusiastic and healthy citizen. At fifty-two years of age, youthful industry and ability had been restored, though nothing seemed less likely during the seven preceding years.

I am happy to report that this healing has been complete. The spasmodic illness affecting my right arm, which occasioned my long musical silence, has never returned. I rejoice that my mental force remains unabated and that I have certainly stayed "outside" for more than five minutes through knowing that God cares for and protects me. I am gratified that the practitioner and his wife witnessed my marriage, which is proving to be a harmonious one.

Most of all, however, I am grateful that I have been able to pursue the study of Christian Science right here in Tenerife in the same spirit of appreciative awe before the relevation of Truth. God has been very good to me since I was introduced to Him through Science. His omnipotence has been clearly proved as I have surmounted apparently insuperable difficulties, such as that of finding a suitable home in these islands before I knew the native language.

"Our heavenly Father never destined mortals who seek for a better country to wander on the shores of time disappointed travellers, tossed to and fro by adverse circumstances, inevitably subject to sin, disease, and death" (*Message to The Mother Church for 1902*, by Mrs. Eddy, p. 11). Thanks to the guide, *Science and Health*, navigation from the adverse circumstances in the hospital in England to the Canary Islands (where the oranges grow), became first a possibility and then an accomplished fact.

Richard Tarrant Bailey, Jr.,
Santa Cruz de Tenerife, Canary Islands.

— *Journal*, Vol. 82, pp. 270–271
(May, 1964).

> Among the "demons" of our day, to be cast out in accordance with Christ's command, are alcoholism and drug addiction. Christian Science literature contains numerous records of such healings, some of them gradual, some instantaneous. The Christian Science approach is never to judge or condemn the individual but to bring him an awareness of his true selfhood as the son of God. This recognition wipes out the desire for drinking, smoking, gambling, narcotics, or whatever the enslaving habit may be. When the desire itself is wiped out, the healing is complete.

I was more or less left on my own at a very early age. My mother died when I was just a year old and my sisters one at a time took care of the house, as they grew up. I got mixed up with a bad crowd, and one thing led to another. I was without God in the world to show me right from wrong. Then I ran away from home. I got arrested and sent to a reform school. Was there sixteen months.

When I was seventeen my father died and I came to Chicago. I was on my own. I ran around and got mixed up with the wrong bunch, and started smoking marijuana. And from there I went to heroin and through the whole list of drugs to morphine, and whiskey on top of it. I wouldn't want to blame it on bad company; I think it was more that I always wasn't satisfied inside.

For eleven years I struggled through all of the tortures of the drug habit. One time I was sent to a U.S. Public Health institution in Kentucky for the cure. When I left the hospital I was pronounced cured by the physicians, but I no sooner got back to Chicago than I was looking for narcotics again. For a period of four or five years after that, things got worse than ever. I just made it one day to another.

Then one day I met this acquaintance of mine at the "Y." I was in pretty bad condition, so he got to talking, and he said why didn't I drop by his place some time. So I was in the neighborhood, and I stopped to see him one evening. We got to talking about religion. He mentioned Christian Science and I asked if he was a Christian Scientist, and he said, "Yes," and he showed me the book, *Science and Health*. After reading the first page I asked him could I have the book. He said no — but he told me where the Reading Room was nearby. So the next day I went to the Reading Room, and I started reading. That was my introduction to it.

This was the opening of a new world to me. Little by little I caught some glimpses of the true meaning of God and man, but I was not then ready to leave off the narcotics. I continued to read, though progress was very slow and painful, and I slipped backwards many, many times.

But one day I was in an office building downtown where a lot of Christian Science practitioners are, and I went into one office, and she said she was busy, so I just went around the corner, and there was this other one, and she could see me. She patiently talked to me about God, and taught me how to apply the truths of Christian Science to help me.

This practitioner stuck with me all the time until I was healed. I would talk with her sometimes twice a week. I would be on a spot some days, waiting all day for narcotics. I would call her and say, "I can't break away." And she would say, "Yes you can" — that God would give me the strength I needed. And then she would help me through prayer.

I learned the meaning through many bitter struggles, of Mrs. Eddy's words in *Science and Health* (p. 5): "Sorrow for wrongdoing is but one step towards reform and the very easiest step. The next and great step required by wisdom is the test of our sincerity, — namely, reformation. To this end we are placed under the stress of circumstances. Temptation bids us repeat the offence, and woe comes in return for what is done."

I started working, — didn't hold onto the jobs right away, but it kept me going. I started to go to church — Sundays. I didn't know if I would make the grade. At first I didn't have any confidence in my ability to do anything constructive about my life. But as I gradually saw myself, in my real being, as the perfect son of God, the way of dominion began to open and I made the effort to leave off some of the drugs. Each day my moral courage improved some, and faith in myself began to become a reality by the work of this faithful practitioner.

Finally the day of victory came and I no longer felt the craving for narcotics. The desire just left me. It was about eighteen months after I'd first gone to the practitioner. I started working steady and going to night school. I attended church regularly. The desire for liquor, tobacco, tea, and coffee also left me with the healing of the other drugs in the habit.

I have had no desire for drugs of any kind for fourteen years. I am a free man. I am gainfully employed as a waiter in a leading hotel. I am an active church member. Words could never express my deep and profound gratitude for Christian Science, and to the practitioner and all others who have helped me on this journey from deep darkness into the light of Truth.

George Francis Langlois, Chicago, Illinois
Radio/TV series, "How Christian Science Heals," 1962.

I FELT terribly lost, lonely — after my husband died, even though I had my three children. My doctor was giving me sleeping tablets I was so upset. Then one evening some friends said they thought it would be better if I'd have a drink to help me sleep. And that was how I took my first drink.

Well, at first it was just once or twice a week. But then I started to drink every night. This went on until I became an alcoholic. Over a period of eight years, I was in the hospital, oh, fifty times

The Tide of Healing

at least. At first I'd stay just a few days, but then it got to be weeks, and then months.

I tried everything — practically every known cure, I guess. And I went to a psychiatrist for three and a half years — every two weeks at first, then every day. But lots of times I'd leave his office and have several drinks before I returned to work.

I operated a lovely beauty shop for many years. But as my drinking became worse it seemed best for me to sell it. And finally the doctor persuaded my mother to have me committed to the state hospital — for a year or more, if necessary.

By this time my children were grown up and living away from home. When all this happened I began to realize I had to do something about my life — it was really a mess. I wondered what I could do and I started praying to God. Then I found a Bible verse in a little pamphlet I had. It's from Philippians (4:8): "Whatsoever things are true, whatsoever things are honest, whatsoever things are just, whatsoever things are pure, whatsoever things are lovely, whatsoever things are of good report; if there be any virtue, and if there be any praise, think on these things." So I started with that Bible verse. And sometimes when I couldn't think of anything else, I'd just look at the sky and see how pretty and blue it was. I'd look at the trees instead of thinking about the unhappiness around me, dreariness and sickness.

Then I began to think about Christ Jesus and how he prayed to God — humbly and deeply just as though God were right there. So I tried to pray that way too — that God was right there and that He could heal me. I just went ahead with that, every single day. And finally I was released from the hospital, after I'd been there only five months.

I wanted to change my way of life and I knew it could only be changed through God. So that's when I finally decided to see a Christian Science practitioner.

I'd read some of *Science and Health* years before. But I hadn't understood it.

So I went to see a practitioner. I told him I had no future unless my whole way of life could be changed. And I knew my only chance was through God. I didn't say too much about the drinking

183

— I was so ashamed of it. And he said, "It never really happened to the man God made." Well, naturally I argued a little — inside of me. But not much, because I had the most encouraged feeling. He kept on talking to me, and I began to feel I'd find my way again. I felt God's nearness. What he told me gave me such a sense of belonging to society again — you lose it, you know, even though your friends are right around you, because you know what you're doing is not right. And by the time I left his office, I was sure I was healed.

There was no more temptation, no more drinking.

There wasn't even a thought of it. I just revelled in the healing. I was so filled with the wonder of it. I had more help from the practitioner and I began to study Christian Science. Little by little I began to understand what it was that had healed me.

Pretty soon I went back to my home in Nebraska. What a wonderful experience it was to go back there! People would come up and put their arms around me and say, "We're so happy for you." There was no question in anybody's eyes, or in their thoughts. And the gratitude I felt to God — well, it was just beyond words.

(Mrs.) Harriet Nelson, Norfolk, Nebraska
Radio/TV series, "How Christian Science Heals," 1958.

I'M A RAILROAD MAN, and for a long time I was a dining car waiter. It seemed to be the thing to do, as soon as you arrived in a city, there would be a group of us that would stop off to bid each other good-bye until the time for going out and discuss different events that happened during the trip and in doing that we'd always stop and have a social drink.

I had been a dependable railroad man for many years, but I had begun to indulge in alcohol to the extent that I became unreliable. I would at the last moment lay off from assignments, and then when I would go back to work I was weak. There were a lot of little things that made me begin to realize that I was just on the verge of skid row and I'd have to do something. Then, after I'd have a few more again, maybe two or three, I'd forget all about it for a while. I never drank on the job, I was wonderful on the job — but they must have wondered, when would he be on the job? I didn't lose any positions, but I lost the opportunity for promotion due to it.

Besides that, I caught what they call a gambling fever. People have told me on my way home about a game that was going to be in progress somewhere. I would go home and take a nap and get up without a quarter and go to someone that had money and borrow some money and go to that game. It got to the place where I was never satisfied unless I was gambling — mostly poker. So the debts piled up.

I came home off this particular trip and this time I came home in very good shape, came right home. I found that my wife had had a bad fall, with severe injury to her kneecap. She had been visiting someone and coming down the stairs and probably looking back, talking, she misstepped. The kneecap had swollen so large that it wasn't flexible at all. She had several small insurance policies, for accident and sickness, so right away she called the different insurance companies and had their physicians come and look her over. About three came and they told her there wasn't anything they could do for her, that it would just be a matter of time for the healing and to stay off it as much as possible.

She became so distressed as she told me, she started crying. Well, I'd never seen her cry before and it did something to me. I started to think about what I could do, and I remembered just five years previous my mother had given me a Christian Science textbook and I had never opened it, it was in my dresser drawer. The wife was lying on the lounge. I told her I would get the book and read to her.

In all of my reading, and I loved to read, even then, I always prepared for it. So I prepared to read the textbook by making a highball, placing it on a tray by a large chair and getting my cigarettes and lighter. I got the textbook and took the wrapper off this beautiful book. Then I sat down and told my wife to relax for I was doing this for her benefit, and her benefit only as I did not need this kind of thing. I started on the first page of the

Preface. Every paragraph I read was so attractive to me that I would stop and think and continue.

On the very first page I saw the statement, "The time for thinkers has come." Well, that aroused my curiosity. What do you mean by "the time for thinkers has come"? Everybody thinks. Then as I read on, like in the chapter on Prayer, the method of praying, then I could visualize things as they should be done and they weren't being done, that is, I hadn't been doing it. And I lost sight of the fact that I was reading for someone else's benefit. I became all in this thing, forgot about everybody else and everything else.

And then I heard water dripping, and looked; the ice was melting in that highball and the water was running over the sides of the glass all over the tray, all over the cigarettes. The wife was sound asleep just as peaceful and quiet. I cleaned up the debris that I had. That was the last highball that I ever prepared or ever drank.

When the wife woke up she asked me what had happened, it was so quiet and peaceful. Then I asked her would she consent to having Christian Science treatment. She said, "Yes." So the next day we had a practitioner, and on the third day she was sitting in a chair opposite me and she got up without her cane or crutches and went down the hall. The hall was waxed, highly waxed, and she made it without any trouble at all. She came back and sat in another chair — her cane and crutches over in the corner.

She started talking to me and finally she said, "Well, where is my cane?" Then she felt her knee. To this day she couldn't tell you which knee it was, the healing was that complete.

I was overjoyed naturally. So this same practitioner I called myself. I wanted to begin the study of the Lesson-Sermon — how to do it. And he came out and showed me how to start and discussed different points of Christian Science. And I told him, "Well, you know, I know I've finished with that liquor, but the cigarettes. . ." He said, "You'll do the same thing with that." The second day I was marking the books for the Lesson-Sermon and the smoke got in my eyes. I had four cartons of cigarettes in my car, used to buy them by the carton. I got right up, gave them away, had no use for them, and I haven't had any desire for a cigarette since. And the gambling, too — that dropped off with me just like you shed an overcoat in the summertime..

When I stopped drinking, and stopped smoking, and stopped gambling, and changed my way of living, my associates in the industry, they made wagers I wouldn't live six months — they said, "You just can't do it." Many still hold to the thought that it was will power, and I tell them, "No, if it was will power I'd be over in skid row, if it was will power. It was Christian Science. It was God's work." Quite a few that have watched have been living a pretty orderly life. They came along the same path, they gave up many things.

I began to read the textbook from the beginning to the last page. The very thought of man's relationship to God — I, like thousands of others have never known that. You see, we've always been told that it's some remote situation, far away, and all we're doing here is preparing for something after we've died. And after reading Mrs. Eddy's book, why the whole picture of living changed — knowing that you're living now — you're enjoying now the truth about God — that He is creator. As well as creator, He sustains you — that His thoughts are your thoughts, if you will permit them to be.

When I got over into one of the chapters later on where Mrs. Eddy states that "one moment of spiritual consciousness is a foretaste of eternity," that explained many things to me. ["One moment of divine consciousness, or the spiritual understanding of Life and Love, is a foretaste of eternity", p. 598.] Then, on page 445, "Christian Science silences human will, quiets fear with Truth and Love . . ." meant so much to me. It meant this: All of my experience, human experience up to that date, the human will, what I wanted to do or what the other person was going to do, what I planned, what you planned — that was it. But after reading the textbook and getting a better understanding of Life, the "I" came out entirely. You were just reflecting what was desired of God's plan. All of your good — not intentions, but your good actions put into practice — that was it.

Within a year or so I received a promotion where I had several men that were under my jurisdiction. The old way of handling men was to demand the first directive — you do this, you do that, or else. But with the love taught me in the study of Christian Science in that short time there came a thought in me to create a desire in the individuals to do the right thing and to become a little closer to them. If things weren't just going right, to find out if I could what was wrong, and maybe I could help. That was one of the ways that we could put Christian Science in practice on the job.

You see formerly you were looking at men from one angle, that is, getting all that you could out of them, or everybody outsmarting the other fellow. It changed the whole picture. The most important thing to me at that time was learning the meaning of Love.

Out of the first promotion there came another one where it was unheard of. I conducted classes every day from nine in the morning until four in the afternoon for the New York Central for the entire Dining Car Department and the Chicago area. I have made progress from waiter, waiter-in-charge, instructor of dining services, steward, assisting in food control, and as of now, System Supervisor.

John E. Johnson, Chicago, Illinois
Radio/TV series, "How Christian Science Heals," 1961.

Christ Jesus declared, "I must be about my Father's business" (Luke 2:49), and Christianity has repeatedly proclaimed that all business, properly regarded and rightly carried on, can become the Father's business in the degree that it is made an occasion to serve God and one's fellow men. To turn to the divine Mind for wisdom in all the transactions and challenges of daily life is to carry Christian healing into those secular activities which are so often put in an entirely different category from the worship of God. To see the complex activities of the modern megalopolis as under the irresistible control of divine law is to begin to bring into evidence the true "city of God." Instead of becoming the helpless victim of increasing complexity, the individual becomes the master of circumstances in so far as he intelligently and faithfully becomes the servant of divine Love.

The Tide of Healing

This happened shortly after World War II. I was sales promotion manager for a large industrial firm in New York. I also handled the trade advertising and public relations.

One of the divisions of the company, a division I was not directly associated with, was busy buying up large industrial properties that had been shut down during the war. Their idea was to put them back into operation so they would be saleable. But one property had defied all efforts to get it into production. It was an old paper mill that had been closed down a long time.

We'd had the property for about a year, and we'd sent engineers out there, efficiency men, expediters, master mechanics — the best talent we could muster. But first a boiler would blow up, then a dynamo would break down, then the electrical system would go out. To make matters worse, we were plagued by a water shortage and a jurisdictional labor dispute.

Reports of the trouble kept coming into the New York office, and when I heard about them, I refused in my own mind to accept them as final. I repudiated the thought that anything could be beyond the harmonious control of divine Mind, because I'd learned in Christian Science that all things are subject to God's intelligent law.

Then one day, very unexpectedly, the president of the company called me in and asked me to fly out to the mill for a 30-day period, to see if I could put my finger on the trouble. I had only a general knowledge about operating a paper mill, and I didn't know a thing about putting a dormant one back in operation, nor about repairing dynamos. The engineers and the local talent in the New York office thought it was a big joke — sending a sales and advertising man on a technical assignment.

At first I was fearful about going. But then I realized this was a challenge — a wonderful opportunity to prove what I'd learned in Christian Science about listening for divine direction — to prove that God's law of adjustment can straighten out any difficulty.

189

A Century of Christian Science Healing

I saw that I had to turn my thought away from all the troubles — the confusion, disagreements, lack, human shortcomings — to the contemplation of perfect God and perfect, spiritual man — man made in His image and likeness, as he is referred to in the Bible. I had to see that fundamentally I wasn't really dealing with dynamos and machinery and conflicting viewpoints. I was engaged in demonstrating the truth — the truth that divine Mind, God, governs all His creation in perfect harmony. I found assurance in Mary Baker Eddy's words in *Science and Health* (p. 283): "Mind is the source of all movement, and there is no inertia to retard or check its perpetual and harmonious action."

Well, after my arrival, it took about three weeks — working 18 hours a day — before there were any real signs of progress. New machinery was practically impossible to get, and for months the used equipment that had been arriving was either faulty or the wrong type. Most of the supervisory help were completely out of patience and had quit — and everybody blamed the New York office for the whole comedy of errors.

During these three weeks I was having conferences every day with people at the mill. And I put in quite a lot of preparation for them — through prayer. Also I had a Christian Science practitioner helping me.

Then one morning I received a letter from the practitioner, quoting a statement by Mrs. Eddy, in which she refers to "the individual, stupendous, Godlike agency of man" (*The First Church of Christ, Scientist, and Miscellany,* p. 14). This awakened me to realize man's God-given dominion. The mesmerism of fear then gave way completely. That very day the labor dispute was settled, and the water supply became adequate. The machinery began arriving in better condition, and the parts fitted together. It actually defied human description or explanation — how everything could fall into place so quickly.

The mill's capacity was a hundred tons of paper a day, running round the clock. Within a week we were operating at full capacity.

The whole thing caused quite a stir in the New York office — in fact, they made me an officer of the firm, and in a few weeks I was elected to the Board of Directors. But the biggest reward for me was the wonderful proof I'd had that we can always turn to God, divine Mind, for the ability and for the guidance we need.

John M. Todd, Leawood, Kansas
Radio/TV series, "How Christian Science Heals," 1960.

THE DAY CAME when I received my first contract as a costume designer with one of the big motion picture studios in Hollywood. Although Christian Science had been a help to me before, the desire for more and more money, more importance, more fame, grew in my thought, shutting out everything else.

I spent much time and effort in pursuit of the people and things which I felt would make me important. I became resentful of other people's success, and began running around trying to do everything I could to get my human personality admired and sought after. I had my office painted shocking pink, and hired a publicity agent. I worked very hard to know all the press people. I would take them to lunch, and cultivated everyone I could think of in this line. I was in night clubs three and four nights a week, because I thought one had to be seen. My husband tried to assist me in everything I wanted. Now, I realize he suffered patiently, silently, and quietly. This went on for about eleven years.

When something didn't go right or I was pushed aside in favor of someone else, I would call a Christian Science practitioner and I'd get out a *Sentinel* or a *Journal* and read a little till things quieted down. Then I would go on. I felt I was being very gay and sophisticated and I did everything that I thought I wanted to do.

When all my "striving and contriving" failed to accomplish all I had hoped for I decided to extend my activities. Designers who had their own business appeared to me to be very successful and sought after, so I decided that I must do this, too. I opened my own wholesale business in better dresses with a big splash and for a little while I had tremendous success. Then the studio decided that my interests were divided, and they certainly were, and so my contract wasn't renewed, which was a great blow to me. The business was on such a shaky foundation that it had to be terminated, amid much bitterness. I was told by a great many stores that nothing connected with my name would ever interest them again. Within a period of about eight months everything in my carefully self-arranged world fell apart. All of it just disappeared under my feet. Not only everything for which I had worked for years was gone, but my name which I had tried so hard to make important now stood for failure.

I couldn't get a studio job, I couldn't get a manufacturing job, I couldn't get anything. For two years I stayed at home without a single offer of work of any kind and struggled with pride and shame and deep regret. I had always cared for my mother and my sister out of my earnings, and my mother, who was not a Christian Scientist, suffered a stroke at this time. She couldn't accept anything but medical care, which soon took all the money I had saved.

With the financial problem we couldn't do any of the gay night clubbing that I'd felt so essential to life. Every single morning I got up and got my Lesson (daily Bible lesson) and sometimes I'd study until noon.

One night I was in utter despair. I picked up Mrs. Eddy's book *Miscellaneous Writings,* and it fell open to the statement (p. 119): "The nature of the individual, more stubborn than the circumstance, will always be found arguing for itself, — its habits, tastes, and indulgences."

I would never read that before, because every time I read it I got resentful, saying, "I can't help my nature, I was born this way." This time I made myself read it and say, "Every single solitary one of your troubles is the result of the 'nature of the individual,' not of the outside circumstances or the people you feel have been so unkind to you and all the things you feel have happened to you." I began to see that what I had wanted was wrong and that I hadn't been willing to be upright, orderly, humble, good, and obedient; and then I was on a better track. The basic uncovering was the fact that I could say, "Yes, 'the nature' — my wants and my desires and my false ambitions and my pride — caused all this and would have to go." It was at last a matter of being willing to

The Tide of Healing

admit that to myself. I think that's probably the hardest thing that one has to do. When I finally said, "Yes, You're right, and I will be obedient," many wonderful things happened.

I received an offer for a job. There were lots of struggles that first year because it seemed to me that many snarls had to be unwound. Every day I would spend noon hours in Reading Rooms in Beverly Hills. And I worked to be loving, something I'd never done before. All those years when I was so filled with resentment at seeing others ahead of me or more important or better, I was always tired. Gradually, I saw that each person is complete, a complete unit of reflection of the divine. I began to turn away from a sense of competition, to look to my true self and say "Thank thee, Father, I have all that I need." I tried to look to Mind, Soul, for the sense of beauty I was created to reflect. I learned just to express the joy that I see and the joy that I feel and the beauty that comes to me.

I have worked with that same studio, off and on, for all the intervening years. In the last few years a way has opened for me to combine world-wide travel and work in a way I would never have thought possible. I do not say that I have completely overcome all false ambition, but I've been taught that the closed fist can't receive. The ambition "to get" has been replaced with the wish "to give." I have a real desire to help others turn to Christian Science to find what it has brought me — the comfort, the joy, and the understanding of God as Father-Mother, Love always.

(Mrs.) *Renie B. Conley, Hollywood, California*
Radio/TV series, "How Christian Science Heals," 1960.

I LIVED and worked in a business block located on a busy intersection in a large city. Serious accidents occurred here weekly. Each time I would silently and audibly declare the truths we are taught in Christian Science, but my prayers seemed of no avail in preventing the accidents. This went on for months.

Then one day another accident occurred. As always I started

fervently declaring God's allness and His perfect government. Then I stopped. I sat down and just listened for God's voice.

Clearly came the solution. I realized why the accidents were occurring. One street was much wider than the other, and those crossing the wider street could not get clear before the lights changed.

If all the traffic was held back for a short time by an all red light period, there would be time to clear the intersection safely for all. I knew this answer to be the result of prayer in Science.

I called the Traffic Safety Department. At first they protested that this could not be done, but at my insistence they listened. In three weeks the lights were set with an all red light period.

This proved so effective that after a six months' trial it was installed on every strategic intersection throughout this large city. I received a card with a gold star for having contributed to the safety of the people of the city.

(Miss) Georgia T. Hale, Los Angeles, California.

— *Sentinel*, Vol. 64, pp. 2109–2110
(December 1, 1962).

WHILE I was driving in a busy city at an intersection where the green signal gave me the right of way, a heavy truck crashed into the right side of my car, doing considerable damage. After the traffic officer disentangled our vehicles and the necessary information was exchanged, I drove to the address of the owner of the truck. On arriving there, I found the driver of the truck, the president of the company, and their insurance adjuster in conference. The president said that according to their driver and the evidence of a few witnesses I was entirely responsible for the collision and resulting damage to the two vehicles, and that he would hold me accountable for damage to their truck. This was all, of course, the reverse of the facts.

Before replying I started to contemplate the spiritual significance of the Lord's Prayer, and I got only as far as "Our Father," when

The Tide of Healing

I realized the significance of God as the only creator of man; therefore man expresses Principle and Truth, and cannot be a false witness; he can witness only to truth. I arose and said: "I am going to tell you the truth about this collision, and I will then abide by your decision. Should you decide that it was my fault, I shall not take you into court; I shall bear you no ill will and shall pay for the damage to the truck and my own car."

At this point the insurance adjuster arose and said: "You do not have to say another word. I authorize you to have your car repaired and send the bill to me, and I will authorize its payment. As for the truck, we will take care of the repair bill." I thanked them and started to leave, when the insurance adjuster called me and said: "How did you ever come to make such a statement? Did you not realize that you were at our mercy as a possible result?" I said, "No, because I was telling the truth and I knew that the truth would protect me from an unjust decision." He then asked me what church I attended, and I replied that I was a Christian Scientist. He said he was convinced that Christian Science was worth looking into.

Carl P. Foeller, Butler, Pennsylvania.

— *Sentinel*, Vol. 53, pp. 912–913
(May 26, 1951).

I'M AN ENGINEER and formerly was manager of a physics laboratory doing applied research. Now I have my own firm. For the past twenty-five years I've been engaged in research and development in the aircraft field — designing and inventing. At first, each time an assignment was given to me, I had the fear that I wouldn't be able to work out the solution to the problem. I think that the fear is compounded in the aircraft industry because the field changes so drastically every few years. The problem always was to get something fast, or we wouldn't get a contract.

Many of these devices that have come to me to be developed have been foreign to my own experience. An example is when I received the problem of designing an angle-of-attack transducer. That's a precision weather vane. It's attached on the fuselage of an aircraft, usually on the side. It tells the pilot which way the wind is blowing past the aircraft. It has special importance for rocket firing and for maintaining proper flight altitude.

The designs that had been tried previously weren't satisfactory and the customer gave us only one more day to come up with something that worked. The device would have to stand the aerodynamic forces of a supersonic airplane and yet be sensitive enough to measure a tenth of a degree change at one hundred miles an hour, which is a fairly low speed for an airplane. Also, the device had to be able to withstand exposure to dust, rain, hail, and so on.

I went back to the office with no idea of how to work this thing out. But then I sat there at my desk with a clean sheet of paper in front of me, and expectantly I turned to God in prayer. I've learned from my study of Christian Science that there is only one Mind. And that the primal quality of this Mind is intelligence, which man reflects. I prayerfully reached out to know that divine intelligence is not limited in any way and that I reflected this all-knowing intelligence. It was quite an interesting thing. The idea came almost instantly and the whole design just unfolded. The heart of this was the bearing, a cantilever design, turned inside out, so the bearings were all inside a tube with a labyrinth dust seal. The whole pattern just came in a few minutes.

The idea seemed so promising we were given several more days to construct a prototype. Then the sand and dust test was run, and on the first test it came out fine, which is somewhat unique. There were little structural problems to work out, but the basic concept was never changed. The unit went into production and is still in use today.

Mrs. Eddy tells us in *Miscellaneous Writings* (p. 307), "God gives you His spiritual ideas, and in turn, they give you daily supplies." Now, the spiritual idea certainly wouldn't be the picture of rivets and bolts and mechanical bearings. The spiritual idea is the complete, perfect, ever-present manifestation of divine Mind, having its being in God. As we see the reality of the spiritually concrete, our human thinking is changed sufficiently so that the solution to the problem becomes apparent. Mrs. Eddy says, "The effect of this Science is to stir the human mind to a change of base, on which it may yield to the harmony of the divine Mind" (*Science and Health*, p. 162). It seems that when we get our thought free from materiality, then things start to happen.

At another time I received an assignment to develop what in the digital computing field is called a "stepping register." I would say that to me that was one of the most amazing examples of how an idea can come when a person's background isn't associated with the problem. It happened in this way. Our firm was a member of a certain defense program. At a meeting our assignment was given to us, and that was to develop this stepping register. At that time I didn't even know what a stepping register was. The fear that presented itself to me was that: first, it was a field I didn't know; secondly, it was a field in which there are a great many highly-trained engineers that had specialized in this type of thing exclusively. Therefore I was afraid I couldn't make any contribution and that our effort would be wasted.

In a situation like this, I've found that just by a very simple turning — by turning first to realize just what God is — the answer has come. I try to realize the infinite nature of Mind, and intelligence as the primal quality of Mind; then, realize that that Mind is mine, by reflection.

It was a rather gradual unfoldment in that first it came in a form which is slightly different from the one we used. Then the complete concept unfolded. It seemed to be a break-through in the digital computing field and won recognition in a national contest.

David W. Moore, Jr., Santa Barbara, California
Radio/TV series, "How Christian Science Heals," 1960.

Through psalm and story the Bible asserts God's power to save men in the most unusual and untoward circumstances — in the wilderness, in a den of lions. Christian Science teaches that as men acknowledge the perfect government of Mind, God, they are able to prove their dominion over all the diverse challenges of human life.

A Century of Christian Science Healing

I SHOULD like to give an instance of an instantaneous healing in my experience. Many years ago I lay in the far-off jungles of Assam in the last stages of dysentery, the only woman in a camp of seventy men. For as long as I was able I clung to the little I then knew of Christian Science, but found myself constantly serving two masters, at one time declaring my oneness with God, ever perfect and harmonious; the next minute overwhelmed by the human conditions.

At last, when I was fast entering the valley of the shadow of death, my husband, who had even less understanding than I possessed, but who had been doing his best to help me, found in a *Christian Science Journal* the name and address of a practitioner in India. A runner was sent with a telegram to the nearest railhead, fourteen miles away, with an urgent request for help. The practitioner received it the next day.

Early the following morning the camp was ordered to move, and I was carried in my bed through the jungle. I was fast losing consciousness and was no longer able to swallow. About midday the camp was passing through a tea estate. The owners, two young planters, seeing my dying condition, suggested that I be left in the bungalow until my husband, after posting the men, could return and be with me. As there was nothing more my husband could humanly do, he gratefully accepted their offer. I was carried into the bungalow unconscious, and my bed and belongings were placed in an empty room. There I was left undisturbed for several hours.

Late in the afternoon I suddenly awoke, found myself completely well, strong, and full of a joyous sense of freedom. I called for a bath, got up, and unpacked my clothes, and when my husband returned shortly after, I was dressed and free of all sense of the dysentery. When dinner was announced, I appeared in the dining room with my husband. I ate a full, normal meal; and after dinner, as the two other young planters had turned up to spend the evening, I sang and played my guitar to them. The next day we had a long and difficult march through leech-infested jungle, but I was not the least bit tired or exhausted.

I have proved that Christian Science is also an instantaneous protection in danger. I was alone in the jungle when confronted with an elephant which had gone wild. Only my knowledge of Science saved me. Within a few hours that same elephant killed a man and two children before it was shot. On another occasion I was protected when in great danger from a cobra attack.

(Lady) Mary L. Giles, Heytesbury, Wiltshire, England.

— *Journal*, Vol. 69, p. 51
(January, 1951).

ONE SUNDAY AFTERNOON my wife and three-year-old daughter and I went out riding with another couple. This happened when we lived in Augusta, Georgia. About ten miles out of town, we came across a small roadside exhibit of a lion that they had at a filling station there. The person who operated the station had been sent this lion by some friends who had gone to Africa to hunt. They sent it to him when it was a cub and he raised it, right out in the backyard. But when the lion got older, he had to pen him up. So he made this sturdy cage, about room-size, out of wooden bars about four inches apart.

It was late afternoon and a little dark in the cage, and we were all lined up, sort of squatting down to see better, and I had our little daughter in my arms. The owner was in the cage. He was going to make the lion do some tricks he said he had taught him.

The lion was at the back of the cage walking back and forth when the next thing I knew he had leaped across the cage, straddling one of the bars, and had me by the head with his two front paws and was gradually pulling me toward the cage. One of his claws was hooked under my right jawbone and the others were hooked in the flesh on both sides of my face and neck. My friend, who was standing next to me, grabbed my baby out of my arms. I pulled the claw out from under my jaw and twisted away from the other paw. His right paw caught my shoulder as I pulled away.

Everyone seemed petrified, and it was all over before anyone could do anything to help me except the owner, who was still in the cage trying to beat the lion off with a small iron rod. I grabbed my handkerchief out of my pocket to cover up the torn places on my throat and face, and everybody started gathering around to see how badly I was hurt. When the owner saw me he said, "Get to a doctor as quick as you can. Don't delay!"

All the way back to town our friends kept insisting on taking me to a hospital or to a doctor. But I was even more insistent that they take me home, which they finally did, although reluctantly. I assured them that I would be all right and would keep them informed as to my condition.

It was about two hours after we got home before we could reach the practitioner. While my wife bandaged the wounds as best she could with cotton and adhesive tape, we talked about the fact that God had given man dominion over all the earth, over the beasts of the field, over the fish of the sea, the fowls of the air, and over every creeping thing, as the Bible says (Genesis 1:24–26). I started to read the daily Lesson-Sermon, but that one thought of dominion just kept ringing in my ears and I couldn't seem to read or think of anything else. As I continued to name everything that man had dominion over, God-given dominion, I became completely satisfied.

By this time, my wife and I were both completely free from fear. We finally reached the practitioner and went over, and when she saw all the bandaging, she felt that we should have the wounds properly covered, so we went to a local physician. When the doctor saw the condition of my jaw and throat, his face paled. Where the lion's claw had hooked under my jawbone, the flesh was torn away exposing the jugular vein. The doctor went ahead and put on the bandages without a word. At our request he didn't use any medication or take any stitches. But when he was through he said quietly, "Son, you're in deep water." The practitioner had gone with us, and when we were finished, he went to the practitioner and told her, "This boy is in deep water. Bring him back tomorrow so I can change the bandages." Of course, we agreed.

The practitioner kept right on helping me. She was up pretty much all night praying. The doctor said later he was up all night, too. He said he just couldn't sleep, thinking about that young man who was going to die, just because he wouldn't have medical attention. I slept quite comfortably, but the next morning I was in quite a bit of pain and I couldn't open my mouth. My jaws were just frozen together tight.

The practitioner laid down the law to me, the law of Truth. Regardless of the pain I did open my mouth and had three meals that day just as I had been in the habit of doing. And by evening, my jaws were free, — no pain, and that was the last of that.

When we went back to the doctor that night, he still didn't say anything until he had finished the bandages, and then he repeated, "Son, you're still in deep water." But he said the bandages needn't be changed until two nights later. But when I went back then — the Wednesday after the accident on Sunday — the wounds were completely healed.

When the doctor took off the bandages he was simply amazed. He said, "Why, those places are well! They're completely healed. If I hadn't seen it, I never would've believed it!" Then he told me that the first night he saw me he never expected to see me alive again, that according to his profession I was a "goner." He was amazed there wasn't any infection of any kind, especially since he hadn't used any medicine.

The doctor was so amazed he just kept talking about it. And he immediately went right out to the practitioner and told her this same thing and said, "I'd like to have a little something to read about this. Things like this don't happen in my profession. Do you have anything that I could read about it?" She did, and sent him some literature. Just what came of it, I don't know.

After that Wednesday there was no need for bandages, of course. I didn't go around telling people about the healing, but the doctor did. I had people that would stop me on the street and say, "Jim, what's this Dr. ——— is saying about you and a lion?"

James M. Chancey, Dallas, Texas
Radio/TV series, "How Christian Science Heals," 1956.

Young people, as well as old, feel the impact of the special moral and intellectual challenges of our age. The definition of man as no more than organized protoplasm or an unstable equilibrium of blind psychic urges tends to drain away all meaning from life. Youth feels this in the attack on a moral order and on the traditional virtues of fidelity and trust, qualities it discovers to be vital in life but often cannot defend. Youth feels the challenge in the emptiness of old religious phrases and the haunting loneliness of spiritual doubt.

At many age levels, at study and play, youth today wrestles with this materialistic challenge. Very young children readily grasp the practicality of the Bible teachings they receive in Christian Science. Many demonstrate the healing power of Love at a very early age. Others as they grow older find the value of anchoring their thoughts in divine Principle, and through experience learn the relevance of Christian values and insights to their secular activities. Still others may drift off into the various currents of contemporary materialism but under the pressure of urgent need turn later to spiritual certainties once glimpsed and now demanding proof.

THROUGHOUT my school experience, I was a mediocre student. I studied very hard to obtain a B average and then sometimes fell short of my goal. However, between grades ten and eleven, I decided to read *Science and Health* from cover to cover. My only motive was to learn more of God. I was surprised to find that when I returned to school I maintained the highest possible marks for the remaining two years without studying as hard as before.

Heber P. Hostetter, Jr., Ames, Iowa.

— *Sentinel*, Vol. 66, pp. 254–255
(February 8, 1964).

ABOUT two years ago, as I was playing at school with a friend, I fell and hurt my arm very badly. When I was in class the teacher saw that my face was white; she asked me what was wrong. I told her, and a friend then took me home.

My mother read "the scientific statement of being" on page 468 of *Science and Health* by Mrs. Eddy, and we both thought about it carefully. It tells us that "Spirit is God, and man is His image and likeness." My mother telephoned my father and told him what had happened. My father helped us to realize that there are no accidents in God's spiritual kingdom, because it is made by Him and controlled by Him, divine Principle. That afternoon the pain had gone, and that night I slept with my arm on a pillow, just to make it comfortable. During the night I knew that "in the beginning God created the heaven and the earth" (Gen. 1:1).

Three days later I was back at school. I was quite happy and contented.

I should like to tell of another healing that took place at boarding school.

There was a boy who kept bullying me. I had enough of him; so I knew the truth that God's ideas always live happily together and cannot harm each other. After I had remembered that God truly loves this boy just as He loves me, the boy did not bully me again.

I am very grateful for Christian Science and for the help we and all others get through it.

Brammie Wantenaar, Sasolburg, Orange Free State,
South Africa.

The above testimony was written by my son on his own initiative. I am pleased to verify that the injury to the bone of the arm, which was quite serious and caused much concern to the teacher, healed quickly, and the healing has been permanent.

Cornelis Johannes Wantenaar.

— *Sentinel*, Vol. 64, pp. 389–390
(March 3, 1962).

A NUMBER of years ago my husband was appointed Christian Science Chaplain at a large reform school for teen-age boys in California — boys from 15 to 21. I was his assistant.

Shortly after beginning this work I overhead some of the boys in my Sunday School class whispering something about the "underground." I didn't think any more about it until later when a large group of very tough-looking boys marched into the room where we held church. They weren't part of the group who regularly attended.

Usually the boys didn't sit in the front, but that morning this group filled all the front rows, just a few feet away from us. You see, my husband and I were conducting the service so we were both in front of the group. For a moment I was overwhelmed with fear. I had heard of some frightening disturbances that had taken place elsewhere in the school when gangs of big boys had started trouble and workers had wound up in the hospital. Our services had a reputation for being orderly, so none of the school supervisors or guards were present.

When my husband announced the opening hymn, some of these boys dropped hymnals and made loud noises. There was every indication that trouble was on the way. I was very frightened, but I rose and walked to my place, looking to God for protection.

As I looked at those young faces it seemed as though I was looking at masks — masks of defiance, malicious mischief, fear, cynicism, sensuality. Then the thought came to me, "These things are not part of the real man. God's perfect children alone are present here." Then I began to feel a great sense of compassion for the boys, recognizing that they felt confused, unloved, and perhaps unwanted. With this the fear began to leave me.

During the Lord's Prayer a few of the boys joined in at first. As it progressed, the noises stopped and more of them joined in.

During the reading of the Christian Science Lesson-Sermon there was a little more noise and elbowing. Occasionally a boy would try to get attention, or start something by making a noise, or mumbling, but it became more and more quiet as we went on. And my fear gradually disappeared. It was wonderful to see calmness and love rule out fear.

At the close of the service all the boys filed out in a very quiet and orderly way. And some of the boys of the underground gang, who we learned later had come to break up the service that day, returned to our services to learn about Christian Science.

The Tide of Healing

During the four years of our appointment, we never had another challenge like this to meet. And while teaching my Sunday School class, I was often alone with as many as fifteen boys in a closed room, but I was never fearful again.

During the time my husband and I were there, many of the boys in our group were healed through prayer. I remember healings of heart trouble, a deformed foot completely straightened, stuttering overcome, and the disappearance of the desire to drink and steal and to be dishonest. We were known as friends of the boys, and were always respected and loved by them. I think largely because we never accepted the belief that they were "bad" boys, but saw through that mask to God's pure and perfect child.

(Mrs.) *Joyce Chandler Parks, Palo Alto, California*
Radio/TV series, "How Christian Science Heals," 1956.

THIS HAPPENED during my senior year in high school. I'd been pole vaulting for three years and I was having one of my best seasons. I hadn't lost a meet and I'd broken a few school records. The league and the city finals were coming up and a lot of pressure was being put on me to win. I was practicing four and five hours a day. Then two days before our big meet, while I was vaulting, I slipped and fell from a height of about twelve feet. I missed the sawdust pit and came down on the metal box at the end of the runway. I sprained my ankle very badly. The coach took me to the school doctor and he taped it up. He said I'd have to stay off it quite a while and I wouldn't be able to pole vault for the rest of the season.

Well, the coach was feeling quite low. But I'd called a practitioner before going to the doctor's office, and I felt absolutely confident.

I guess the best way to explain it is to go back to when I first started pole vaulting. One day I'd be good and then next I'd be just terrible. It seemed that every day there'd be a new problem. This went on until I began getting rid of the thought of self-glory and started realizing my true goal should be to glorify God, by expressing man's God-given dominion. Not until I really found my goal did I begin to improve. You see, I believe that our purpose in doing things such as athletics is to express divine qualities as best we can — qualities like intelligence, exactness, control.

So when this problem with my ankle came up, I knew it was just another opportunity for me to prove God's care. It wasn't a case of wishful thinking — or trying to use will power. I went to that meet with a feeling of confidence even though the ankle was still quite painful. I felt I'd be taken care of, and that there could not be a cause or effect apart from God that could touch me.

I didn't do any warming up that day, and I by-passed the first jumps until I felt I was perfectly ready. And when I decided to go, I walked out on the runway and prayed for God's guidance. I jumped and I never jumped better in my life. I vaulted all afternoon without any feeling of pain or hindrance, and I had no more trouble with the ankle after that. I took second in the event — but it was because of a minor difference in form. It had nothing to do with my ankle. And even though I didn't win that day, I had a tremendous feeling of satisfaction. To me this proof of God's care was a far greater victory than just winning a medal. I felt it was a true victory because it showed me how we can rely on God in everything.

Richard D. Kemp, San Diego, California
Radio/TV series, "How Christian Science Heals," 1959.

DURING FOUR YEARS of college and two years of graduate study in social work, I found Christian Science to be of tremendous help in my studies and in making the adjustments required in college life.

When I first went away to college, I joined my friends in occasional smoking and drinking, because I felt it was a sign of good fellowship. Also, it seemed that those who didn't drink or smoke weren't as popular as those who did, and too, I wanted to be a good sport. Belonging and being accepted were very important to me, as they seem to be to all college students. I justified my actions by saying I wanted to be a part of "the crowd." But I was attending the Christian Science Sunday School, and through my study of the Bible and *Science and Health*, I got a different slant on the subject of social adjustment. Through this study, as well as through my own application of Christian Science to problems in connection with my schoolwork and with health, I learned that man, as God's likeness, includes all right ideas, such as strength, perfection, loveliness, and purity. Little by little, I began to see that the understanding of God brings satisfying activities and friendship, as well as poise.

During my junior year I stopped smoking and drinking completely. At first I felt rather uncomfortable, particularly when my friends made critical comments; but I realized it was an act of courage and common sense to stick to my convictions. On these occasions I turned to God, divine Mind, to tell me what to say. This led me to say what seemed right at the time, so that I didn't leave the impression of being either self-righteous or prudish. I also earnestly prayed to know that man can only express love and kindness. In this way I got rid of any resentment. As I progressed in my understanding of Christian Science and consistently refused to use tobacco or alcohol, gradually my friends came to accept this. In fact, from time to time several of my friends would confide in me that they didn't care for the habit but didn't have the courage to give it up. And as a result of applying my religion, I found I enjoyed the respect of others. I had a sense of belonging and I was active in a number of campus organizations.

One thing that helped a great deal was my attendance at meetings of the Christian Science Organization which was conducted entirely by Christian Science students on the university campus. There, of course, I met many congenial friends. I especially enjoyed hearing the experiences of fellow students and how they used Christian Science in college life.

This has been an extremely valuable lesson for me, and since leaving college it has been much easier for me to take a stand. I'd like to say also that Christian Science has answered the questions about life that have occurred to me, and it has given me a religion that is not only inspiring but extremely practical.

(Miss) Betty Jane Thwaits, Milwaukee, Wisconsin
Radio/TV series, "How Christian Science Heals," 1954.

The following dialogue is from an interview with Miss Julia W. Willis, Washington, D.C., and F. Karl Willenbrock, Cambridge, Massachusetts, from the radio/TV series, "How Christian Science Heals":

MISS WILLIS:

In the middle of my freshman year at William and Mary when I first read *Science and Health* I began to realize that intelligence comes from divine Mind or God, not from a brain. So intelligence is never limited, never a question of human struggle, but rather of spiritual unfoldment. It is always constant, always available.

This understanding gave me a sense of freedom and joy that I'd never known before. It freed me from the strain and struggle in my school work and my grades improved. I had such renewed interest in my studies. I was able to engage in sports, maintain an outside job, and hold offices on the campus, like house president. I also served as Reader in our Christian Science Organization. But at the same time my grades went up in spite of all the additional activity.

They'd always been poor — or I shouldn't say poor, but average with a struggle. For example, I was failing physics. I was working every spare hour, day and night on it. I didn't have a very strong background in mathematics and had been getting 30's and 40's in tests.

Then one day a test was assigned. I'd studied the subject matter thoroughly. This time I decided to really apply what I'd been learning in Christian Science. I knew that understanding came from God, the divine Mind, and was expressed everywhere, and therefore it could be expressed in my experience.

I passed the test — in fact I got 100, and I passed the finals. I raised my average in the course from an F to a B.

DR. WILLENBROCK:

I wonder whether I could ask you some questions about this. From the standpoint of teaching, the important thing is whether you understood the subject matter. Just passing a test doesn't necessarily prove it.

MISS WILLIS:

Yes, I felt that I'd really gained a foothold in the understanding of physics. I enjoyed the second semester very much.

DR. WILLENBROCK:

But what was the subject at the turning point? Many liberal arts majors have difficulty with the mathematical parts of physics although they do very well in the more qualitative aspects.

MISS WILLIS:

This test was in mechanics, which included a lot of derivations and formulas.

DR. WILLENBROCK:

Well, mechanics is often a difficult subject for people who don't have much interest in physics.

MISS WILLIS:

Yes, I think it was the annihilation of fear and limitation in my thinking that did it, because I always thought myself hopelessly stuck with limited ability. But the understanding of God gave me a sense of freedom, joy and dominion. You see, when I grasped the teachings of Christian Science I felt that it had fundamental truth. There was a fundamental logic there that satisfied me. As I utilized it, it freed me from self-imposed limitations of intelligence, ability and endurance.

DR. WILLENBROCK:

Your experience reminds me of one of my own, connected with the work toward my Ph.D. degree. It happened when I was finishing my thesis. I was working in electron physics and my thesis included both the theoretical and experimental work.

A Century of Christian Science Healing

The thesis was due at five o'clock on a Monday, and on Saturday night, I was stuck. The theoretical part was typed up — 100 pages of equations and graphs and so on. But I'd gotten some experimental results which didn't agree with my theory. I thought the theory was right, but these results didn't seem to fit in at all. It looked as if it might take weeks to straighten it out.

But that night while I was working in the lab my wife was doing some especially clear work for us in Christian Science. There had been a sentence in one of our recent Lesson-Sermons from the book of Daniel that illumined our thinking about the situation. It gave us a sense of the infinite intelligence which the divine Mind, God, constantly makes available to man. It was Daniel 9:22: "O Daniel, I am now come forth to give thee skill and understanding."

This seemed to meet my situation exactly. There was a need for skill in performing the experiments, and then for understanding in interpreting the results. I saw that I could rely on divine intelligence for the direction I needed.

So the next day I went back to the lab. And pretty soon a couple of ideas came that looked worth while. I tried them and they supplied what was missing. In other words the right ideas came and I was able to knit things together.

MISS WILLIS:

What about the experiments that didn't fit in?

DR. WILLENBROCK:

I found there was an additional factor which I hadn't been aware of, which accounted for the difference. And so the theory was right and the experiments were right. I gathered some more data that day and wrote my final chapter that night. I don't want to make it sound as though my thesis could not have been improved upon — but the experience did show me how Christian Science can help us "to exceed our ordinary capacity," as Mrs. Eddy says.*

(Miss) *Julia W. Willis, Washington, D.C.*
F. Karl Willenbrock, Cambridge, Massachusetts
Radio/TV series, "How Christian Science Heals," 1955.

* "The term Science, properly understood, refers only to the laws of God and to His government of the universe, inclusive of man. From this it follows that

The Tide of Healing

I was coming home from a party in San Francisco. I was in college then and lived across the Bay. As we were driving along, another car smashed into us. The door flew open and I was thrown out. I landed right on my head on the curb. I was unconscious, and they called an ambulance and took me to an emergency hospital in the city of Oakland. The hospital called my parents and told them that I had a very severe basal fracture of the skull, that both optic nerves had been severed, that I had about two hours to live, and asked them to come down immediately. Right away my parents called a Christian Science practitioner who had helped us many times, and the three of them came down to the hospital.

I was in the operating room when they arrived. Some stitches were taken in my head, and my parents were told that was the only thing they could do for me. No other medical treatment was given. The doctors repeated their statement that I had only a few hours to live.

I was told afterward that, even though I was unconscious, as I came out of the operating room, I kept repeating over and over the words of Jesus: "Father, I thank Thee that Thou hast heard me" (John 11:41).

They took me into another room in the hospital. My parents and the practitioner continued to pray as we're taught in Christian Science — to know the ever-presence of Life, God, that God was the only Life and that that was my life. So I got past the crises. I remained unconscious for a week. The doctors said that if I lived, I would be an invalid for life, and would probably be blind.

My parents kept on having Christian Science treatment for me, and one of them stayed with me all the time. The second week I gradually regained consciousness and started asking them to read me various things from the Bible and *Science and Health*. I remember the definition of man from the textbook and the eighth

business men and cultured scholars have found that Christian Science enhances their endurance and mental powers, enlarges their perception of character, gives them acuteness and comprehensiveness and an ability to exceed their ordinary capacity (*Science and Health*, p. 128).

Psalm, especially those two things. Part of the Psalm is, "What is man, that thou art mindful of him? and the son of man, that thou visitest him? For thou hast made him a little lower than the angels, and hast crowned him with glory and honour" (Ps. 8:5, 6).

To the question, "What is man?", Mrs. Eddy answers in part: "Man is not matter; he is not made up of brain, blood, bones, and other material elements. The Scriptures inform us that man is made in the image and likeness of God" (p. 475). It came out later that those were things that I had learned in Sunday School years before when I was just a small child, and had really thought I didn't have. I had gone to Sunday School faithfully and learned my lessons, but I couldn't really say that I sat down with Science seriously very often unless something was seriously the matter with me.

This was really a turning point in my experience. I was getting a clearer sense of the fact that man actually is spiritual, not at the mercy of material injury — because he is the image and likeness of God, Spirit. I knew that in spite of the appearances, this was the truth, and it would heal me.

When I had regained consciousness my eyes were badly crossed, so that I couldn't read, but the doctors were surprised that I could see at all. At the end of the second week in the hospital, they moved me to the college infirmary. Still no medication was given.

Each day one of my parents came to read and work with me. One of my Dad's favorite hymns is No. 412, and we prayed through the words together: "O captive, rise and sing, for thou art free." I could see that I was just captive to mortal sense, and that in reality I could rise and sing, for I was free. I sang all the hymns I could remember and learned some new ones. I continued to improve, and at the end of four weeks I went home. My eyes became completely normal the next day. The doctors had expressed surprise that there was no damage to the brain or nervous system. One physician was Dr. ———, a famous brain surgeon on the Pacific Coast. As I left to go home, he said to my parents, "Prayer healed your daughter!" Every single injury was healed, and I had full use of all my faculties.

Later I was required to have a complete physical examination in order to re-enter college. The doctor that examined me didn't know anything about this case. She just gave me a cursory examination, and I felt disappointed that she hadn't been impressed by the healing. So I asked her if she wasn't going to examine my head. She said, "What's the matter with your head?" and turned over my medical record. She saw this list of predictions about various disabilities. Then she gave me a very thorough examination, including my eyesight, and found that everything was perfect. About three years after this time, I wanted to teach school, and I had to have another thorough examination. They found my eyesight completely perfect and no trace of any trouble at all. This took place eighteen years ago and there have been no after effects.

Christian Science has been a continuing help. During the Korean war, my husband was in Korea and I was alone with our two older boys. Later we were together in Japan. During all these experiences we have had strong proofs of God's loving care. The idea that there is just one Mind, and that we all reflect that Mind and are governed and united by it — I think really that means the most to us of anything in Christian Science.

(Mrs.) Adele R. Ranck, West Bradenton, Florida
Radio/TV series, "How Christian Science Heals," 1959.

IT HAPPENED in Germany, during the Second World War. A shell hit in front of my jeep, and a large fragment of it went through my right arm. It took away a piece of bone, leaving just a sliver between the upper and lower portions.

I could take my arm and move it around, just like I had a third joint between the shoulder and the elbow, and move it in all directions. So there wasn't any union there. The shell fragment had gone in the front of the arm and come out the back of the arm, and in so doing had just completely shattered the bone.

I was cared for there for a few days, and then taken to a hospital in England. The doctors there said I'd never have the full use of my right arm. In fact, they said I would undoubtedly be retired from the Army for physical disability. Certainly I would never be able to raise my arm higher than my right shoulder, and I might just as well get used to being left-handed.

After about a month in England, I was sent back to the United States, down to an Army hospital in Virginia, near my home. All they did was just change the cast on my arm, and I was sent home on convalescent leave. During that time I went up to West Point and arranged to get a job up there teaching math. I was assigned to the hospital, but was permitted to go up to West Point on temporary duty. Meanwhile, I was reassigned to a closer hospital in New York and had to report in for examinations periodically, about every six months. There was no medication or anything of that sort. They would just take X-rays.

On one occasion the doctors wanted to put a plate in my arm, because they said it was very unlikely the bone would ever be strong enough to support the arm. I even went before a Retirement Board at one time. But I told them I had no desire to retire. I wanted to be active, and stay in the Army.

Well, after I really got settled at West Point, I got the Bible and *Science and Health with Key to the Scriptures*, by Mary Baker Eddy, and began to study earnestly. You see, I wasn't an active Christian Scientist at this time, although I'd attended a Christian Science Sunday School for several years when I was a young boy. When I was eighteen, I enlisted in the Army, and I began to drift away from the earnest study and application of the truths I'd learned in Sunday School. There was social drinking, smoking, and the use of profanity. Later I got an appointment to West Point, and graduated from there during the middle of the war. At that time I'd made the excuse that I was busy fighting a war, and didn't have the opportunity to study.

But all this time I still knew Christian Science had given me the correct explanation of God, and I always had in the back of my thinking that some day, when the opportunity presented itself, I was going to be an earnest student of Christian Science again.

It was this experience with my arm that really resulted in a deeper awakening and realization of my responsibility and my opportunities. When I was up at West Point, in the winter of 1946, I felt, oh — somewhat despondent, and wondered just exactly what was my purpose in life. I began to kind of reflect on what I was doing, and what I ought to be doing. And all of the things I learned as a boy in Sunday School would come back to me, and I would think of my experience in the war, and would think, there really wasn't any sense in this foolish indulgence in the so-called material pleasures — I wasn't really getting any enjoyment out of it, anyway.

It was about this time that I decided that I would go up to the Reading Room in Newburgh, which I did, and got myself a Quarterly. I had my books with me, the Bible and *Science and Health* — I'd had them right along — and started studying again. I didn't ask a practitioner for help, just studied and prayed on my own.

One morning, I came across this passage from *Science and Health*: "Christian Science brings to the body the sunlight of Truth, which invigorates and purifies" (p. 162). And the passage goes on to say: "It changes the secretions, expels humors, dissolves tumors, relaxes rigid muscles, restores carious bones to soundness." I can remember as I read that passage, I just sort of thrilled that this was indeed what Christian Science was doing for me — invigorating and purifying me, uplifting and elevating my thought to see God, myself, and my fellow man, as they really are.

As I read those passages — especially "the sunlight of Truth invigorates and purifies . . . restores carious bones to soundness" — I can remember as I read that — it was like a light dawning in my consciousness. I realized that the healing was taking place. And I knew that the medical reports that my arm couldn't be healed, that it was very doubtful that it would be healed, just had no basis in Truth at all. I realized that a transformation was not only taking place in my thinking, but in my experience. I felt confident as I continued my study, that the healing certainly was taking place. I didn't feel despondent, I didn't feel lost. I felt cheerful — sure that I was on the right track and that everything would work out fine.

Shortly after this, the X-rays showed that callus had started to deposit along this sliver of bone between the upper and lower portion, where it had been shot away. I remember the doctor was quite surprised to see this callus was depositing. The last X-rays showed the bone had completely filled in.

I was restored to full general duty, and reassigned to Annapolis, to teach math. I was completely healed, and had the full use of my arm. I would go out sailing with some of my friends and what not — handling the ropes, I guess they call them "sheets." That was in 1947.

It was approximately six months from the time I began to really study Christian Science, until the complete healing. And by this time the smoking, drinking, and the use of profanity, were all overcome, too.

I think probably the most outstanding feature of it all was that prior to this experience I felt I was just sort of drifting, and rather useless. I wasn't quite sure what my purpose in life was, I felt that all my experiences were superficial. I was doing some interesting work, but it wasn't satisfying. And my spare time, well, I was rather wasting it with attending cocktail parties and talking silly small talk that really didn't amount to anything. I just wasn't happy. Whereas after I began to study earnestly, I had a satisfying experience. I realized that I had an opportunity every minute of every day to see myself and my fellow man in the true light. This not only contributed to my own well-being, but I was able to bring it to others, which was more important. Also, it has enabled me to be of much greater service in my Army career.

(Lt. Col.) Wayne L. Bart, Haymarket, Virginia
Radio/TV series, "How Christian Science Heals," 1959.

The world today faces new frontiers in its thinking about race, nationality, political and social barriers, mass poverty and ignorance. While the best collective efforts of organized society are challenged to solve these problems, the best thinking of the individual Christian is needed in order to correct and heal the basic attitudes at the root of the problems. Christian Science emphasizes that man is not a biological organism shaped by ruthless hereditary and environmental forces beyond his control but is the spiritual image and likeness of God. Each individual demonstration of this fact is a contribution toward that wider emancipation of the human race for which all men of good will hope.

The Tide of Healing

O N pages 476 and 477 of *Science and Health* Mary Baker Eddy tells us clearly how Jesus healed. She says: "Jesus beheld in Science the perfect man, who appeared to him where sinning mortal man appears to mortals. In this perfect man the Saviour saw God's own likeness, and this correct view of man healed the sick."

These beautiful lines from Science and Health came often and strongly to the thought of the writer when she was living for a time in one of the countries of the Near East where many of Jesus' followers once walked and performed great works, but where, today, even those who would call themselves Christians are very few, and where the visible scene seems to have fallen into a deplorably impoverished, unhappy state. At times the writer was tempted to be quite overwhelmed with the immensity and the apparent hopelessness of the problems that seemed everywhere apparent, and she spent a great deal of time struggling over them, trying to do something humanly about improving them.

Among the importuners who often followed her on the streets was a young boy with lovely brown eyes and a quick warm smile, who presented a most unhappy picture of the lack of all good things and one of indescribable dirtiness. He could speak but a few words of English, and she could speak but little of his language. "Houseboy?" he kept asking of her. She was glad that he wanted to work rather than to beg, but she realized that in his condition no one would possibly take him as a houseboy. There were things she would have liked to tell him, but there were no words for the telling, and even had there been words he would still have lacked the background to understand the import of them. There seemed no way of helping him with any degree of permanence.

Then one day as she handed him a few coins, aware of their inadequacy to touch his real need, the lines quoted above from *Science and Health* flashed into thought. It came to her that Jesus must have encountered many people who looked much like those around her, like this very boy, and she began to think of what Jesus did about it. Surely he did not stand helpless, offering a few coins, mentally listing the human things that needed correction and searching for a means of communicating the truth. Instead, he turned completely from the picture before him and spiritually beheld man as he is, in all his beauty and cleanliness and health. He "beheld in Science the perfect man," and, in this beholding, the change which was called healing spontaneously took place. He sought God, accepted only the presence of God, and the "things" necessary to the change of the scene were added. Out of the depths of her heart the writer prayed: "Lord, open Thou mine eyes that I too may see! Let there be light!"

And suddenly there was light. There was nothing but light — the light of spiritual reality. So bright was the light that she was no longer conscious of the boy or the place; she was not aware of saying good-by or of walking away from him. She was aware only of God's presence and of His spiritual, perfect universe.

For several days the boy did not even come into her thought. And then one day she again met him on the street, and she could scarcely believe her eyes. He was truly a new person. There were no sores on his face. He was clean — his clothes, face, teeth, hands, hair. In her delight she exclaimed excitedly over his changed appearance and pointed to his clothes. "New!"

"No new," he said. "Wash."

The words came out: "Who? Who told you to do these things?"

It took him a moment to answer: "No man. No man tell." Then, still searching for words, he looked upward, his gaze slowly following a great semicircle above. Then suddenly, joyously, he explained, "I" — and he pointed, not to himself, but upward — "I! I tell me."

"I tell me." That was all he could say, all he needed to say. His whole expression proclaimed eloquently that the message had come to him from on high. He was using "I" as Mrs. Eddy correctly defines it for us on page 588 of *Science and Health* where she says in part, "There is but one I, or Us, but one divine Principle, or Mind, governing all existence." The universal Mind, that Mind which was in Christ Jesus, had spoken to him, directed him, healed him, possessed him.

That was the beginning of a complete transformation for the boy. Shortly he found work with a French family, and he continued

The Tide of Healing

to appear healthy and radiantly happy; he was always clean, and soon he began to show forth many little marks of French courtesy. He even became a man of property, buying himself a bicycle out of his earnings.

The experience was also the beginning of a changed attitude for the writer toward the entire country.

Velma Lewis Ingraham, Berkeley, California

— "Spiritual Discernment," *Journal*, Vol. 72, pp. 4–5
(January, 1954).

I BELONG to a minority group. I was confronted not with one label, but a confusion of labels. My maternal grandmother was Scots-Irish. She married a mulatto. My grandmother on my father's side was a Cherokee Indian. She also married a mulatto. As a result of this mixed background, there were feelings of pressure and insecurity. I felt I had no particular niche, not knowing what group I really belonged to.

Some members of the family living in the South are very fair. I'm brown. They're on one side; we're on another. This can produce little hurts and resentments.

I'd gone to an all-white school in Michigan, and my playmates were all Dutch. My family accepted a white standard. But then I ran into barriers. I wanted to be a doctor, and so I took a pre-medical course. But when I applied for medical school, I found there were limitations on the number of women accepted. Also I learned there was a flat ban on Negroes. So that door was shut. I found similar barriers in the business world, though fortunately there were good opportunities for progress.

But then in an hour of great need, I began to study Christian Science. Gradually I began to emerge from the mental turmoil. My whole viewpoint on life began to change. Humanly speaking, there just wasn't any solution; but through this religion I gained a whole new concept of man, and it brought me a sense of freedom.

A Century of Christian Science Healing

What appealed to me most of all was the explanation Christian Science gives that God is divine Principle, unchanging Love, including all within His care. Also, that man's real self isn't Irish or Indian or colored or white, because man is spiritual, made in the image and likeness of God. I stuck to the wonderful truth that my real self is a spiritual idea of God. I began to see others in this light too.

This has given me an understanding of my real origin in God instead of in material ancestry, community, or race. I've learned that the real answer is spiritual enlightenment. As a result, I'm not only freer — I'm *free*.

(Mrs.) Wylodene Govia, Bronx, New York
Radio/TV series, "How Christian Science Heals," 1962.

As a boy in my teens I witnessed much injustice, wickedness, and cruelty during World War I, and I asked myself for what reason the people were suffering from these crimes and for what reason I was experiencing them too. So I started then to think the question over. I also asked: What is the aim of man's life? What is the end for myself? Neither home, school, society, nor church gave me an answer. For a few years I looked for the solution to that problem; but the harder I tried to find it, the more I was confused. Being disappointed, I started to seek satisfaction in sports. It was long before the opportunity to find the solution came, but thanks to God my questions were at last answered in a satisfactory way.

A few years before the Second World War I noticed that my wife was interested in the Scriptures and in other religious books, but she never talked of them to me. I thought it was right for women to be interested in religion, but not men. Nevertheless, on the day the war broke out my wife asked me to pay a visit to her best friend, and I agreed. This woman spoke to me for nearly half an hour of God and Christ Jesus, but in a way that was quite strange to me, and I could not understand her point of view exactly.

A week later I was forced to leave my home and go to the country, where I stayed in a little town. The first day the air raid alarms sounded I hid myself in a small house. In a few minutes a bomb was dropped, and the house was demolished. For a while I lost consciousness. Although I was thought to be dead, I did recover. During that time, however, I had only one desire, namely to return home, to see that woman, and to speak with her of God. Nearly two months I stayed in the country, but at last I succeeded in returning home. The next day my wife led me once more to the woman, who was a Christian Science practitioner, and from that time I started to study Christian Science.

I should like to relate one particular experience too which took place four years ago when I was traveling from my country to England to have class instruction. I had crossed two frontiers when I was forced to stop my journey because I was told my passport was not in order. I was told I must take a train going back. At first I was exasperated at the injustice, and I was afraid. It seemed, at that moment, that all the efforts of my friends, of my teacher, and of myself were to be annihilated. Having only pocket money and no idea what to do or where to go for help, I despaired greatly.

I was deprived of my return ticket to England, and I was put down on the railway station in this strange city at night. But the Saviour was at hand. My despair lasted not long after I awakened and started to think rightly. I began to dig into my consciousness to find the reason for my misfortune, and after a short time I found the fault which was the source of my misery. I began to correct my thinking immediately. I wrestled all the night in prayer, and the story of Daniel, who was thrown into the lions' den, offered an example for my guidance. When the king came to the den in the morning and found Daniel alive, Daniel greeted him by saying (Dan. 6:21), "O king, live for ever." By the time the morning came I was completely at peace and could approach everyone with as much charity in my heart as Daniel expressed to the king. No wonder that the solution came soon.

I got the necessary seals to my passport in that city. A woman of that country took me by the hand and led me to the station-master, who gave me my ticket back. The same lady put me on the train, and I was able to reach my destination place twenty-four

hours later, having learned the lesson for all my life to hold un-
tiring watch over my thinking all the time. The experience showed
that God's love and protection are actually ever present although
they may seem not to be.

I wish to express my gratitude to God for Christ Jesus, the Way-
shower. I am extremely grateful too for Mrs. Eddy, the Discoverer
and Founder of Christian Science. I feel very fortunate to have the
privilege of working in a Christian Science Society.

Jozef Ciszewski, Warsaw, Poland.

— Journal, Vol. 81, pp. 558–559 (October, 1963).

> A basic factor in Christian Science healing is its view
> of material appearances as being without real substantial-
> ity, permanence, or validity. This is more than a statement
> of "philosophical idealism"; it is a corollary of the practi-
> cal grasp of Spirit as true substance. In coming to grips
> with such a proposition the demands of the skeptical
> modern mind for both rationality and proof must be met.
> The following experience illustrates one of the ways in
> which men and women of skeptical temperament have
> sought an answer to their doubts and have found it:

IT SEEMED to me many things in the world were so very wrong.
It was my firm conviction that if there was a God, He had made a
real mess of creation, and left man ill-equipped to put things right.

I'd been affiliated with two or three faiths at different times but
being dissatisfied, I began a study of the philosophies. But that
didn't satisfy me either. I found that in order to accept the conclusions of these philosophies, you first had to accept the premises.
And the premises were by definition just hypotheses or suppositions.
No matter how far you followed them there was no point where
you could stop and say — this is it, this is the truth. It just wasn't
there.

I was impressed by the rigorous standard of logic I encountered, but there was no reason to accept the conclusions of these philosophies as being any more valid than the assumptions. And the assumptions about God, if nothing else, seemed a bit confused. At the same time, I wondered why Christianity, as I knew it then, wasn't explained with the same faultless quality of reasoning.

I became an atheist, and I thought if I could find nothing more satisfactory than atheism, at least I wanted to be a good one. So for ten years I studied and thought in that direction.

My wife had always been a Christian Scientist. Of course, I didn't readily accept her views — in fact, I'd always argued with her about it. But I saw several good healings through Christian Science, right in my own family, and I had to admit there was something there — something I needed very much. So I set myself seriously to the task of trying to understand Christian Science.

Christian truths are beautiful in their simplicity, but I was still arguing on the side of matter. To me matter was substance and basis of all life. You see, I'd spent many years studying it, weighing it, measuring it, considering its uses, limitations, handicaps. It seemed much more real to me than God, about whom I knew little or nothing.

At first I couldn't accept Christian Science. I remember one day while driving a farm tractor I was thinking about a statement in *Science and Health* (p. 468) where Mrs. Eddy writes: "There is no life, truth, intelligence, nor substance in matter. All is infinite Mind and its infinite manifestation, for God is All-in-all."

This seemed impossible to accept, when the sun was blazing down, the transmission case was burning my feet, a choking dust was boiling up from the plows, and the exhaust was roaring in my ears.

Then there was another thing that struck me as utterly impossible — the Bible statement that man is made in the image and likeness of God. How in the name of logic, I wondered, could each individual in the diverse multitude of humanity be the image and likeness of the one alone God?

Well, it was soon after this I had a healing myself through Christian Science treatment. That's when my thinking began to change completely. It was a crippling back condition. As a young lad, I'd fallen about twenty feet from a tree when a limb had broken off. I'd injured some of the vertebrae in my back and had trouble with it ever since, including sometimes extreme pain.

One day I was driving a heavily loaded truck, and the pain became so bad I had to ease the truck to the side of the road and stop. After some time I managed to get home and into bed. Then I agreed my wife should call a Christian Science practitioner. The practitioner came to the house. One of the things he discussed was how very much God loved me. He spoke with such deep conviction that I found myself really believing that there was at least that possibility.

On about the second or third day, after a little nap, I woke up with a very warm sense of light. It was a wonderful inward glow of light and love. Apparently it was that my consciousness was opening up to the real presence and meaning of divine Love. But anyway, I knew right then that I was healed. And I was healed. Never again did I feel any pain from this back.

Actually, though, the physical healing wasn't the most important part of it. The really important thing to me was this. I now was satisfied there is a God, a very loving God, and that I could turn to Him again and again, in perfect trust, no matter what the problem might be.

I had to come to firm grips with this business of matter. I had to move my thinking over into an area where I could recognize God, divine Mind, as the starting point. I had to see that Spirit, God, is All, completely supreme, as Christian Science teaches. Therefore that matter is an illusion, or false concept, is actually unreal.

Steeped in materialism as I was, this was a long distance to travel. And it wasn't easy. But I could see that there isn't an experience we have that is outside of our thinking. To accept matter into our thinking as real is to surrender our thinking to material limitations, material impositions and laws. So to break away from material concepts is not only a perfectly intelligent but legitimate thing to do. It's not only the honest and good thing to do, but ultimately we are virtually forced to it because the propositions of matter lead to such an ultimate dissatisfaction that we just throw up our hands and give them up, recognize them as being utterly useless.

The Tide of Healing

I saw that when we accept into our thinking the real import of God's infinitude, God's ever-presence — and consequently when I recognize that I am the expression of God's selfhood and have no other identity — this rules out materialistic thinking and the discords it imposes on the physical body. If man is made in the likeness of God, as the Bible says, then he can only express divine intelligence and wisdom — in fact all the spiritual qualities of God. In other words, the image of God must be a spiritual idea and not a mortal material being.

This was certainly a very new concept to me and there isn't a part of my life that hasn't been blessed. The pessimism and confusion disappeared. I was led into a useful and interesting career, as an electronic scientist doing systems engineering work for the Government.

Above all, I'm grateful to have found a completely satisfying answer to my search for God.

Cleo N. Lawrence, Rome, New York
Radio/TV series, "How Christian Science Heals," 1960.

A scientific age asks whether Christianity can be scientifically demonstrated in coping with the problems of the age. An affirmative answer is given by many Christian Scientists who today are doing advanced work in physics and chemistry, in mathematics and electronic research, as aeronautic engineers and jet pilots, as participants in nuclear projects and space programs. The following testimonies illustrate the sort of individual experiences which confirm them in this conviction:

MY INTEREST IN CHEMISTRY began in high school, and I've worked as a chemist for many years. At the time of this experience I was in charge of radioactive waste treatment and the high level Gamma irradiation facility in an atomic energy establishment.

When I took the position, I had to submit to a physical examination. Later, to my surprise, I was called in and asked if I'd been exposed to radioactive materials, or if I'd been in an accident recently. These questions were asked because the examining doctors said my hemoglobin count was dangerously below normal, and they said it was a wonder I was even alive. They asked detailed questions about my health, none of which applied to me, for I felt excellent. They strongly recommended that I see a specialist and take immediate steps to correct this condition.

This whole thing was a challenge to me. I'd been brought up in Christian Science and I was accustomed to turn to God for healings. From the time I was a student in the Christian Science Sunday School, I'd known and proved many times that there is no power apart from God, who is divine Love, the only cause and creator.

Once before in my work as a chemist I'd been faced with the necessity to prove God's all-power. My hands and chest had been badly burned in a laboratory accident. Fear was expressed that I would die of shock or be permanently disfigured. Then as now I relied solely on Christian Science.

I prayed steadfastly, holding to the spiritual fact that God does not afflict, therefore men cannot be afflicted. The very next day I was able to go back to work without any pain. The burns healed very quickly, and new skin emerged from the burned area within a very short time without the feared complications, and without leaving any scars. This was accomplished entirely through prayerful treatment by a Christian Science practitioner.

So again I turned to God for the healing of this blood condition, realizing I could lack nothing needful because God supplies all good.

I realized that God is actually man's true life, and man is not dependent on material conditions. And so the symptoms predicted at the time I was examined never appeared, nor was I ever fearful about their possible appearance. I began to feel the peace which comes from understanding that God is divine Love, the Principle of all existence, and that the real man is actually spiritual and is maintained eternally in God's loving care.

Within a year the hemoglobin count was normal, and it has remained so. I had made no use of the material means recommended, but relied only on Christian Science to meet the problem. This experience happened in 1948 and there has been no return of the condition.

(Miss) H. Gladys Swope, Madison, Wisconsin
Radio/TV series, "How Christian Science Heals," 1957.

I'D JUST JOINED a major aircraft manufacturing company as an engineer, and this was the first assignment they'd given me. What they wanted me to do was to design a compact but rugged gearing mechanism to control the elevators on the tail of a jet plane. They'd encountered some rather difficult control problems with this particular airplane, occasioned by exceeding the speed of sound — going through the so-called sound barrier. And so they required a gearing mechanism to remedy the difficulty.

I found out later they'd had other men working on this problem for almost a year, but they hadn't been able to find a satisfactory solution. After studying the problem for two or three weeks, I realized that probably there was no analytical solution for it. The problem was very complicated — it involved the location of several linkages in the proper relationship to each other, and to the airplane. Primarily I had to locate three main centers around which the links would operate. That was the crux of the problem.

Mathematically there seemed to be an infinite number of possible locations for these centers, but there was probably only one set that would satisfy all the requirements. There just wasn't any way to work it out mathematically, so far as I could see. So finally, I decided to try for a solution on the drafting board, but after I had put all the basic information on my drawing I began to feel overwhelmed — just helpless. There just didn't seem to be any way of arriving at the answer by any engineering knowledge I had. So I went back to my usual way of working out difficult problems — through prayer, the prayer of spiritual understanding, the way I'd learned in Christian Science. Back while I was working my way through college I'd found how necessary it is to rely on God in everything we do. So I knew that if I were faithful to the study and application of Christian Science, I could find the right answer. I knew that God provides everything we need — if we are alert enough spiritually to discern it.

So that day I leaned back in my chair — I was sitting there at my drafting board — and I prayed. I started by thanking God for His goodness. I realized the ever-presence of the divine Mind — His all-power, His infinite capacity. I reminded myself that the Bible says that man is created in the image and likeness of God, the likeness of divine Mind, or Spirit. So I reasoned that man actually reflects the intelligence, the capacity, of the divine Mind.

I sat there trying to become more aware of my close unity and relationship with this Mind — the unchanging relationship; that all true intelligence comes from God, not from any so-called human mind; that man is the expression of the divine intelligence.

I just sat there praying this way for — oh, half an hour or so. Then I picked up my pencil and went back to my drawing. It soon came to me where the first point ought to be, so I marked a center there. Then, I saw where another point should be, and I put my pencil there. And a few moments later I made a mark where it appeared the third pivot point should be. I was led to mark down these three points without any calculations.

Then I worked several days drawing in the mechanism around these three points. I ran it through all its operations, to be sure it cleared everything, and did what it was supposed to do for the elevators. Well, it worked perfectly — on paper at least. So I went to my supervisor and asked him to look over my solution. But he was busy and he just gave me a skeptical look and said, "I don't see how you could have an answer this soon — you go back and study it a little longer."

So I did — then I went back to him — twice, in fact, but he still couldn't believe that I could have the answer so soon. Finally, I made a working mock-up — a full-sized model in which all the parts function. When I showed this to him, he worked the mechanism several times, then his face lit up and he said, "I can't understand it. I had a man working on this for almost a year, and I worked on it some, and others did, too, and we just couldn't get the thing to work out — but this one looks as if it might work." So he finally approved having parts made for flight tests. And the very first test showed that the mechanism functioned perfectly. So it was put into production, and the basic design is still flying today.

I never had to change the location of those three main pivot points. And when you realize there's an infinite number of possibilities where they might have been located, you can't help but see that it was relying on divine intelligence that brought the right answer. To me this was a clear proof that when we listen for God's guidance humbly and prayerfully, we can be led to the right answer, even though from a human standpoint the problem appears to be without a solution.

Dwight S. Mills, Felton, California
Radio/TV series, "How Christian Science Heals," 1958.

I GOT MY WINGS as a naval aviator in 1956, and was assigned to a jet fighter squadron on the West Coast. The jet planes of today are very complex machines. So, every day I'd do some prayerful thinking in regard to my flying. I really tried to understand that the divine Mind, God, is always present to supply the intelligence needed to meet any emergency.

I had several opportunities to prove this understanding of God while I was a pilot. For instance, there was the day I was on a practice gunnery hop over Nevada. I was flying a single-seat, single-engine plane when my engine quit. I had a flameout, a complete loss of power, and I began to lose speed rapidly. I must confess that my first thought was: "A flameout! It's happened to me now." I called my flight leader on the radio and told him what was the matter. The other planes immediately stopped the exercise we were going through. One of the pilots flew up beside me to spot the place — if I crashed.

I was about 100 miles from the nearest landing field. The mountains below me were very rugged — a crash landing seemed out of the question. I guess I was pretty frightened at first. But I did start saying aloud: "God is my Life. I cannot be afraid because I know infinite Life cannot be destroyed." I also recalled part of a verse from Isaiah, "In quietness and in confidence shall be your strength." After a few seconds, I calmed down.

I was flying at around 28,000 feet, so I decided to try and get the engine started again instead of bailing out of the plane immediately. I told my flight leader what I planned to do, and set about preparing the engine for the relighting procedure. By this time, I was calm enough to recall every step of the rather involved process. I got all the switches set right, tried for the relight, but the engine failed to respond. This cost me about 6,000 feet in altitude. But I was still high enough to try again. It took a couple of minutes for the engine to drain before I made another attempt at an airstart.

All of this time I could hear excited chatter over my radio — emergency calls going out, a nearby base being alerted to stand by with rescue equipment. Well, this wasn't helping my thinking any, so I turned off the radio and forced myself to sit back and earnestly pray. I became conscious of the nearness of God to man, the nearness that comes because of man's spiritual relationship to God. In other words, I knew that the real man is the expression of infinite Spirit and is therefore spiritual, and can never be separated from God's loving care.

With these thoughts in mind, I tried again to relight the engine — but still nothing happened. I lost more altitude, and was down to 15,000 feet. There was still time for one more try before I would have to abandon the plane.

Again, I had to wait for the engine to drain, and I continued to pray. When I first went into flight training, my mother had pointed out a helpful passage from *Science and Health* where Mary Baker Eddy writes (p. 399), "If Mind is the only actor, how can mechanism be automatic?" It became apparent to me that God, divine Mind, is ever present, supreme, all-powerful.

I tried to start the engine the third time, and this time it responded. I got almost full power and climbed to 30,000 feet. I flew back to the air station and made a safe landing.

The maintenance men found that through an oversight one of the two fuel boost pumps had not been hooked up and that the other pump had burned out while I was flying. They said that under these conditions it might be possible to get the engine relighted, but it seemed pretty unlikely I would have gotten back as much as 95% power and that I was able to climb to 30,000 feet. There was a general feeling in the squadron that something extraordinary had happened.

Later on, my skipper told me he had never heard anybody sound so calm in an emergency. This really made me grateful for the spiritual understanding of God that enabled me to overcome my momentary panic and calmly think along both spiritual and practical lines.

Ralph Burr, Wilmette, Illinois
Radio/TV series, "How Christian Science Heals," 1960.

In facing the challenges of the future, Christianity draws rich sustenance from the past. Every spiritual step forward, whether in the experience of an individual or of humanity as a whole, is in a sense a resurrection — a rising above old standpoints but at the same time a lifting higher of old truths. At the threshold of the space age, the world still hears those words from the apostolic age: "Lo, I am with you alway, even unto the end of the world" (Matt. 28:20).

The Church of Christ, Scientist, as already explained,* was organized in part to "commemorate the word and works of our Master," as well as to "reinstate primitive Christianity and its lost element of healing." On Easter Sunday, 1960, a special radio program was produced for the purpose of explaining to those of other faiths or of no faith the Christian Science understanding of the resurrection. An excerpt from that program may serve as a fitting conclusion to the present chapter.

I T IS SAID that when the early Christians met they would greet each other with the salutation, "Christ is risen!" Their lives were

* See editorial comment on page 6 of this book.

illumined by the fact that Jesus had triumphed over death and in that act had revealed to them the infinite power of good to overcome all evil.

This was the gospel, or good news, which they took to a world plunged in misery and frustration. As Paul said of Jesus in his second Epistle to Timothy, he "hath abolished death, and hath brought life and immortality to light through the gospel." In other words, he has shown us what life really is, not under the curse of mortality, but indestructible and eternal — the radiant expression of God's own being.

Was this good news too good to be true? Does it have any meaning for our own day and age, almost two thousand years removed from that far-off Easter morning, so far removed, indeed, that many people today question the resurrection of Christ Jesus?

Probably to no body of Christians is the resurrection more important than to Christian Scientists. Certainly it is to them a living, practical, immediate truth which has a bearing on every aspect of their lives.

Such resurrection is a progressive experience. It does not come all at once. An individual healing or awakening may come in an instant, but the full emergence from mortal limitations into spiritual freedom takes immense time and growth. Christians are not spared trials of their faith any more than Jesus was spared the cross; but, following his example, they use such experiences as opportunities to prove God's love. They do not resign themselves to the adverse circumstances that may face them; instead, they overcome them by understanding God's will to be life not death, victory not defeat. This is sharing in the Saviour's resurrection.

In this series of programs, "How Christian Science Heals," we have presented week after week concrete, carefully verified cases of healing of all kinds — healings, for instance, of cancer, tuberculosis, blindness, deafness, broken bones, pneumonia, as well as of emotional disorders, false character traits, inharmonious personal relations, business difficulties, and so forth. These have all been examples of the resurrecting power of a spiritual understanding of God, the understanding that God bestows. They have shown how a right apprehension of God lifts man out of the tomb of material-mindedness, of mortal thinking, into what St. Paul describes as "the glorious liberty of the children of God."

Today, instead of inviting a guest to give another such personal experience of the healing power of God, I am going to read to you a poem from *The Christian Science Journal* entitled "Easter Certainty." This poem makes specific reference to the testimonies of healing which are published each month in the Christian Science periodicals. I think you'll see its appropriateness when I read it.

"Christ Jesus rose from the tomb. This is no empty story,
remote and far away.
In an actual year on a certain day
Jesus rose from the tomb and spoke in a garden with Mary.

"Then he showed himself again
to Peter and James and John,
seafaring sane young men,
not easily put upon,
and to more than five hundred others,
eating and breaking bread,
not a ghost, but flesh and bone.

"Once and for all he proved
that Life is stronger than death;
once and for all he proved
that Spirit is master of flesh.
Knowing the utter lie
of material law and rule,
not turning to drugs for aid
nor needing a surgeon's skill,
he proved that God is the Life of man,
not to be bound by death or pain.

"Because Christ Jesus rose, we may speak with men today
here in our own city, perhaps in our own street,
who have seen the eternal Word rise up in power and dispute
the fable of death and force it to let its captives go.

A Century of Christian Science Healing

"Here in these very pages, turning on, we may read
the verified simply written testimony of those
who have turned from matter to Spirit in their hour of utmost
  need
and have risen from beds of sickness — because Christ Jesus
  rose.

" 'Lo, I am with you alway,' the ascending Saviour said,
'to the world's end.' As he promised, the Christ is with us still.
And, like the obedient Marys turning from their dead,
we too may turn from our sorrows to be healed by the Christ's
  'All hail.'

"If any have waited long
for husband or wife or child,
father or mother or friend,
to rise from a sickbed healed
by the power and the spirit of Truth,
they need not doubt, but can know
that it can and it will be so,
as surely as Jesus rose from the tomb
on a spring day long ago."

Chapter Three

The Horizon of Healing

Chapter Three

The Horizon of Healing

HEALING AND SALVATION

"AND AS YE GO, preach, saying, The kingdom of heaven is at hand" (Matthew 10:7).

In the New Testament narratives, the first impact of the good news of the kingdom is repeatedly felt as physical healing in the life of a particular person — a cripple waiting hopelessly at the pool of Bethesda or sitting at the gate of the temple day after day. The man healed of blindness by Jesus, pressed by his neighbors for a "proper" explanation, fell back on the tangible evidence, on what he himself had experienced. "One thing I know," he said, "that, whereas I was blind, now I see" (John 9:25).

To a Christian Scientist the real importance of a healing is the light it lets through. The change in physical condition or personal circumstance is only the outward and visible evidence of an inward and spiritual grace — a hint of a perceived spiritual fact. In looking back on a healing, the Christian Scientist is likely to think, not "That was the time I was healed of pneumonia," but "That was the time I learned what real humility is," or "That was the time I saw so clearly that all power belongs to God."

It is not the purpose of this book to discuss the metaphysics of Christian Science. The authoritative presentation of that subject is to be found in *Science and Health,* the textbook of Christian Science. But many of the testimonies included show the healing insights into the metaphysical implications of the Christian gospel which individuals have found through their study of the textbook, and they indicate why metaphysics is a living discipline, not merely an abstract study, to the Christian Scientist.

It is within individual consciousness that all Christian Science

237

healing takes place. The outward results are regarded as among the added things of which Jesus spoke in Matthew 6:33. The real meaning of even the most remarkable bodily healing is not in the observed physical change but in what it indicates about the unseen structure of reality. Again Christian Scientists find this implied in Jesus' words: "The kingdom of God cometh not with observation: Neither shall they say, Lo here! or, lo there! for, behold, the kingdom of God is within you" (Luke 17:20, 21).

The real change, as Christian Scientists understand it, is from material-mindedness to spiritual-mindedness, from self-centered to God-centered thinking. This is illustrated by many of the testimonies in this book and by thousands more like them. A single comment by a woman healed of arthritis of the spine may stand as a typical example:

"My healing was not immediate. But 'man's extremity is God's opportunity,' and this was my opportunity for spiritual growth. I studied with a thirst I can hardly describe, month after month. At first I looked daily for a physical healing, but it didn't come. Finally I realized that, healing or not, Christian Science was the Science of all Being, and the most important thing in my life. And I studied for the joy of unfoldment and the quenching of that great thirst. I no longer anxiously looked for a physical healing, for I had forgotten the material self in my joy and discovery of my real self.

"I really don't know exactly when during those weeks the complete healing came. But I know that the pain began to fade as I searched avidly for Truth, forgetting to search for physical healing." *

Today there is a growing recognition of the identity of healing (in its broadest sense) and salvation, an identity made clear by the root meaning of the two words. The phrase in Luke 1:77 which is translated "knowledge of salvation" in the King James or Authorized Version of the Bible was rendered by Wycliffe in the fourteenth century as "science of health" (or in some printings as "science and health"). This is sound etymology and sound metaphysics, for sal-

---

* (Mrs.) Mary M. Terryberry, Grand Rapids, Michigan, in the Radio/TV series, "How Christian Science Heals," 1962. The complete healing occurred seventeen years before the testimony was given.

vation necessarily means the rescue of men from all that would separate them from the fullness of being.

It is in this context of full salvation that Christian Science views the healing of disease. And it is from the concrete vantage point of bodily healing that the broader implications of salvation and the full magnitude of the meaning of healing can perhaps be best explored. The next section of this chapter is therefore devoted to some of the practical therapeutic aspects of Christian Science.

PRACTICAL ASPECTS

A NUMBER of testimonies in this book have told of healings that were delayed while the individual, in Paul's words, learned to "put off the old man with his deeds" and to "put on the new man, which is renewed in knowledge after the image of him that created him" (Col. 3:9, 10).

The purpose of spiritual healing is never simply to produce physical ease. It is rather to put off the limited, physical concept of man which binds thought to matter, and thus bring to light Paul's "new" man. This is the man whom Christian Scientists understand to be the "real" man, created by God in His own image, spiritual and whole.

Here is the reason Christian Scientists do not turn to a doctor if they are not quickly healed through their own or a practitioner's prayers. Bodily conditions they view as effect rather than cause — the outward expression of conscious and unconscious thoughts. On this premise what needs to be healed is always a false concept of being, not a material condition. The purpose of turning to God for healing is therefore not merely to change the evidence before the physical senses but to heal the deeper alienation of human thought from God.

This is a purpose which, as Christian Scientists view it, deserves the most rigorous effort. Their very persistence in holding to what they call the truth of being in the face of alarming physical evidence to the contrary may be what is needed to bring about a healing. Testifiers sometimes express special gratitude for a long-delayed healing which has forced them to search their hearts, discipline their thoughts, and spiritualize their motives more thoroughly.

When a Christian Scientist fails to demonstrate the healing power of God in a given situation, he does not question the goodness of God. Instead he asks himself where he needs to bring his own thinking and living into closer conformity with God's law. Like the student of mathematics who may fail to solve a difficult problem through improper application of the relevant mathematical principle, the Christian Scientist does not blame the perfect Principle of being for the faulty result but seeks through the experience to grow in understanding and obedience to divine law.

The willingness to yield to the demands of Principle in a given situation — or even to recognize them — may sometimes come only after bitter experience. In some cases a relatively minor physical ailment may require a longer struggle with ingrained traits of character than does an acute need which turns the individual more wholeheartedly to God. The newcomer to Christian Science who has experienced a remarkable healing discovers, as he progresses in his study, that the blessings are inseparable from the demands.

On the other hand, the student of Christian Science who has accepted its mental and moral discipline and demonstrated for himself the unfailing goodness of God is not likely to look elsewhere for help. It is no sacrifice to forego medical treatment when one has repeatedly proved that "the word of God is quick, and powerful, and sharper than any twoedged sword" (Hebrews 4:12). Puzzling as the Christian Scientist's confidence may be to others, it is rooted in concrete experience and reasoned conviction as well as in the Christian promises.

When due allowance has been made for the inevitable imperfections in the human practice of Christian Science and for the abuses of it by those who may claim its name without accepting its spirit or its discipline, the fact remains that it has restored the healing of primitive Christianity to a recognized place in modern society. What seemed to most people like a preposterous claim when it was made by a single Christian woman one hundred years ago has been accepted since then by increasing numbers, many of them professional people trained in modern scientific method and the critical examination of evidence. Whole families have relied exclusively on Christian Science for healing through several generations.

Today the legality of the practice of Christian Science is firmly established in the United States and in many other countries. Increasingly its practice has won recognition as an acceptable alternative to medical treatment in the eyes of public and private agencies concerned with health, despite the natural preference of these agencies for orthodox methods.*

In addition to this pragmatic recognition, based on actual long-term experience with Christian Scientists, there is of course the more basic acknowledgment by law of the constitutional right of Christian Scientists to practice healing as part of their religion. On this more fundamental ground, Christian Science practitioners in the United States are exempted by statute from the provisions of the medical practice acts of the various states, since they are engaged not in the practice of medicine but of a religious ministry including healing. This is also the basis of their practice in other countries.

Christian Science healing is in fact one way of worshiping God. It is an integral part of a deeply felt and closely reasoned view of ultimate reality. This very fact sometimes causes its use of the words "real" and "unreal" to be misunderstood. For when Christian Scientists speak of sickness as unreal, they do not mean that humanly it is to be ignored. They mean rather that it is no part of man's true, essential being but comes from a mortal misconception of being, without validity, necessity, or legitimacy. Like a mathematical error which has no substance and no principle to support it, sickness is not to be ignored but to be conscientiously wiped out by a correct understanding of the divine Principle of being. This is the metaphysical basis of Christian Science practice.

The Christian Scientist constantly distinguishes between what

* See "Recognition of Christian Science Treatment," *The Insurance Law Journal*, January, 1963; "Legal Position of Christian Science Healing Appraised," *The Spectator* (Philadelphia), October, 1963; "Legal Status of Christian Science Treatment," *Medical Trial Technique Quarterly*, December, 1963. Hundreds of insurance companies recognize and pay for Christian Science treatment and care in lieu of medical treatment in their group as well as individual contracts.

he calls the absolute and the relative — the absolute facts of spiritual being and the relative needs of human existence. On the one hand Mrs. Eddy writes, "The Christlike understanding of scientific being and divine healing includes a perfect Principle and idea, — perfect God and perfect man, — as the basis of thought and demonstration" (*Science and Health,* p. 259). On the other hand she writes, "Imperfect mortals grasp the ultimate of spiritual perfection slowly, but to *begin* aright and to continue the strife of demonstrating the great problem of being, is doing much" (*ibid.,* p. 254). The absolute reaches the relative at the point of healing.

It follows that although Christian Scientists do not use medical methods they by no means neglect human suffering. Their treatment is wholly spiritual, but it would not be Christian if it did not involve compassionate attention to human needs. Special provision is made for those who may require nursing care while receiving treatment. The Church of Christ, Scientist, conducts two sanatoriums and certifies others which are privately run. Here such care may be received, but without medication. It also accredits and lists Christian Science nurses who have completed a three-year training course at one of the sanatoriums. These services are recognized in various ways by law and by various public and private agencies.*

Yet beyond the scaffolding of legal rights and institutional aids which mark the present position of Christian Science stands a total commitment to the power of divine Love. Prayer reaches out to God as the very Life of man, the eternal Truth transcending and embracing every human circumstance, the Father-Mother of a flawless spiritual universe. This is the vision of reality involved in metaphysical healing.

Christian Scientists, like all Christians, have a long way to go humanly to reach the standard set by their Master: "Be ye therefore perfect, even as your Father which is in heaven is perfect" (Matthew 5:48). Like practitioners of other systems of healing, they learn from their mistakes and failures as well as from their

* For example, Public Laws 89–97 (Medicare) and 86–382 (Federal Employees Health Benefits Act). See also Public Laws 86–724 and 86–778: 42 U.S. Code, Sec. 422 (b) (1); Railroad Retirement Board Order No. 49–187, May 23, 1949. In the United Kingdom, Public Health Act, 1936, Sec. 193, makes provision for Christian Science houses (nursing homes).

achievements and victories. They learn, too, that Christian discipleship never permits them to settle down complacently on past proofs of God's care. But they have reason for immense gratitude in what they have already proved of the omnipotence of good, and they are challenged to higher proofs in the future.

THE WHOLE MAN

Traditionally salvation has been thought of in connection with sin and healing in connection with sickness. The "soul" has therefore been assigned to the clergyman and the "body" to the physician.

Today, with the growth of psychosomatic medicine, chemical-controlled behavior, and a pastoral counseling movement which has been conditioned to a large extent by psychological and medical disciplines, the distinction is breaking down. The "miserable sinner" of yesterday is the "sick" man of today. It is often a question whether he will turn to the doctor, the psychiatrist, or the minister for help in his trouble.

The common element in many diverse and even contradictory trends in medicine and theology is a sense of the interrelatedness of physical, mental, and spiritual health. Christian Science is posited on such an interrelation, though it maintains a common-sense distinction between sickness and sin. These are seen as variant manifestations of the belief that man has a finite, material existence apart from God. Both are to be healed by understanding man's true unity with his divine source.

The concept of wholeness plays an increasing role in modern thinking, which has been so fragmented by specialization that it now seeks anxiously a unifying principle to bring the pieces together again. To the Christian Scientist the "whole" man is St. Paul's "new" man, the man who is wholly united through Christ with God. Since reality is centered in Spirit, healing becomes a matter not of manipulating the human mind or body but of turning unreservedly to the divine Mind, in which man has his true, essential being.

In one place Paul writes of the new man "which after God

is created in righteousness and true holiness" (Ephesians 4:24). Wholeness and holiness are etymologically related, and in Christian Science they are understood as synonymous. A contemporary theologian, Paul Tillich, recognized the same point when he wrote: "The word salvation is derived from the Latin word *salvus,* which means heal and whole. . . . But saving also means delivering, liberating, setting free. . . Saving is healing from sickness and saving is delivering from servitude; and the two are the same." *

To many people this implies a closer cooperation between the doctor and the minister. For instance, a leaflet of the American Medical Association which stresses the need to treat the whole and not the part recognizes that "the faith of the individual patient is a vital factor in total health," but it interprets this aim in terms of better communication between physician and clergyman.† This is the explicit objective of the association's recently established Department of Medicine and Religion.

By contrast, Christian Science emphasizes entire reliance on spiritual means for the healing of both sickness and sin. It sees these as products of the "carnal mind" which Paul describes as "enmity against God" (Romans 8:7) and the answer to both as being found within the divine Mind, or God. The healing of bodily conditions and of human behavior follows as the natural result of exchanging the false suggestions of the carnal or mortal mind for the true facts of being as they are known to the divine Mind.

This radical position rules out the possibility of dividing faith between prayer and drugs, or between spiritual discipline and psychiatric techniques. In much pastoral counseling today the answer to disease-producing hates and fears is sought chiefly through the human mind's gaining insight into itself. By contrast, Mrs. Eddy writes in *Science and Health* (p. 151): "The human mind is opposed to God and must be put off, as St. Paul declares. All that really exists is the divine Mind and its idea, and in this Mind the entire being is found harmonious and eternal."

Physical healing experienced on this basis never leaves the individual mentally and morally just where it found him. Even if,

* Paul Tillich, *The Eternal Now* (New York: Scribner's, 1963), pp. 113, 114.
† *The Physician, the Clergy, and the Whole Man,* leaflet of the American Medical Association (1964).

as sometimes happens, he starts out with a blind faith in the practitioner who is helping him, he learns in time that it is always God who does the healing, not man. What is involved is a yielding of human character to divine influence, never a yielding of one human mind to another.

While a practitioner may help a patient to progress step by step, giving him friendly encouragement, counsel, and inspiration to meet the different phases of a particular problem, thousands of testimonies show that healing can take place when patient and practitioner are far apart. They may never even have met or communicated, beyond the initial request for help. While this phenomenon is unknown in psychological counseling, it was familiar to Jesus, as when he healed the centurion's servant at a distance (Luke 7:6–10), and it is natural enough if the divine Mind is not localized. Genuine Christian healing is never projected from person to person through space but flows freely to all who understand that infinite Mind is no respecter of persons.

This rules out the concept of "suggestion" which plays a key role in much psychological counseling. The word is reserved in Christian Science to describe the kind of thinking that seems to shut one off from the presence and power of God. A Christian Science practitioner does not "suggest" health to his patient any more than he would try to make the sun shine. His task, as he sees it, is simply to rise into that altitude of thought in which the unobstructed light of Truth shows him man as he really is. This is not a matter of mystical transport or the result of repeating esoteric formulas; it is a humble and rational turning to Mind for light.

When the skeptics of Jesus' day insisted that he healed — "cast out devils" — by Beelzebub, the prince of the devils, his reply indicated that this might indeed be the method used by some of his critics. "But," he added, "if I cast out devils by the Spirit of God, then the kingdom of God is come unto you" (Matthew 12:28).

Instead of rejecting this as a reference to an obsolete demonology, the Christian Scientist sees in it a figurative description of two ways of handling the evils that bedevil human existence. One way would use the powers of the human mind to control the evils arising from the human mind's own shortcomings. The other way endeavors simply to "let this mind be in you, which was also in Christ Jesus" (Phil. 2:5) — and understands this to be the eternal Mind or Spirit called God.

On this latter basis the healing of sickness and the healing of sin are closely related, as Jesus showed when he healed the palsied man (Matthew 9:1–8). Christian Scientists do not, however, imply that all sickness is the result of sin, in the narrow sense of that word. Perhaps the most common cause is fear, and behind that they see ignorance of the true nature of being. Yet in the root sense in which sin is defined as a missing of the mark, all belief in a life apart from God is ignorantly sinful. Christian Science insists that such belief is a slander on the pure and sinless man of God's creating.

Sin may have disappeared from the vocabulary of modern psychology but it remains an essential term in the Christian Scientist's spiritual arsenal. The higher mission of the Christ-power, writes Mrs. Eddy in a passage already quoted on page 6 of this book, is "to take away the sins of the world."

HEALING IN THE CHURCHES

THE REVIVAL of Christian healing in this century has been quietly gathering momentum. A considerable body of lay and clerical literature bears witness to the steadily growing interest in the subject. In recent years one denomination after another has taken official cognizance of the challenge offered religion by the ministry to the sick.*

A Presbyterian minister who has conducted healing services at his church for several years remarked at a conference on spiritual healing in 1965: "We're only a handful now and we're not yet theologically respectable. But in twenty years they'll all be won over

* See, for instance, the report of the Archbishop's Commission of the Church of England (1958) on "The Church's Ministry of Healing"; report adopted May, 1960, by the 172nd General Assembly of the United Presbyterian Church in the U.S.A. on "The Relation of Christian Faith to Health"; report of the Committee on Anointing and Healing, United Lutheran Church in America (1962), and of the Commission on Church and Ministry, United Church of Christ, Evangelical and Reformed (1960).

to it." * This is typical of the enthusiasm of many of those in the traditional churches who are now actively exploring the possibilities of spiritual healing.

More than seventy years ago Mary Baker Eddy wrote in *Pulpit and Press* (p. 22): "If the lives of Christian Scientists attest their fidelity to Truth, I predict that in the twentieth century every Christian church in our land, and a few in far-off lands, will approximate the understanding of Christian Science sufficiently to heal the sick in his name." Though there are wide divergences in doctrine, method, and scope among those who are now endeavoring to practice spiritual healing, their common aim is to heal the sick in Christ's name. To that extent at least, Mrs. Eddy's prediction is already being realized.

Yet both Christian Scientists and Christians of other denominations would be quick to point out the distance which still separates their methods. The revival of the Protestant ministry of healing is taking place within the organizational patterns and historic doctrines of the respective churches. Thus priests or pastors of denominations with a strong emphasis on ritual, conduct services featuring laying-on-of-hands and anointing with oil. Others, with less of a liturgical heritage, have maintained that such ministrations are better carried on in private or after appropriate psychological counseling. Still others contend that healing is a special gift, a charisma, and seek to exercise it in the tent-meeting atmosphere of the evangelical crusader.†

What is common to all these methods as well as to Christian Science treatment is a deep conviction that disease is contrary to God's will. There is a general repudiation of the older disposition to believe that God sends pain and disability to man as a necessary discipline — in which case it would seem illogical and even impious to seek to contravene His will by means of a pill or serum.

That God in His inscrutable wisdom should torture a small

* Boston Conference, April 27, 1965.
† The differences in the history and methodology of the pastoral counseling movement, the liturgical healing movement, and the metaphysical movement represented by Christian Science are explored in an unpublished doctoral dissertation "Religious Healing in the United States; 1940–1960" by B. Crandell Epps (Boston University, 1961). Dr. Epps, who has served as a Protestant chaplain in the United States Army, is himself a Christian Scientist.

child, for instance, in order to punish its parents is repugnant to moral sense and unthinkable of the loving Father revealed through Christ. While Jesus himself prayed for submission to his Father's will, Christianity rests on the conviction that God's will for him was to triumph over the agony and death imposed on him by men — to triumph spiritually, morally, and physically. His whole ministry of healing involved intelligent conformity to God's will.

As the Christian Scientist understands it, such conformity includes the overcoming of faith in matter and of reliance on material means of healing. For the Christian traditionalist who believes that God works through matter it may be possible to combine some measure of reliance on prayer with some measure of reliance on medical skills. Generally it has been accepted that God creates both germs to cause disease and drugs to cure it, and many Christians are not troubled by this appearance of a house divided against itself. But the more uncompromising position of Christian Science reflects the radicalism of Jesus' words: "It is the spirit that quickeneth; the flesh profiteth nothing" (John 6:63).

Thus the differences of method between various types of religiously-oriented healing reflect more profound differences of religious conviction. Christian Science in particular rests on metaphysical postulates which rule out any sense of healing as miraculous, in the sense that a miracle is a supposed violation of law. Christian transformation from sin to grace in daily living might appear a miracle from the standpoint of the psychiatrist. But orthodox Christianity does not usually put repentance and rebirth into the category of miracle. In the same way, physical changes following a changed relationship to God do not seem mysterious to the Christian Scientist for whom matter is an expression of thought.

Despite all the differences which mark the various forms of religious healing, a common core of Christian faith — a shared spirit of service — unites them at their best.

The writer of a popular survey of present-day healing developments in the churches * comes to the conclusion that they all have in common an outreaching love and the recognition of a power or

* Will Oursler, *The Healing Power of Faith* (New York: Hawthorn Books, 1957), p. 330.

force beyond oneself, to which one can turn in total humility and trust. This is essentially the Christianity of the Sermon on the Mount, with its faith in God's love overflowing in love for one's fellow man. This is at the heart of Christian Science, as of all genuine Christianity.

The opening sentence of the first chapter of *Science and Health* reads: "The prayer that reforms the sinner and heals the sick is an absolute faith that all things are possible to God, — a spiritual understanding of Him, an unselfed love." Christian faith and Christian love are both essential to Christian healing. And if Christian Science also demands an *understanding* of Spirit which shows healing to be logically consistent with universal law, this does not make faith unnecessary, it merely makes it absolute.

THE HEALING OF THE NATIONS

A CENTURY ago the emphasis in the Christian churches was almost entirely on individual salvation. Apart from a few reform groups, there was little pressure for the involvement of the church in social action. A future heaven was still thought by many to be sufficient compensation for the present iniquities and inequities of society.

Today there is widespread suspicion of any religion that is merely personal. A pietism that turns its back on the enormous collective problems of mankind is felt to have little relevance to a society in which corporate action plays so essential and pervasive a role.

It is said of the tree of life, in the Book of Revelation (22:2), that "the leaves of the tree were for the healing of the nations." Christian healing must necessarily extend to the collective aspects of living. But the deepest spiritual intuitions of mankind have always pointed to the fact that it must start with individual regeneration.

An individual healing, physical or otherwise, may include the healing of racial or class prejudice, of economic injustice, political bigotry, social indifference, or any one of a thousand forms of moral myopia. If the healing proceeds from a clearer view of man's relation to God, then it is inevitably a step toward a more unselfed attitude to human life, toward engagement with broader issues.

Mrs. Eddy's own concern with public affairs grew rather than diminished through the years in which she was founding the Church of Christ, Scientist, and it culminated in her establishment of *The Christian Science Monitor.** Here was an indispensable link with the world in all its unregenerate multiplicity. Quite apart from the *Monitor's* normal functions as a responsible news journal of international scope, the paper would serve as a valuable instrument to educate Christian Scientists to their larger social responsibilities. Acting as a guide among complex issues rather than as a dictator of opinion, it would stand as a constant reminder to its readers that the world at their doorstep desperately needs all the healing insight and practical intelligence they can bring to it.

Like members of other groups, Christian Scientists come from widely diverse backgrounds. All sorts of social and political views are to be found among them. The individual who turns to Christian Science for healing possesses inevitably a whole set of likes, antipathies, convictions, and temperamental characteristics.

To start thinking from the standpoint of Spirit as the only reality is to discover for oneself a new identity. It is, in traditional Christian terms, to be "born again." But as Mrs. Eddy writes in her *Miscellaneous Writings* (p. 15): "The new birth is not the work of a moment. It begins with moments, and goes on with years; moments of surrender to God, of childlike trust and joyful adoption of good; moments of self-abnegation, self-consecration, heaven-born hope, and spiritual love."

This new sense of being cannot help but overflow in active love for others — first, perhaps, in one's more immediate relationships, eventually in new awarenesses, insights, and outreachings to society at large. Sooner or later it must result in shaking up those entrenched personal predilections which breed intolerance and are so often mistaken for eternal truths. When Spirit is accepted as the only absolute, the relativity of all human positions becomes gradually evident.

* See Erwin D. Canham, *Commitment to Freedom: The Story of The Christian Science Monitor* (Boston: Houghton Mifflin Co., 1958), pages 3–17.

The Horizon of Healing

This no more inhibits a Christian Scientist from being an ardent fighter for a particular social cause than it does any other Christian, but it should and can allow him to fight with charity rather than bigotry, with a desire to heal his opponents rather than to crush them. Where a common Christian concern for society exists, even antagonists on a crucial issue can find mutual respect — and learn from each other.

Whether a Christian Scientist participates in the social battles of our day as a liberal or a conservative, a fighter or a reconciler, a partisan or an independent, a private or a general, his ultimate purpose is to *heal*. Yet most Christian Scientists would probably agree that up to now only a small fraction of the healing dynamic of their religion has been utilized in relation to the urgent collective problems facing the world.

The whole human race cries aloud for the healing of its dividedness. "Love hath one race, one realm, one power," Mrs. Eddy writes in her *Poems* (p. 22), and from the vantage point of that realization many of the most anguished struggles of the present can be recognized as the birth throes of a higher concept of man.

Everywhere men blindly strive for a manhood that is more than an accident of biology. Like the prodigal son among the swine, who "came to himself" and thus came to the unchanged love of his father, they are summoned to wake to their true identity as the valued sons of God. Those who have glimpsed even a little of what that means are called to demonstrate their faith to their fellows.

CHRISTIANITY AND SCIENCE

O<small>UR PRESENT AGE</small> is sometimes characterized as the post-Christian era. For good or for ill, the natural sciences wield much of the intellectual authority that once belonged to the historic church.

On the one hand atomic physics has made possible the total extinction of the human race; on the other hand molecular biology has made plausible the indefinite prolongation of human life. In this situation the implications of spiritual healing have a great deal more importance than may be recognized at first.

A Century of Christian Science Healing

If man is mere organized matter, governed in the last analysis by laws of physics and chemistry, then his position in the universe is a very precarious one indeed. Inhabiting a planet which itself is the merest mote of dust in astronomical space, chance product of a blind evolutionary process, he faces the eventual annihilation of his whole kind in the inevitable death of the solar system, if not by some earlier man-made catastrophe.

This is the cosmic destiny which awaits the most ambitious hopes and achievements of the scientific materialist. This is the sense of ultimate meaninglessness which haunts even his jauntiest assurances. Beyond tomorrow's scientific utopia lies the shadow of ultimate cataclysm.

To this existential situation Christian Science brings a radical but reasoned conviction that Life is Spirit, eternal and indestructible. This is something different from the traditional religious hope in a heaven beyond the grave. The three-decker universe implied in older conceptions of heaven was one of the early casualties of modern science. The kingdom of heaven announced by Christ Jesus and revealed by Christian Science is the presence of Spirit here and now; it is the infinite order and harmony of the universe created, maintained, and beheld by divine Mind. It is spiritual reality as opposed to material appearance, immortal being as opposed to temporal self-delusion.

In the context of today's physics, matter eludes understanding by the ordinary layman. Its seeming solidity dissolves into a shadowy whirlpool of energy which he finds himself unable to comprehend or to imagine. He is told that matter can only be understood mathematically, and he knows that this mathematical understanding enables the physicist to control it far more effectively than when it was regarded as impregnable substance. He knows that what his forebears would have regarded as miracles are now achievable by what those same forebears might have regarded as mathematical magic, but with unhesitating faith he accepts these miracles as the natural result of scientific understanding.

The Christian Scientist goes a step farther. As he sees it, a metaphysical understanding of matter — derived from the recognition of Spirit as true substance — confers a power over material appearances surpassing anything achieved by natural science. For, metaphysically understood, matter is seen to be an impossible limit on the power of Spirit, an insubstantial belief that substance, or being, is finite and mortal. It is a false mode of consciousness, with no more power than belief gives it. Viewed in this light, material limitations inevitably yield before spiritual understanding.

Such a view is not to be confused with traditional forms of philosophical idealism. Plato and Hegel can rescue man from the tyranny of phenomenal appearances only by theory, never by healing, and a merely theoretical rescue is no rescue at all. To find one's roots in the Life that is Spirit is something quite different from taking a philosophical stance on the primacy of ideas.

Christianity has always been a way of life, not merely a way of thinking. Christian Science, as its very name implies, draws life and thought together.

This, as the Christian Scientist sees it, was the way of Jesus of Nazareth. His purpose, he said, was to bear witness to "the truth," and the truth, he promised, "shall make you free." Truth *acts*. Through every act of his earthly ministry Jesus brought the truth of spiritual being to bear, precisely and predictably, on the error of material appearances.

Of his healing work Mrs. Eddy writes: "Jesus beheld in Science the perfect man, who appeared to him where sinning mortal man appears to mortals. In this perfect man the Saviour saw God's own likeness, and this correct view of man healed the sick" (*Science and Health,* pp. 476, 477).

A child who sees a straight stick lying halfway in a puddle and halfway out may believe that the stick is bent at the point at which it enters the water. A better informed adult is able to explain that the stick is not really bent, for he "looks" not at the visual image of the stick but at his scientific knowledge regarding the refraction of light. Then he lifts the stick out of the water to prove his point.

This rough analogy suggests something of the way in which a Christian Scientist looks beyond the temporary evidence of the physical senses into what he calls the Science of Being for a true explanation of man. He does not wishfully imagine a perfect human being where a sick and sinning mortal seems to be, but he thrusts beyond all material appearance to the truth of spiritual being. To perceive the truth of any situation is to have that situation grasped by Truth. To perceive man as the expression or idea of Spirit is to reshape human experience closer to the spiritual idea.

The healing of physical disease is one of the most concrete proofs that can be offered of the substantiality of Spirit. It is not of itself conclusive, and in the nature of things it cannot be offered under the conditions of controlled experiment. But in conjunction with all the other evidences of spiritual power furnished by Christianity understood as Science it offers a substantial challenge to materialistic assumptions.

In the nature of things the propositions of Christian Science cannot be affected by new developments in natural science — for instance, the possible discovery of other forms of life on other planets or the synthetic creation of human life on this planet. For if reality is pure Spirit, material existence at best can be only a series of attempted approximations of reality. As Mrs. Eddy puts it, "Whatever seems to be a new creation, is but the discovery of some distant idea of Truth; else it is a new multiplication or self-division of mortal thought, as when some finite sense peers from its cloister with amazement and attempts to pattern the infinite" (*ibid.*, p. 263).

Christian Science rests on an absolute premise, even though it appeals to verification by experience. Christian Scientists often speak of prayer as "knowing the truth," and Truth itself towers far above any particular instance of its power. The worship of God is in its highest sense an absolute commitment to Truth, regardless of the consequences to oneself.

This is illustrated in the testimony of a woman who turned to Christian Science after the doctor told her he could do no more for her.* Suffering from an internal growth, totally blind, almost completely paralyzed, and finally in a semi-coma, she heard her husband say to the practitioner who had been called in, "If Christian Science heals my wife, I'll be the best Christian Scientist you

* Mrs. Lois B. Estey, Geneva, New York, in *The Christian Science Journal*, December, 1955, and the *Christian Science Sentinel*, March 23, 1957. Also in Will Oursler, *The Healing Power of Faith*.

have in your organization." The practitioner answered: "Don't say that. If Christian Science is not the truth, you do not want it, even if it heals her. If it is the truth, you want it, even if she is not healed." Suddenly, as the woman later explained, "the fear of dying left me in my realization that what I really wanted was to know God better — to know Him as He actually is — to know the truth." The same night she was instantaneously healed.

This is an example of the scientific spirit, the love of truth for its own sake, though the practical proof was "added." That Christian Scientists who are working in the physical and biological sciences have been able to improve the quality of their contributions to these sciences through their understanding of Christian Science is not without significance. There is no hostility between their religion and the scientific spirit, but Christian Science operates from a position beyond the calculations and categories of material sense.

"The kingdoms of this world," we read in Revelation 11:15, "are become the kingdoms of our Lord, and of his Christ; and he shall reign for ever and ever." The sciences of this world caught up into the universe of Mind are transmuted into that spiritual Science of Being which lies beyond all finite questionings.

THE SECOND CENTURY

IN A BOOK so largely devoted to healing, it may be appropriate to return to a concrete example of a healing experienced, a life lived. The following testimony by Mrs. Mina L. VanDam of Concord, N. H., appeared in the *Christian Science Sentinel* of January 23, 1965:

"According to the world's way of counting, I am now over one hundred and two years old. Christian Science found me when I was a young woman of twenty-three. I had been given up by the doctors, who said I had quick consumption. Each day I was wrapped up well and put on the porch.

"One day a lady came by and asked me if I knew anything of Christian Science. I said I had heard of it, but knew nothing of its teachings. She brought me literature and talked to me. I accepted all she told me of God wholeheartedly.

A Century of Christian Science Healing

"I had no definite Christian Science treatment, but simply read a copy of *The Christian Science Journal*. I lived with that *Journal* for one month. After that time I walked out to the barn; then I went upstairs — a thing I had not done for a long time. I obtained a copy of *Science and Health* by Mrs. Eddy. Within a year, much to the amazement of my neighbors and my husband, who later took up the study of Christian Science, I was completely well. I drove the horse and cut the lawn and was quite normal again.

"For the past twelve years or so I have had the privilege of living in The Christian Science Pleasant View Home. I study the Lesson-Sermon from the *Quarterly* daily: I read all our periodicals regularly. I love *The Christian Science Monitor*; as I read it I do prayerful work for the world. Also I do prayerful work for our Home here. I enjoy walking up the broad corridor to the sun-room in the wintry weather. I like the out-of-doors.

"I am more grateful than I can say for all the blessings that have come to me through the study of Christian Science; and for our Leader, Mrs. Eddy, my gratitude knows no bounds, because she unlocked the treasures of truth in the Bible for us all to know and use."

This quiet tribute looks back over much of the past century. The same year that it was printed, the sixth biennial meeting in the interest of Christian Science Organizations at Universities and Colleges was held in Boston, with some forty-five hundred students from thirty-four countries attending. At the final session, a period was set aside for spontaneous testimonies.

Among those who sprang to their feet to speak was a young Negro who told of his healing of tuberculosis, then went on to express his joy and gratitude for the unlimited spiritual freedom he was discovering. His testimony ended with the words of a song which he described as "about the same age as Christian Science." In their unaffected simplicity the words of this old freedom song might stand for the larger and deeper rejoicing of all who have found their citizenship in the kingdom of God: "Free at last, free at last, thank God Almighty, we're free at last."

In this spirit Christian Science faces its next century.